FROM THE AWARD-WINNING WEBSITE, AISH.COM

ISRAEL

LIFE IN THE SHADOW
OF TERROR

Personal Accounts and Perspectives
from the Heart of the Jewish People

Edited By
Nechemia Coopersmith and Shraga Simmons

TARGUM/FELDHEIM

First published 2003
Copyright © 2003 by Aish.com
ISBN 1-56871-237-5

Published by:
TARGUM PRESS, INC.
22700 W. Eleven Mile Rd.
Southfield, MI 48034
E-mail: targum@netvision.net.il
Fax: 888-298-9992
www.targum.com

In conjuction with:
AISH.COM
1 Western Wall Plaza
P.O.B. 14149
Jerusalem, Israel
E-mail: israel@aish.com
www.aish.com

Distributed by:
FELDHEIM PUBLISHERS
202 Airport Executive Park
Nanuet, NY 10954
www.feldheim.com

Printed in Israel

Dedicated to the

victims of Arab terror

בקרובי אקדש

ויקרא י:ג

Dedicated to our beloved

Rabbi Noah Weinberg

When one drops a pebble into a body of water, rings spread out to the edge and beyond. This is your work of 30 years: one pebble, one Jewish soul at a time, each creating waves of energy that go beyond the measurable boundaries of time and space.

May the Almighty continue to give you strength of mind and body to continue your work. May you continue to experience pleasure from your family, which is the entire Jewish people. And may you merit to behold the Mashiach from the roof of Aish HaTorah!

With great love and respect,

Robin and Dennis Berman

CONTENTS

Introduction 13

Acknowledgments 17

LIVING WITH TERROR

Victim of the Media War 21
Tuvia Grossman

On the Front Line 24
Danny Verbov

Jerusalem and Her Lovers 28
Sara Yoheved Rigler

The "Good" Terrorist 32
Seth and Sherri Mandell

Children of Death, Children of Life 35
Sara Yoheved Rigler

Remembering "Shema Yisrael" 42
Ben-Zion Nemett

Intersecting Lives 46
Rabbi Shalom Schwartz

"I Am a Jew..." 51
Liba Pearson

A Tale of Two Families 55
   Sara Yoheved Rigler

At One in the Fire 65
   Liba Pearson

Survivors in Netanya. 70
   Anna Yakobovitch

Shiri, My Song 74
   Tova Lebovits

Awaiting the Wounded 77
   Dr. Avraham Rivkind

Why I Am Not Afraid 82
   Liba Pearson

Tears on Gray Cement 87
   Vadim Sirotnikov

Laughter in a Time of War 94
   Sara Yoheved Rigler

Preparing for War 102
   Sarah Shapiro

On the Bus with Mayor Bloomberg 106
   Rabbi Nechemia Coopersmith

Our Heroes and Theirs 110
   Jon Medved

ISRAEL PERSPECTIVES

To Restore Our Destiny 115
   Rabbi Noah Weinberg

Murdering Our Hopes 119
   Elie Wiesel

Ramon's Legacy 121
   Rabbi Shraga Simmons

Home for the Soul 127
    Rabbi Ahron Lopiansky

What Are We Dying For? 132
    Sara Yoheved Rigler

The Power of Freedom 139
    Natan Sharansky

Land of Spiritual Acquisition 143
    Rabbi Noson Weisz

Learning from Sadism 149
    Lawrence Kelemen

When Humanism Becomes Fundamentalism 154
    Sara Yoheved Rigler

Israel Independence Day: Pain and Blessings 161
    Rabbi Emanuel Feldman

Feeling the Loss 165
    Rebbetzin Tziporah Heller

A Zionist Manifesto 169
    Sara Yoheved Rigler

Why Israel Fights 177
    Yossi Klein Halevi

Israel's Strength 181
    Rabbi Berel Wein

The True Face of Israeli Youth 184
    Sara Yoheved Rigler

Why Jerusalem Matters 189
    Rabbi Nachum Braverman and Rabbi Shraga Simmons

ISRAEL DIARIES

Virtual Tourism in Israel 195
    Dvora Levin

Coffee with My Enemies 199
    Sarah Shapiro

Fighting for Israel 206
    Alan Leventen

Tears at Rachel's Tomb 211
    Ester (Ellen) Katz Silvers

A Place to Sigh 215
    Yaffa Ganz

His Name Was Nachshon Wachsman 219
    Esther Wachsman

Preserve the Vessel 226
    Sarah Shapiro

Mother Brigade 232
    Liba Pearson

Insidious Palestinian Television 236
    Sue Tedmon

A Different Kind of Independence 240
    Mara (Frei) Goldblatt

The Flowers 243
    Sarah Shapiro

Missing in Action 247
    Rabbi Shraga Simmons

Dear Jewish Studies Faculty at San Francisco State . . . 254
    Professor Laurie Zoloth

Hidden Hero 258
    David Arenson

Birthday for the Bereaved 261
    Sherri Mandell

THE MIDEAST CONFLICT

Twenty Facts about Israel and the Middle East 267
William J. Bennett, Jack Kemp, and Jeane Kirkpatrick

The Root Cause of Terrorism 273
Benjamin Netanyahu

Jerusalem: Jewish and Muslim Claims 276
Rabbi Ken Spiro

History of the Territories 286
Efraim Karsh

Faisal's Trojan Horse 299
Memri.org

The Problem, Not the Solution 303
Dan Gillerman

Anti-Globalization and Anti-Semitism 308
David Arenson and Simon Grynberg

Except When You're Targeting Jews 312
Jeffrey Dunetz

Seven Principles of Media Objectivity 315
Rabbi Shraga Simmons

Jeningrad 321
Tom Gross

Why Are They Saying All Those Terrible Things about Israel? 326
Lenny Ben-David

Dishonest Reporting 332
Israel H. Asper

Can the Whole World Be Wrong? 337
Sara Yoheved Rigler

Peace at Any Price Equals War 340
Jeff Jacoby

"Occupied" Territories?. 343
    Dore Gold

The Refugee Issue. 353
    Rabbi Shraga Simmons

Children Under Fire 357
    John Wiggins

One Hundred Years in a Nutshell 366
    Ben Blicker

15 Things I Don't Understand about the Peace Process . 370
    Ephraim Shore

COMING HOME

Still Crazy: Why We Made Aliyah 377
    Sol Jakubowicz

Should I Stay or Should I Go? 381
    Nathan Morris

Israel Now. 386
    Tefilla Buxbaum

Mom, I'm Moving to Israel. 390
    Jenna Ziman

Fifty-five Ways to Help Israel. 393
    Aish.com Readers

To Live as Jews 406
    Rabbi Shalom Schwartz

Loving the Land of Israel. 410
    Sara Yoheved Rigler

Introduction

וידום אהרון.
And Aaron was silent.....

(Leviticus 10:3)

After the sudden, tragic death of his two sons, Aaron's only response was silence.

Two youths destined for leadership and greatness, cut down in the prime of life, leaving behind a vacuum impossible to fill.

For Aaron, words were totally inadequate. When your world has been suddenly upended and thrown into a freefall, you're left reeling in pain and gasping for air. Words become useless. It is impossible to describe the unfamiliar darkness of tragedy and despair that envelopes you, supplanting your previous, ever-so balanced world.

And Aaron was silent.

Over the past three tumultuous years in Israel — from the launch of the concerted Arab war of terror in September 2000 to the disintegrating "road map" in September 2003 — 870 people have been murdered by Arab terrorism and 5,794 wounded in a relentless onslaught of terrorist attacks, including 103 suicide bombings.

Words are insufficient to express the scope of the pain and tragedy in the shattering of thousands of families, which have been plunged into a daily struggle of survival, adversity, and aching loss.

Words can never describe the kind of evil that straps a belt of explosives and detonates it in a hotel filled with elderly Jews celebrating Passover, in a pizza parlor, a shopping mall, at a bar mitzvah celebration, a café, a disco, a city bus, a university cafeteria; an evil that places a nine-month-old baby in the crosshairs of a rifle and pulls the trigger; an evil that publicly lynches two reserve soldiers who made a wrong turn into Ramallah; an evil that murders children and parents on their return from prayers at the Western Wall; an evil that stones to death two teenage boys to the point where dental records are required to identify the bodies.

This book should not be written with ink, but with tears.

So it is with trepidation and recognition of the inherent limitations that we offer this book, because words, despite their inadequacy, are all we have.

Our hope is that the words in this book will convey to readers an inside look into the daily terror Israelis have been facing. It is all too easy to distance ourselves from the enormity of the pain and to go on with our routine lives, especially for those who live across the globe. By identifying with the real life victims of terror, we can feel their pain and truly care, the way we ought to when a family member suffers a tragedy. We cannot carry on our lives as usual while our brothers and sisters are being blown to bits on buses.

This book also portrays another aspect of daily life in Israel: the remarkable courage, perseverance, and faith of everyday Israelis.

Words are particularly important in describing recent events because, in addition to a war of terror, Israel is in the midst of a war of words. The Arab world and international media have distorted the very language of the conflict, promoting false jingoisms like "one man's terrorist is another man's freedom fighter" and "cycle of violence" that obscure the truth of who is the aggressor and who is the victim.

Beyond this, terms like "terrorism," "occupation," "refugees," "anti-Semitism," "racism," "excessive force," and even "jihad" have been subverted, turning the meaning of these words on their head, robbing Israel of the ability to persuasively present the validity of her cause to the world and to ourselves with confidence and clarity.

This book aims to dispel many of the falsehoods, by presenting clear definitions and carefully constructed arguments, enabling us to regain our confidence in Israel's mission and proactively fight for her cause.

And finally, words are needed to give these events some kind of spiritual context. This is not an attempt to explain "why"; the pain is still too raw and no one today is a prophet. But that does not preclude us from trying to understand some of the Torah concepts that give general contours to these events.

Indeed, these 1,000 days are as baffling as any 1,000-piece jigsaw puzzle. We can look at any particular piece, such as the deaths of Dr. David Applebaum, the head of the emergency department in Shaare Zedek Hospital, and his 20-year-old daughter Nava, murdered on the eve of her wedding, and we cannot possibly understand what we are looking at or how it fits into the larger picture.

This perplexity is not new. Even Moses, who reached the highest levels of wisdom, could not understand one aspect of existence: why tragedies happen.

"You can see My back, but you cannot see My face" (Exodus 33:23). God told Moses that in looking forward, humans cannot comprehend God's ways; but ultimately by looking backwards in history, we will understand the reasons why.

The Jewish people know that history is not haphazard. We know that God runs the world. And God's finished picture will not have paint splashed all over the canvas willy-nilly. No, God's finished picture of human history will be a picture of exile and redemption — clear and precise.

As Isaiah (11:9) describes: "The earth will be full of the knowledge of God, as the waters cover the seas." In the age of the final redemption, everyone will realize that neither chance, nor economic factors, nor political powers, nor military superiority, but God alone is the definitive causal factor behind everything, and the ultimate source of our solution.

Israel is under attack. In response, we need to deepen our devotion to and love for the land and its people. We need to recommit ourselves to the ideal of Israel as the place where the Jewish people can best fulfill their mission of *tikkun olam* — embodying God's moral message and being a light unto the nations. We must stand up and support her — economically, spiritually, and politically. We must become educated on the issues and counter the misinformation that seeks to undermine Israel's legitimacy.

The Hebrew word for peace, *shalom*, comes from *shalem*, which means whole and complete. This entails more than a mere cessation of hostilities. We yearn to see all the pieces of the puzzle fit. This is the true *shalom* that Jews have always prayed for. May we merit to see it speedily in our days.

Acknowledgments

Our endless gratitude goes to the talented team at Aish.com: David LeVine, Yitzhak Attias, Jack Kalla, Mike Cooper, Ben Buxbaum, Sara Yoheved Rigler, Chaya Sorcsher, Malkie Sender, Chavie Miller, Emuna Braverman, and Chaya Richmond. Your dedication and expertise have made Aish.com the largest Jewish educational site online.

To Kalman Packouz, Nachum Braverman, Tuvia Hoffman, Pinchas Waldman, Leah Miller, Shmuel Kaffe, Shmuel Silinsky, and the Aish HaTorah administrative and executive offices for their important assistance.

To Rabbi Noah Weinberg, the dean of Aish HaTorah International, whose vision, wisdom, and encouragement continue to serve as a beacon of light, guiding, and inspiring us to set our sights higher and tackle the challenges that come our way.

To our loyal and dedicated readers — your feedback, enthusiasm, and support has been instrumental in shaping Aish.com.

To all the supporters of Aish.com for their generous financial assistance and invaluable guidance. In particular we thank Yuri and Deana Pikover for their unwavering commitment and indispensable guidance, and Dov and Nancy Friedberg, Bob and Michelle Diener, Art and Sally Klein, Meir Vaisman, Dennis and Robin Berman, and Mitch and Joleen Julis for their tremendous support and dedication.

To all the writers and contributors to Aish.com for their inspiring, insightful, and exceptional content that makes the website a treasured resource for hundreds of thousands of readers.

To our wives, for being true partners in our efforts to impact *klal Yisrael*.

To Sarah Shapiro, whose formidable editing skills enhanced this book.

To Rabbi Moshe Dombey and the staff at Targum Press.

And to the Almighty, who sustains us with His undeserved blessings and unceasing miracles. We are forever grateful for the privilege of sharing His infinite wisdom with so many.

Nechemia Coopersmith and Shraga Simmons
Jerusalem, October 2003 / Tishrei 5764

LIVING
WITH
TERROR

Tuvia Grossman

Victim of the Media War

September 30, 2000 — Palestinian violence erupts with such sudden fury that many Israelis are caught in the bloodshed before they even know it is happening. One young man tells how he ended up nearly lynched — and on the front page of The New York Times.

I was thrust into the international limelight on September 30, 2000, when *The New York Times* published a front-page photo of me — bloodied and battered — crouching beneath a club-wielding Israeli policeman. The caption identified me as a Palestinian victim of the intifada. In fact, however, I am a 20-year-old Jewish student from Chicago, studying at yeshiva in Jerusalem.

Here's how it all happened:

It was the eve of Rosh Hashana, and I hailed a taxi with two of my friends to go visit the Western Wall. Along the way, the driver took a shortcut through one of the Arab neighborhoods of Jerusalem. We turned a corner and suddenly there were about 40 Palestinians surrounding the car. Before we knew it, huge rocks had smashed all the windows of the taxi.

Some of the Palestinians pulled open the door and dragged me from the vehicle. About 10 of them jumped on top of me, punching and kicking me. I crouched to the ground and tried to cover my face to protect myself as much as possible. All I could see were a flurry of sneakers kicking me in the face.

Then I felt a strong pair of hands grabbing me, and I uncovered my face because I thought someone was trying to help me. But it was just another Arab; he held the back of my head and punched me square in the face. I fell flat on the ground and the Palestinians jumped on top of me again. One of them stabbed me in the back of my leg, ripping through muscles and tendons. Two other Arabs held my head so I couldn't move, while two more bashed rocks onto my head... again and again and again.

By this time the beating had gone on for about eight minutes. I had already lost three pints of blood and was losing consciousness. I said *"Shema Yisrael"* — the declaration of faith that a Jew says before he dies. I tried not to black out, because I was sure if I did, it would be the end.

Because it was the eve of Rosh Hashana, the image of a shofar flashed through my mind, and I recalled a biblical story I'd learned in yeshiva. The prophet Gideon and his 300 men were badly outnumbered against the Midianite army of 130,000. So Gideon's troops banged pots and blew shofars, hoping that the noise would scare the enemy. With God's help, the ploy worked, and Gideon won the battle.

So I yelled at the top of my lungs. The Palestinians were startled momentarily, and I was able to get up and run. But I am heavily nearsighted and my contact lenses had fallen out. So there I was — barely able to see anything, with blood pouring down my face, and my leg badly wounded — being chased up a hill by 40 Arabs throwing rocks at me.

It was a miracle, but somehow I outran them and reached a gas station where Israeli soldiers were posted.

I collapsed on the ground, and that's when a group of freelance photographers started snapping pictures. An Israeli policeman was protecting me, yelling at the Palestinians to back off from finishing the lynching. But the photo — sent to 15,000 news agencies throughout the world by the Associated Press — identified me as a Palestinian. The obvious implication was that the Israeli policeman had just beaten me. In truth, it was the total opposite. I was a Jewish victim of Arab attackers.

When a photo gets published, there are many links in the chain, and in this case, I don't know where the fault for the garbled caption lies. But it is deeply disturbing that when there's a victim, the media assumes it must be a Palestinian.

It's bad enough to be beaten bloody, get stitches up and down my head, and have my leg so severely stabbed that therapy was required to regain use of it. But to be used as a pawn in the media war, as part of Palestinian propaganda to gain international sympathy, well, that hurts even more.

There is a great struggle in Israel and this event highlights the power of the media to influence public opinion. If truth is to prevail, we can't just "read" the newspaper. Be discerning and become part of the process. Otherwise, you're just as I was — a victim of the media war.

Danny Verbov

On the Front Line

October 12, 2000 — More than any other incident, the lynching of two Israeli reserve soldiers in Ramallah transformed the nation's consciousness. The mask had been torn off. If Palestinian mobs could resort to such barbarism, then we were clearly far from the dream of "peaceful coexistence."

I'm a quiet, well-mannered Englishman. One month each year, I drive army jeeps as an IDF reserve soldier. In September 2000, on the holiday of Rosh Hashana, my unit was positioned at Ayosh Junction on the edge of Ramallah. The army's aim was to keep the situation under control and not allow the riots to overflow into endangering the lives of Jewish residents nearby.

At about 9 a.m., about a dozen Palestinians began placing tires on the road and then set them on fire, laying a screen of thick black smoke. This was the way every day began.

I sat in the jeep, tightly gripping the steering wheel, waiting to see what would happen next. Within 10 minutes, hundreds upon hundreds of Palestinians streamed toward the junction, placing me on the front line, as a target for stones, rocks, iron bars, glass

DANNY VERBOV is originally from Liverpool, England, and now lives with his family in Ma'ale Michmas, north of Jerusalem, where he creates personalized calligraphic artwork.

bottles, Molotov cocktails, and, later, live bullets.

Under bombardment, thoughts of panic raced through my mind: Am I going to die? Who's going to tell my wife? What will be with my kids? I felt utterly hopeless — a speck in the universe, totally exposed and vulnerable.

On the other hand, I felt a strange power of responsibility. It was my challenge from Above to do what I had to do: help my fellow soldiers, obey orders from the commanding officer, engage in serious soul-searching, and pray like I'd never prayed before.

Our Bible is filled with stories of how military strength is a secondary factor in winning the war. Our wars are won in our hearts and in our spirits, and nowhere else. That Rosh Hashana morning, I had a shofar with me, and I fantasized about taking it out, standing on top of the jeep and blowing the shofar to disperse the stone throwers. (I thought better of it, however.)

Out there in the jeep, I felt that my actions could make the difference between life and death. Not just for me, but for the whole of Israel.

With that realization, everything takes on a new dimension. One is more careful with every word of speech. The mind becomes totally alert, aware of the consequences of every move. The senses are fully charged; you see and hear things you never noticed before. You can exist on two hours of sleep and minimal food — and yet remain totally alert. Because your life is at stake.

If only we could maintain this high level of alertness in everyday life.

∽◌∾

The last day of my reserve duty started "normally." I sat in my jeep, waiting for the hundreds of Arabs to throw boulders.

At about 10 a.m. a call came over the army radio. Some soldiers had disappeared into Ramallah. My first response was a downcast shudder of "Oh, no," and I immediately called my colleagues at Aish HaTorah to tell them to drop everything and start praying.

There was ominous silence in our jeep as we awaited news. Our orders were to cordon off Ramallah, not allowing any Arab vehicle in or out, while the army, through air reconnaissance and communication with the PA, attempted to locate the men.

But it all happened too quickly. "We need a doctor... Get a helicopter here now.... We have one body and one seriously wounded.... Where's the doctor?!"

And then silence. A long, painful silence.

There was a lot more silence, and painful sobbing, as I sat in that jeep for the next 12 hours. Details of the brutal lynchings trickled in. Two Israelis were bludgeoned, thrown from the window, burned, disemboweled, and then dragged through the street.

I sat in the jeep, numb. I saw the tank reinforcements come in. I heard the Apache helicopters whirring in the sky. But it was not until late afternoon that the IDF bombed. And even then, we gave a warning of exactly when and where we were going to bomb, in order to prevent unnecessary loss of life. No other army would do such a thing. But we are a Jewish army, and we place the value of life on the highest pedestal. There were no injuries or deaths as a result of those bombings.

And then, ironically, amidst the horrors, my final image of that day was a stunning sunset — a deep blue sky, traced with streaks of red, as another Israeli night drew mercifully closer.

Maybe that is the message we should extract from this day of anger, blood, and tears. Every day there is a sunset, and every morning there is a sunrise. Sometimes we're not aware of it, but it's there, always, with the Almighty's quiet, guiding hand: "And it was evening and it was morning..." (Genesis 1).

Our Supreme Commander created the world and sustains it on a daily basis. He knows the complete picture. He is not influenced by anger or repugnance; neither is He swayed by the world media or the UN.

We are God's soldiers, entrusted with 613 commands. We may not always understand them. Some may not be particularly convenient, and others may get us frustrated or embarrassed.

But on a day like this, a soldier must obey orders. Whether he agrees or not; whether it's convenient or not; whether he understands or not. His life, and that of others, is at stake, and he must accept the word of those who see the big picture. Though we seem

to lack political and military solutions, we do have a Supreme
Commander.

The timing of these events was no coincidence. On Rosh Hashana, the Books of Life and Death are open in the heavenly court.
It was obvious to me why these disturbances began at this crucial
time of the year. The Almighty is trying to tell us something.

I left the army a few days before Sukkot, the festival when Jews
all over the world leave their comfortable permanent homes and
move into flimsy, temporary huts, with only branches as a roof. It's
a symbol of trust in God, of total reliance on His protection.

The main theme of Sukkot is *simcha*, joy. How is it possible to
have joy in such perilous times?

Sometimes in the darkest of hours, the brightest light is seen.
The entire 18 days, our battalion had only three minor injuries.
Should we explain this through the law of averages? Or rather that
God performs miracles for us, morning, noon, and night?

The Almighty brought us out of Egypt "on eagle's wings," and
He has not let us down since. In spite of everything the world has
thrown at us — Crusades, Inquisition, pogroms, Holocaust —
we've survived it all. And I believe we'll pull through this, too. Because the Supreme Commander has promised that we will.

Those 18 days of reserve duty were the most harrowing of my
life. And in a strange sense they were among the most satisfying.
True "happiness" is knowing you're doing the best you can do, in
the circumstances designed precisely for you.

In such situations, God is telling us to figure out what we're
here for. We're given tests of extreme stress, to prove to ourselves
that we can do it. How many of us know why we are here in this
world? When faced with death, life becomes real. You get priorities
straight. If you ever get thrown into a war, make good use of the
opportunity. Figure out what you're living for.

Sara Yoheved Rigler

Jerusalem and Her Lovers

January 8, 2001 — 300,000 Jews gather outside the Old City walls to express loyalty to Jerusalem as the capital of the Jewish nation.

It was great to be a Jew in Jerusalem today.

More than 300,000 Jews from throughout Israel and the world — the largest rally in the history of modern Israel — gathered together to express their loyalty to Jerusalem as the eternal, undivided capital of the Jewish nation.

The rally began at eventide when Jews from all over Israel, holding torches and Israeli flags, formed a human chain around the Old City. Hebrew songs of love and longing for Jerusalem blared from mammoth speakers set up along the 16th century walls. By nightfall, the crowds stretched from Jaffa Gate for more than a kilometer up Jerusalem's main street.

As Mayor of Jerusalem Ehud Olmert said: "This is not a demonstration. This is not a political rally. This is simply the natural expression and outpouring of the love and fidelity of the Jewish people for Jerusalem."

SARA YOHEVED RIGLER is a featured writer on Aish.com. After 15 years of practicing and teaching Eastern philosophy and meditation, she became a Torah-observant Jew and moved to Israel, where she now lives in the Old City of Jerusalem with her musician husband and two children.

Most of the speakers were simple citizens, representing the gamut of Israel's society: from a 13-year-old boy to a retired general; from a woman who had made aliyah only three years ago to a man whose ancestors had walked to Israel from Yemen a century ago; from a secular left-wing kibbutznik to a rabbi who was a member of the paratroops division which liberated the Old City in 1967.

The crowd itself was even more diverse than the speakers. They had come from every corner of the country: the Golan, Eilat at the southernmost tip, the northernmost town of Kiryat Shemona, and all the towns along the coast. Planeloads of supporters had flown in from England, France, the United States, and Russia. Sympathetic Christians also attended. There were Ashkenazim and Sephardim, Ethiopians and Russians, American students and fourth-generation sabras.

No signs representing any particular party were held up. No statements were made against any political figure or group (except Bill Clinton, whom the Mayor of Jerusalem called upon not to be the first president in American history to seek to divide Jerusalem). No negative notes were sounded.

Israel is a nation of only 6 million people with two dozen political parties, where the adage, "Two Jews, three opinions," proves itself in constant divisiveness and strife. But this night we were united around a common love. This night all hearts beat in unison. This night witnessed the strength of the unity of the Jewish people.

Together we felt invincible. Nothing could overwhelm us — not international pressure, not CNN's caustic censure, not Arab terrorism and violence, not post-Zionist despair. Standing there along the brightly lit walls of the Old City, we were a nation united in resolution, true to our Jewish history, committed to our Jewish future.

The rally had been organized by Natan Sharansky, the Soviet refusenik who spent 14 years in the gulag and is now a prominent Israeli politician. True to his own definition of the event as apolitical, Sharansky himself did not speak. Instead, his wife Avital addressed the crowd.

Before thousands of us who believe that only a miracle can save the Jewish state, Avital Sharansky stood there — a living example of how faith and persistence can make a miracle happen. She left the Soviet Union the day after her wedding and did not see her bridegroom for 14 years. With her dissident husband imprisoned by the Communist authorities, Avital took on the Soviet system, publicizing the plight of the refuseniks and garnering support for them all over the world.

Angered by this sprightly young Jewish woman, the Soviet government decided on the ultimate revenge: they would keep Sharansky imprisoned until Avital was past child-bearing age. But Avital could not be cowed nor silenced. She made her husband's name into a household word, and eventually she won his release. The couple now has two daughters.

Avital, a petite woman with wire-rimmed glasses and a scarf covering her head, compared the relationship between Jerusalem and the Jewish people to that of the heart and the body.

Just as only a healthy heart can effectively pump blood to all the extremities, so Jerusalem's reunification in 1967 heralded a spiritual awakening among Russian Jews like Avital, distant from their Jewish heritage. In fact, the worldwide *teshuva* movement of tens of thousands of assimilated Jews returning to their religious roots traces its beginnings to the aftermath of the Six Day War, which liberated and reunified Jerusalem. A healthy heart feeds even the most distant limbs.

Publicity for the rally said that it would culminate in a mass swearing of allegiance to Jerusalem. All the speakers, including the mayor, assembled around the podium.

The emcee pronounced the words: "If I forget you, O Jerusalem..."

The crowd roared in response: "If I forget you, O Jerusalem."

The emcee continued the words of the 137th Psalm: "Let my right hand wither..."

"Let my right hand wither," more than 300,000 voices cried out in unison.

"Let my tongue cleave to the roof of my mouth," the emcee intoned.

The man with the pony tail in front of me, together with the Hassid with the long *peyos* to his left, shouted out the words: "Let my tongue cleave to the roof of my mouth."

"If I fail to remember you..." led the emcee.

The religious family to my right and the old Sephardi couple behind them fervently repeated: "If I fail to remember you..."

"If I fail to elevate Jerusalem..." the emcee continued.

"If I fail to elevate Jerusalem..." the three punk-haired teenagers on my left cried earnestly in concert with a group of young yeshiva students.

"Above my foremost joy!" the emcee concluded.

"Above my foremost joy!" the words rose up into the moonlit night and echoed off the Old City walls. Or perhaps the walls themselves were joining in our ancient oath.

And we, who had turned out more than 300,000 strong for the sake of the unity of Jerusalem, experienced Jerusalem bestowing on us a unity we had not known.

The Jewish people at one — at last.

Seth and Sherri Mandell

The "Good" Terrorist

May 9, 2001 — Two Israeli teenagers are found stoned to death in a cave near Tekoa, their community south of Jerusalem. A grieving couple questions the media.

Palestinian terrorists slaughtered our son Koby, 13, and his friend Yosef Ish-Ran, 14. The two boys, who played hooky from eighth grade to go hiking in a dry riverbed a half-kilometer from our home, were found with their heads crushed and bodies mutilated beyond recognition. The killers dipped their hands into the boys' blood and smeared it on the walls of the cave where the boys were found.

Koby was both an American and an Israeli citizen. He loved Cal Ripken, Michael Jordan, making chocolate milk shakes for the whole family, and studying the logic of the Talmud. He was almost finished with eighth grade and had just started to care about the way he looked. He was kind and athletic and funny, and he was smart, smart enough to understand the way that language affects perception. What we call or name an action often determines how we perceive it.

SETH AND SHERRI MANDELL made aliyah five years ago and live in Tekoa. They are founders of The Koby Mandell Foundation, dedicated to creating and funding programs to help children and families struck by tragedy or trauma heal their emotional wounds and improve their quality of life.

In a stunning and painful development, many American newspapers, including *The New York Times* and the *Washington Post*, have bought the Palestinian propaganda line whereby murderers who kill innocent Israelis such as Koby are not terrorists trying to instill fear and to demoralize a civilian population, but rather are "militants" engaged in a campaign of warfare against a repressive government.

According to this line of reasoning, our son — and other children like him — are killed not by cowardly and immoral terrorists, but by brave and honorable Palestinian militants. Militants are engaged in combat, in military action, ready to give up their lives to attack the enemy — even if the people they are fighting aren't old enough to shave.

Calling Palestinian terrorists militants justifies the actions of people like Sheikh Yassin of Hamas and Marwan Barghouti of the Tanzim, who eagerly send Palestinians to die "nobly" for their cause, targeting Israeli children — such as those recently killed in Jerusalem, on their way home from school, riding a public bus filled with other students. A terrorist opened fire with an M-16, killing two teenagers and wounding 50 others.

On the day of the shooting, the headlines in *The New York Times* and elsewhere reported that the attack had been perpetrated by Palestinian militants. By morning, those militants had been transformed into "gunmen" — an even more offensive, more neutral term, with its old-fashioned atmosphere of gung-ho bravado. The word is blameless, a description rather than a definition. A man with a gun, engaged in illegal activity. Illegal, but not necessarily immoral.

What has happened to the word "terrorist" — one who inflicts terror, horror, and pain, and brings about overwhelming fear? Why are these men called by innocuous labels when their goal is to kill and maim as many innocent people as possible? And what about the word "terrorism" — a system whereby cruel horrors are inflicted upon a particular population? Why has that word suddenly been excised from the political rhetoric about Palestinians?

Let us not excuse leaders who extol death by suicide bombing, or who encourage their people to spray bullets into crowds of innocent children on their way home from school. And let us not mistakenly define terrorism as random events, rather than as an institutionalized system of intimidation.

Palestinian leaders consciously inculcate their society with the culture of terrorism. That's one reason why polls indicate that more than 75 percent of the Palestinian population favors suicide bombings. That's why, on the evening of September 11, Palestinians were dancing in the street, celebrating the 3,000 people struck down by a "militant" plot on American soil. (Reuters still refuses to label September 11 as "terrorism.")

That's why Palestinians accord rock star status to suicide bombers who die a "martyr's" death. It's a message that legitimizes terrorists such as the one who blew up the Sbarro pizza parlor, killing our friend Frimet Roth's 15-year-old daughter, Malky, a flute player and poet.

Palestinians celebrated the Sbarro bombing by opening an exhibition at an Islamic university. The display consisted of a cardboard cutout of the Sbarro storefront, fake blood spilled upon the ground, and pizza and limbs strewn about. This is how the Palestinian students learn to glorify the systematized "martyrdom" of good "militants."

Make no mistake about it. Our son Koby was killed by terrorists. We beg you: do not whitewash that fact. Do not justify our son's murder.

And do not jeopardize America's moral fight against terrorism by calling the Palestinians who killed Koby, Yosef, and all the other Jews who have perished at their hands "resistance fighters." No. Call them what they are: cruel, callous, child-killing terrorists. People who have blood on their hands and hate seared into their hearts.

Sara Yoheved Rigler

Children of Death,
Children of Life

*June 1, 2001 — 21 Israelis — mostly teenagers — are killed
when a Palestinian homicide bomber blows himself up on
the seafront promenade near the Dolphinarium disco in Tel
Aviv. The road for the survivors is long and arduous.*

Headlines around the civilized world decry the loss of innocent life at the Dolphinarium disco. But those headlines
are gone by tomorrow, leaving behind another, forgotten
story: the 100 injured victims who survived.

Eighteen-year-old Polena Vallis was at the Dolphinarium that
night. Following is a free translation, from the original Hebrew, of
Polena's account:

> For months I had not gone out because of the pressure of
> high school finals. I had just passed the civics exam and the
> math exam was yet far off. So I deserved to go out and have a
> good time, didn't I? Apparently God thought otherwise. I
> had always known that the ways of God are strange. But this
> night, I understood that the ways of God could also be dan-
> gerous and fatal.

For biography of SARA YOHEVED RIGLER, see p. 28.

As usual, we went to the Dolphinarium disco. On the way, my friend Emma and I joked about the catastrophes that had befallen Israel lately. Jokingly I said that perhaps the stage in the disco would collapse, as had the floor in the Versailles wedding hall disaster. With a giggle, Emma retorted that it wasn't funny.

As we approached the disco, we saw that the line was long.... I looked around in hopes of seeing familiar faces. The chattering and giggling continued. Suddenly a loud and deafening noise shook our eardrums. The boom was followed by the sharp smell of blood and burning. Human flesh flew in all directions. Quickly the floor was covered by blood and bodies.

I felt like I was inside an oven. I have always complained about Israel's hot weather, but even that could not be compared to the heat that surrounded me. From the force of the mighty wave, I fell hard on the ground. When I was able to stand up and flee, I felt that the ground was burning around me. In the midst of it, boys and girls were on fire.

I began to run like a crazy person. Together with my friends, we ran and collapsed together behind a car. I looked at my legs, completely covered with blood. "Oh, it's just blood," I said to myself. "I'll go home and wash it off. It will be okay...."

"Your legs! Your legs! Oh my God!" My friend Toma's screams roused me from my thoughts.

What's she screaming about? I said to myself. *It's just blood.*

But suddenly I saw a gaping hole in my right thigh. I started to shriek like a maniac, until a man came and took me to an ambulance.

All the way to the hospital, I prayed that I would faint and lose consciousness, so I would not have to hear the groans of the girl dying beside me.

I passed the first night in the hospital screaming, worrying, and praying for Emma. They transferred me to the department of plastic surgery where I underwent two operations.

Three days after the bombing, I was shocked to find out that Emma was in critical condition. Two nails which the terrorist had packed into the bomb had lodged in her brain. The doctors removed one nail, but the other they dared not touch. I constantly prayed for Emma's recovery.

Finally God heard my prayers. Emma is here with me now in the rehabilitation unit. Another eight kids are here with us, too. We have all made friends and support each other, all of us joined in the deepest bond of our shared trauma. Often we remember that night, and we speak and cry about the friends who are no longer with us.

I will never forget that night, the night which brought with it deep disappointment in Arabs, who are supposed to be our brothers, but who killed 21 innocent young people. A human being does not do such a thing. We Jews must support each other because terrorism does not distinguish between persons.

✖

Tanya is a petite 17-year-old who looks like a girl I went to Hebrew school with. She was also at the disco that night. Born in South Africa, she and her parents made aliyah from Canada three years ago. I try to focus on her face, but my gaze is repeatedly drawn to three hideous scars on her neck.

"A bullet, a huge bullet," she curls her index finger onto her thumb, making a circle almost one inch in diameter, "went in one side of my neck and out the other side."

"And it missed your carotid artery?" I ask, appalled.

"By microns. The doctor said it was a miracle," Tanya answers. Two other large bullets, which the terrorists pack their bombs with to maximize the fatalities, hit her thin neck. "The doctor said it was like being shot three times in the neck and still being alive. It was a big miracle.

"When the bombing happened, I was praying to God the whole time. I stopped breathing. From the force of the bomb, I literally flew through the air. I landed on my feet. Then I saw blood and body parts everywhere. I fell down and starting screaming. I didn't lose consciousness. I knew that if I closed my eyes, I would never open them again. I just kept praying."

Eerily, several months before the Dolphinarium bombing, Tanya had her right arm tattooed with a leaping dolphin. She wears an eyebrow ring on her pierced right eyebrow.

How has the bombing changed her attitude toward life? Tanya reflects for a few minutes, then replies, "I have a new life now. New things to think about. Life is more precious to me now. I've stopped drinking. I was never a heavy drinker, but now I don't want to lose even one minute to being drunk.

"My parents and I used to fight a lot. Now we don't. Since the bombing, we're a lot closer. We talk more. Of course, my mother still has rules. We used to fight over the smallest thing, like whenever my room was dirty, which it always was. Since the bombing, she doesn't yell anymore. She just says nicely, 'Please clean up your room.' "

As a mother who has yelled at her daughter over a messy room, I wonder what it must be like, every time Tanya's mother looks at her daughter, to see her grotesquely scarred neck, reminding her how close she came to not having a daughter to reprimand.

In 1997, 17-year-old Noam Rozenman was walking down Jerusalem's Ben Yehudah pedestrian mall when a terrorist bomb went off. The force of the bomb propelled him toward a second bomber. The blast perforated both his eardrums and burned his face, arms, legs, and back. When he looked down at his left foot, he saw it facing the opposite direction, hanging by a thread.

Doctors at Hadassah Hospital managed to sew his foot back on. After two months in the hospital, five operations, and many months of crutches and cane, Noam today can walk and run. One eardrum is still perforated and his body is still full of shrapnel splinters, too numerous to be removed surgically. The doctors told him the shrapnel would work its way to the surface, but today, four years after the bombing, he still feels metal under his skin. "It only hurts when it pinches a nerve," remarks Noam offhandedly.

"The injuries are just the beginning," says Noam. "Then it's a whole long saga." The son of a computer scientist, Noam never went back to high school. "For an entire year after the bombing, my life was shadowed by the bomb. I was constantly at the hospital for treatments. I became lazy, got into bad stuff, bummed around. Then there was the guilt factor — the guilt that I survived when five people right next to me were killed."

Noam chose not to enter the army, feeling that he had paid his dues. The decision left him isolated, since all his friends were inducted at the age of 18. "I was a complete outsider. There was a wall between me and my friends in the army."

Overcome by a sense of his own mortality, it took Noam a long time to become motivated toward any long-range goals. Finally, three years after the bombing, Noam earned a high school equivalency diploma. After drifting through several different jobs, Noam has returned to his old love, photography. He is working regularly now as an apprentice to a professional photographer.

As a friend of Noam's mother for 10 years, I cannot help but remember my impression of young Noam before the bombing: a nice ordinary kid, a handsome jock. Now, sitting across from him on the veranda of his parents' Jerusalem home, I am struck by the profundity and extraordinary sensitivity of this young man.

"I am blessed," he claims. "Every morning when I look in the mirror and see my scars, I realize what could have been. I could have been permanently crippled, or dead."

Looking back on how the bombing changed his life, Noam reflects, "I'm a more spiritual person because of it. The bombing brought me closer to God. It made me realize how precious life is. It also made me more sensitive, more aware of other people's suffering."

As we converse, it becomes clear that Noam made a conscious choice to use the bombing to propel himself forward as a human being. "I realized that I could look at the bombing in two ways: 1) I was a healthy, strong kid, and God gave me a bad deal, or 2) I went through all that horror, and I'm alive thanks to God.

"I chose the second way."

I am visiting Tel Aviv's Ichilov Hospital, one month after the Dolphinarium bombing. I am standing beside the bed of 16-year-old Victoria, a pretty brunette with large brown eyes and metal fixtures protruding from her left arm and left leg.

"They are holding my arm and my leg together," she explains.

"Are you in pain?" I ask.

"All the time," Victoria smiles weakly, "except when I have visitors."

Suddenly the atmosphere is shattered by blood-curdling screams. Seventeen-year-old Katya, from the bed across the room, is taking her first steps since the bombing. I turn to see a petite blonde figure bowed over a walker, flanked by her mother and a nurse.

"Just 10 steps to the door and 10 more steps back to your bed," the nurse is saying.

Katya takes a second step and shrieks in pain. I feel like crying, but that would do Victoria no good. With panicked eyes, she watches Katya. I paste a smile on my face and try to distract Victoria. "Have you been up on your legs yet?"

Her large brown eyes riveted on Katya, she shakes her head. "My turn is next."

Two months after the Dolphinarium bombing, three victims remain hospitalized: Victoria, 15-year-old Ziva, who was severely burned, and Alona, who suffered brain damage which wiped out her memory. She does not recognize her parents and cannot speak.

Of those who have been discharged from the hospital, most return regularly for additional operations. Three weeks after being discharged, Polena is back for surgery to remove shrapnel from the sole of her foot, which leaves her in excruciating pain. At the same time, Oksana, who has lost feeling in one hand, is back for an operation to remove nerves from her foot and transfer them to her hand.

In Bat Yam, 10 minutes down the beach from the site of the bombing, I speak with another victim, 18-year-old Faik.

"How nice," I remark, gazing at the magnificent Mediterranean view. "You can go to the beach every day."

Faik, who was severely burned on his arm and stomach, looks at me as if I'm crazy. "We can't go into the ocean at all!" he exclaims. "The salt water would kill us."

Faik's family came to Israel from Khavkaz (Former Soviet Union). While his body is healing, his psyche is not. He is plagued by nightmares and fears — afraid of places with crowds, afraid of every Arab he passes on the street.

Yet the worst part for the "Dolphinarium kids" is the death of their friends. Tanya shows me a photograph of her and her best friend, 16-year-old Liana. "We were going to open a hairdressing salon together." Liana was killed in the bombing.

❧

In the midst of their agonizing recuperation, all of the Dolphinarium victims report a new sense of the preciousness of life.

"There is nothing more important than life," Faik asserts. "I always wanted to be a musician, to go study music in Italy. But it was too expensive, too difficult to make happen. Now I feel that I have only one life, so I must use it to fulfill my dreams. I feel an urgency to fulfill my dreams because you do not know what will be tomorrow."

Although all of the Dolphinarium kids made aliyah, most of them from Russia, not one of them regrets coming to Israel. Nor do any of them consider moving to a "safer country."

Faik, four years in Israel, declares, "I feel more like I belong to the Jewish nation than before the bombing. I feel like we are one people, and together we will overcome this crisis."

Noam, whose family made aliyah from Los Angeles six years before the Ben Yehudah bombing abruptly ended his youth, says: "My suffering is the suffering of the Jewish people. I was chosen to be the body."

The Dolphinarium headlines have come and gone. But for Noam and Faik and Tanya and Emma and Victoria and Katya and Alona and the hundreds of other victims of Arab terrorist bombs, the boom will continue to echo, endlessly, in their bodies and souls.

Let us not forget them.

Ben-Zion Nemett

Remembering
"Shema Yisrael"

August 9, 2001 — 15 Jews are killed and 130 wounded in a homicide bombing at the Sbarro pizzeria on the corner of King George Street and Jaffa Road in the center of Jerusalem.

F riday night, after Shabbat evening services, my daughter and I were discussing the weekly Torah portion. What does the commentator Rashi say at the beginning of the portion? I asked. My daughter Shira (Hebrew for "song") answered me, paraphrasing Rashi. I breathed a contented sigh.

Why would I burden you with such a description? It is such a common sight — that of a father discussing the weekly Torah portion with his child. Except that everything here is new: the person, the time, and the place.

The place: Intensive Care Unit, Shaare Zedek Medical Center, Jerusalem.

The time: 24 hours after the terrorist attack at Sbarro's in Jerusalem.

The person: my daughter. Her body is bruised, battered, and

BEN-ZION NEMETT is a school supervisor in Jerusalem.

broken after a long surgery that bestowed upon her the gift of life. A new Shira, a new song.

Shabbat evening at the recovery room. The color white dominates every corner, so different from the Shabbat white that we are used to. The white of the operating room feels nerve-wracking and threatening, compared to the white of the Shabbat with its soothing aura of splendor and sanctity. Until then, I had no idea there could be such a different significance to the color white, depending on where you are.

Shira is alternately sleeping and awake. She is drowsy from the many painkillers she is being given. At one point she wants to ask me something. I lean down to listen. "Daddy, what about that family that was right in front of us in line for pizza? What happened to them?"

I know who she is talking about. The Schijveschuurder family. Both parents and three of their children were killed. In a choked voice, I tell her that God willing, the Almighty will help them. I thought to protect my child from the bitter news until a later stage. Fortunately, the humming of the machines around her drowns out the emotional storm that encompasses me.

But after several minutes, Shira asks again, "Daddy, how is that family?"

I ask her why she is asking specifically about them.

Shira tells me that when the terrible explosion occurred, the children were seriously injured. They were actually burning. Then one of the small ones cried, "Daddy, Daddy, save me!" And the father yelled back to him, "Don't worry, say with me *Shema Yisrael* — Hear O Israel, the Lord is our God, the Lord is One."

"And suddenly there was quiet, Daddy." She stares at me. "What happened to them?"

And I — whose father was almost the sole survivor of his family destroyed in the Holocaust, I who grew up on the *Shema Yisrael* that Jews said before they were murdered, and know well the spine-chilling stories of Jews led to slaughter, losing their lives at the end of that phrase, "the Lord is One" — now hear from my little girl the same story. The Treblinka death camp and the Sbarro restaurant become one.

Grandfather, granddaughter — and I the father in between. A genetic code — mysterious, painful, deep — connects the holy victims of the Holocaust and those of Sbarro, holy victims whose only sin was to be part of the Jewish people.

Images merge.... The child then and the child now, wanting his father to save him, and the father who knows where they are going and cries to our Father in Heaven, *"Shema Yisrael,"* together with his dying son. *Shema Yisrael*, then and now, from within the flames.

I can hardly choke back the tears. The heart refuses to believe. And I hear Shira's voice bringing me back to the present. "Daddy, I will never forget those voices. Never."

A difficult thought passes through my head. Maybe I myself have forgotten? Maybe I fell asleep while on guard? Maybe my father, because he was there and felt the Holocaust, has always remembered, "In every generation enemies rise up to destroy us." But my friends and I, members of the generation of Israel's revival — could it be that having sensed the light at the end of the tunnel, the vision of peace and humanity at our doorstep, we have not remembered?

The images of flames and smoke, the voices crying out *"Shema Yisrael,"* have been heard by the generations before me, and after me.

Shira, I want you to be able to forget those horrible images. I want you to have peace of mind. But I don't want you to forget the significance of those voices. Because faith from within the flames is refined, pure, unrestrained, firm, and burning.

Yet how can I ask you not to forget when I myself lapsed into forgetfulness and allowed myself to be led astray by illusions of a new Middle East?

When a doctor showed me the preoperation X rays, I saw nails, bolts, and screws from the bomb, intended to increase the magnitude of injuries and deaths. Now they were all in your small body. You had become a veritable hardware store. Materials used by people to build and construct are used by savage murderers to wreak havoc and destruction.

I recognized one of the screws. I recognized it at once. It was mine. (My friends and I used to tease each other, "Hey, you've got a screw loose!") I saw the screw in the X ray and recognized it as the screw that had become loose in my head. The screw that caused me to forget.

Maybe I can prevent the excruciating pain and unbearable suffering from others in my generation. Maybe others could tighten their loose screws in order to better comprehend whom we are dealing with. In the pantheon of horrors that will be remembered for all time, there is a place reserved for those terrorists and their handlers in the east of hell, together with their Nazi predecessors.

"*Shema Yisrael*" is heard, blood flows into blood, and we here in the Land of Israel will continue to raise a generation with a healthy soul and with faith, a generation that can live without fear.

A generation that remembers all.

Rabbi Shalom Schwartz

Intersecting Lives

December 2, 2001 — 15 people are killed by a homicide bomber on an Egged bus in Haifa. One month earlier, two teenagers were killed when a terrorist opened fire at a public bus at the French Hill junction in Jerusalem. The victims of those two tragedies strangely intersect.

I woke up today to the news of another suicide bomber, and I feel that my capacity to bear the pain of any more losses is reaching its limit.

Last week I spent a day with Boris and Alla, the parents of Tanya Boravik, who was killed in Haifa by a mass murderer (suicide bomber sounds too romantic). Their pain is deeper than words can convey, because for them, every parent's unspoken fear has become reality.

Tanya, 23, whose deep eyes belied her youth, was a talented photographer who first came to Israel in 1995 on a program for high school students from the Ukraine. She wrote home about how wonderful life in Israel was. A year later, her parents, brother, and grandmother joined her in her new home.

RABBI SHALOM SCHWARTZ is the founding director of Aish Toronto and the Aish Russian Program. He currently serves as Director of Leadership Development for Aish HaTorah Jerusalem and is executive producer of the documentary film, *Relentless: The Struggle for Peace in Israel.*

At the cemetery, Tanya's father placed a large framed photograph on her grave. My eyes were drawn again and again to hers as the Deputy Defense Minister's words were drowned out by the torrential rains. Speech after speech filled the air, but the words found no hearts. The sense of bewilderment was too profound.

Tanya had participated in the Aish Haifa community, coming for the holidays to be with other students and young families. They, like her, were immigrants still suffering the effects of Russia's 70-year campaign to destroy Jewish life. It was a group of people who knew how to appreciate the opportunity to build a Jewish community tailored to their needs.

For 70 years, Russian Jews had been denied the right to know or practice Judaism. Study of Torah was seen as such a serious ideological threat that even teaching Hebrew was punishable by imprisonment, or worse. Rabbis and leaders were persecuted or killed; schools, synagogues, and all manifestations of Jewish community life were eliminated.

After the funeral, Tanya's father pleaded with me to stay. "Please understand. We are victims of the Soviet war on Judaism. I don't even know how to mourn as a Jew."

I had once attended a Soviet-style mourner's meal in Minsk, but to see it in Israel was much more unsettling. It is painfully tragic that after 70 years of forced assimilation, we have brought Russian Jews home to Israel, but not yet home to their heritage.

That day, after spending time with Tanya's family, I left for Jerusalem. Upon my arrival, I went straight to the memorial service marking the 30-day mourning period for Shoshi Ben Yishai.

Shoshi, born in America, was murdered by a terrorist as she traveled home from school with her friends on Jerusalem's Egged bus #25. That is the bus that travels to my neighborhood. Shoshi was a schoolmate of my daughter Nitza.

I was in the United States when Shoshi was killed. I immediately realized from the first reports that the terrorist had targeted a bus full of girls from my daughter's school. I trembled with fear as I tried to get through the busy phone lines to reach my home. When I finally got through, Nitza answered with a calm and strong voice. "Yes, my friends were on the bus. But we don't know the whole situation yet."

Later, after Shoshi's funeral, Nitza's depth and confidence were remarkable. "I'm okay, Abba," she tried to reassure me. "Are you?"

I reflected on how deeply my daughter lives with an awareness of life and death, seeing them through the prism of Judaism. For her, Torah concepts are not abstractions, but rather, reality, and the concepts found expression naturally in her response to this tragedy.

❦

At the memorial service, Shoshi's parents, together with Shoshi's younger siblings and her 200 schoolmates, listened to eulogies given by rabbis, teachers, and friends.

A 40-page booklet with stories, pictures, and lessons learned from Shoshi's life was distributed. We read how she always had a smile on her face and was the first one to greet a new person or guest. She would sense whenever a friend had a problem and would initiate a conversation to help that person open up, to see how she could help.

The rabbi made a point that rang so true. To mourn the death of a young person is to mourn the loss of potential. The life that could have been lived. I looked at Shoshi's smiling face on the cover of that booklet and saw the joy she could have brought, the family she could have built, the dreams that would have one day been fulfilled.

We are not here to lessen the pain, the rabbi told us. No one can do that and no one should try. The family's pain is real and will not go away for a lifetime. This pain is real and is meant to be felt and learned from.

Shoshi died *al kiddush Hashem*, in sanctification of God's name, killed because she was a Jew. Those who hate Jews and seek to destroy goodness testify to our purpose as a nation. God's covenant with the Jewish people beckons us to teach the world about goodness — and to carry the burden as the target of evil.

In our response to death, we can teach the meaning of life. We tune into the reality of an eternal soul. We understand that the Jewish response to tragedy is *teshuva* — individual and community change. And we have confidence that God is with us in our sorrow as in our joys.

I thought back to my experience at the home of the Russian immigrants, Boris and Alla. I wished they were here. Or that we were there for them.

Tanya, born in Russia, and Shoshi, born in America — the eldest children of two different families, both of them young women whose smiles and personalities had brought light wherever they went.

They never met. But their lives, at this moment, had intersected.

In difficult times, the Jewish family is one. At all times, we need to act more as one family. Jews are being murdered in the streets. How much do we care? What will we do?

Shoshi's family could take comfort in the way their daughter's death had moved her friends to undertake a greater commitment to life. Tanya's family, on the other hand, and hundreds of thousands like them, are painfully lacking the Jewish knowledge, and a sense of Jewish community that could be a source of wisdom and support in these very trying times.

To change in some meaningful way, no matter how small, in the merit of a person who has died, is an affirmation that her soul lives on, eternally benefiting from the positive deeds she continues to inspire.

It is also a response that says: I am not indifferent to suffering. By changing ourselves, we express the belief in God's involvement in our lives, and the belief that everything happens with meaning and purpose. When tragedy touches us, we are called upon to wake up and change the state of affairs within us and around us.

I looked at the list of things undertaken by Shoshi's schoolmates: "I will improve my use of speech." "I will try to greet everyone with a smile." "I will be more sensitive to others and their problems."

I asked myself: *What am I prepared to do? How will I change for the better? What can I undertake that will really make a difference?*

When Natan Sharansky was locked in a KGB prison, his wife Avital was asked, "How can we help?" She responded: "If he were your brother, your son, your husband, you would figure out a way."

I believe that if we would appreciate our shared destiny as Jews, we would begin to reach out to each other differently, to treat each other more as family. For the next 30 days, I am going to work at improving that sensitivity in myself. Those whom I wouldn't normally see as part of my community, I will now try to view as my extended family.

Perhaps, we — you and I — can undertake to be part of Tanya's family and community, by doing something in the merit of the souls of Tanya and Shoshi.

Perhaps the Jewish people can grow closer together.

Perhaps we can find an end to this horrible suffering.

Liba Pearson

"I Am a Jew..."

*February 21, 2002 — Wall Street Journal reporter Daniel
Pearl, in Pakistan to retrace the steps of "shoe bomber"
Richard Reid, is abducted in Karachi on January 23.
Weeks elapse without word of his fate, before a macabre
video confirms his death.*

These days in Israel, I've noticed that cab drivers no longer
say, "Have a nice day" when you get out of the cab. Instead they
say, "Have a quiet day." By that, they mean: "Let's hope no one
dies today." Because it seems that with almost every day comes another horror — two teenagers blown up in a pizza shop, an old man
bludgeoned to death in a soccer stadium, a mother and her devel-
opmentally disabled daughter shot in their home by a terrorist
who will later be proclaimed a hero by people who live a half-
hour's drive from me....

When I saw that Daniel Pearl, the *Wall Street Journal* reporter,
had been killed by his captors, I can't say that I was surprised. But,
still, I had a moment — longer even than usual — where I grieved.

LIBA PEARSON is a writer who grew up in Phoenix, Arizona, and now lives
in Jerusalem.

I read the obituaries: about his joviality, his love of music, his propensity for walking around the newsroom in bare feet. And the reports were now "releasing" the information that Daniel Pearl was Jewish. To us — to Jews — this came as no surprise. His name, his face.... We already knew that. And as silly as it seemed that his captors might not know it themselves, I understood why his family had asked that it not be reported.

Then I read Daniel Pearl's last words: "My father is Jewish.... My mother is Jewish.... I am a Jew."

That was apparently the last thing he uttered before one of his captors stepped up behind him and slit his throat. Then they beheaded him, videotaping the entire grisly spectacle. Those words — they beheaded him — must be said in a whisper. They don't make sense, even to me — and I live in a place where children are killed for eating pizza.

They beheaded him.

Things like that don't happen. The gruesomeness of it, the barbarism....

But that's not what stuck in my head.

He was a Jew and his mother was a Jew.

I don't know what "kind" of Jew Daniel Pearl was — if he went to synagogue regularly or thought about keeping kosher, if he considered himself a member of any particular "stream" of Judaism or not, or if his pretty wife is Jewish, or if he planned on giving the son she is carrying a bris.

And right now it doesn't matter.

This is something that the wicked men who killed him understand, sometimes, much better than we do. Whether he was right or left, whether he was completely assimilated or fervently observant — Daniel Pearl was a Jew.

As I sat reading eulogies, with tears brimming in my eyes, Mordechai's admonition to Esther came into my head: "Do not imagine that you will be able to escape in the king's palace any more than any other Jew."

Just like the old man beaten to death in a soccer field, like the teenagers eating pizza, the mother and daughter.... They all committed the same crime: being a Jew.

I try to comprehend how this happens, how can they do this. But I understand that I cannot understand.

The Torah exhorts us: "Remember what Amalek did to you on the way..." (Deuteronomy 25:17).

The nation of Amalek attacked the Jews as they wearily made their way out of Egypt. Their deeds were most dastardly: They attacked the Jews' rear, where the old and sick and weakest were. Ironically, Amalek's forefather was a grandson of Esav — and therefore not-so-distantly related to the Jews. And yet they attacked just after the miraculous splitting of the Red Sea; they feared neither the Jews nor God.

Why did they do it? Our Sages answer simply: because Amalek was evil.

Remembering what Amalek did to us means remembering that there is such a thing as simple wickedness, and remembering Amalek rebukes the notion that everyone is motivated by some sort of rational self-interest.

Thousands of people were slaughtered as they sat in their offices in the World Trade Center, and there are those who say we must "understand" why those who perpetrated the deed did so.

Evil cannot be simply explained by reason. Evil deserves not to be understood, twisted into some shape that we recognize as rational behavior. Evil deserves only to be eradicated. Our charge to remember Amalek confronts us with that.

We so want to rationalize evil into something we can wrap our intellects around. We want to believe that Hitler had some sort of gruesome Jewish kindergarten teacher and acted out his frustrations on the whole Jewish people. Mordechai set off Haman's dreadful inferiority complex. And maybe the nation of Amalek had appallingly low self-esteem?

No.

Nor can we any better understand the actions of the men who stepped in front of a video camera and murdered Danny Pearl.

"My father is Jewish.... My mother is Jewish.... I am a Jew."

When he said that, they killed him. We know for what he was executed, what crime he committed.

The Torah's discussion of Amalek concludes: "It shall be that when God lets you rest from all your surrounding enemies in the land that God gave you as a heritage to bequeath, you are to erase the memory of Amalek from beneath the heaven. Do not forget."

And, just like the old man in the soccer field, and the mother and daughter, and the kids in the pizza shop, we must never forget what the spirit of Amalek did to Danny Pearl.

And we must never forget that refusing to be cowed by the fear the modern-day Amaleks spread and continuing to live life as a proud, committed Jew — that is the truest victory we can understand.

Sara Yoheved Rigler

A Tale of Two Families

March 2, 2002 — 11 Israelis are killed and 50 injured in a homicide bombing outside a synagogue in Jerusalem where people had gathered for a bar mitzvah celebration. Months later, two Israelis are killed and 28 injured in a homicide bombing at the French Hill intersection.

THE FRANKLINS

Rachel Rosenberg was 15 years old in 1944 when the Nazis shoved her and her parents into a cattle car and deported them to Auschwitz. Dr. Mengele immediately dispatched her parents to the gas chambers, but Rachel, the precious only child born to them after 16 years of marriage, was chosen for life.

Rachel survived. She survived nine months of forced labor in the Birkenau section of the camp. She survived the Death March on which hundreds of prisoners were herded out of Auschwitz in January 1945, and trudged over snow-covered Polish countryside until a bleeding, starved remnant reached Germany. She survived returning to her village, 90 percent of whose Jewish residents had been murdered, and knocking on the door of her family's house, only to be rudely rebuffed by the gentile who had moved in.

For biography of SARA YOHEVED RIGLER, see p. 28.

The petite 16-year-old made her way to Budapest and enrolled in a school for religious girls. In May 1948, Rachel heard a newsboy shouting the headline: "Jewish State Is Declared." She immediately applied to go to Israel because, as she explained more than 50 years later: "They were killing us in Europe. I wanted to raise a family in Israel, where it was safe to be a Jew."

Two years later Rachel married Moshe Yitzhak Herczl. Moshe came from an intensely religious Hungarian family of nine children. Only three of them survived the Holocaust. Moshe came to Israel in 1948 in order to fight in the War of Independence. After their marriage, swept up by Ben Gurion's dream to make the desert bloom, the young couple moved to Tifrach, a tiny settlement in the Negev Desert.

Although a brilliant scholar who would later write a book on Christianity and the Holocaust, Moshe was so enthralled with the new land that he gladly worked building roads and plastering houses. Three daughters were born to them: Tova, named after Rachel's mother; Sarah, named after Moshe's mother; and Miriam, named after one of Moshe's five murdered sisters.

In 1961, the Herczls were sent by the government of Israel to South Africa to teach Hebrew and otherwise serve the Jewish community of Cape Town with Moshe's considerable knowledge of Judaism.

In Cape Town, Sarah Herczl met Avner Franklin. They were married in 1977, and the next year came on aliyah to Israel, settling four years later in the Jewish Quarter of Jerusalem's Old City. Moshe and Rachel Herczl also returned to Israel at this time.

On August 26, 1980, with great elation, Moshe and Rachel celebrated the birth of their first grandchild, a daughter born to Sarah and Avner. Moshe asked that the child not be named after any of the murdered relatives. This was a new generation, far away in time and place from where Jews were killed for being Jews. Sarah and Avner obliged; they named their daughter Michal.

Michal grew up to be an intense, earnest, intelligent, inquisitive, and hard-working girl. She loved music, had a beautiful singing voice, and played the guitar. A sensitive person, she was easily hurt, but never struck back. "Michal never in her life hurt any human being," a lifelong friend testified.

Sarah Franklin devoted herself full-time to her six children, keeping up with the latest research on nursing and nutrition, studying with them, and spending hours talking to her beloved firstborn Michal. The result was a family so mutually loving and close-knit that when Michal enrolled in a religious women's college a 90-minute ride from Jerusalem, she chose to commute from home daily rather than live in the dorms.

Michal applied her own sensitivity to the way she treated other people. During college, she volunteered for Perech, an in-school tutoring project for children with learning disabilities. In order not to embarrass her charges by singling them out, she designated the whole fourth grade class as a "Perech project" and invited whoever wanted to spend private time with her.

On the morning of Wednesday, June 19, 2002, Michal, who was characteristically a slow riser, bounded out of bed and announced to her mother, "Today is going to be a great day." It was her last day of college, having completed a four-year degree in counseling and Jewish history in three years.

It was to be Michal's last day in another way as well.

Late in the afternoon, after her last class, Michal boarded the regular transport which daily took her back to the entrance of Jerusalem. For some reason, she got off the transport and caught a ride with a classmate who was driving to Jerusalem and who offered to drop her off at the French Hill junction.

On the drive home, her friend turned toward the Modi'in Road, a route where several Jews have been killed during the wave of violence. Michal protested. Why take such a dangerous route?

Michal and a friend alighted from the car at the French Hill junction. Having been the scene of two fatal terror attacks in the last year, the intersection is guarded 24 hours a day by two pairs of border policemen, one on each side of the intersection.

Michal called her mother on her cell phone to ask if anyone wanted to pick her up. Avner, who works as a bookkeeper at an accounting firm, had just arrived home, and Sarah was busy preparing a special dinner to celebrate Michal's final day of college. She told Michal to take the bus.

While waiting for her bus, Michal decided to say goodbye to her college friend Hadas Jungreis, who was standing at a bus stop on the other side of the intersection. Michal crossed the street and hugged Hadas, just as an Arab terrorist got out of a car and sprinted past the guards toward the crowd at the bus stop. The guards chased him, but in a flash the bomb exploded.

⬦⬦⬦

Most of us who live in the Jewish Quarter heard the sirens. "It's more than three sirens," my eight-year-old son sagely announced, knowing that three sirens are a tell-tale sign of a terrorist attack.

Sarah and Avner turned on their radio and heard that the suicide bomber had attacked the French Hill junction. Immediately they called Michal's cell phone. There was no answer. This was strange and worrisome, because eminently responsible Michal always called home after every terror attack to assure her family that she was okay.

She must be wounded was the obvious, terrifying conclusion. Avner called the hospital hotlines which, with long, tragic experience, go into action after every terror attack. It was too soon for them to have the names of the injured.

Avner and Sarah decided to split up and each go to a different hospital to search for their beloved daughter. Leaving the celebratory dinner on the kitchen table, Sarah and her good friend Penny raced to Shaare Zedek Hospital. At the emergency information center there, sitting across a desk from a specially trained social worker, they pored over lists of the injured from all four Jerusalem hospitals. Michal's name did not appear.

Then, with rising dread, they combed the waiting areas outside the operating rooms. The terror victims undergoing surgery were a five-year-old girl, her one-year-old brother, and a 15-year-old. (The five-year-old died within minutes.) Meanwhile, the workers cleaning up the scene of the attack had found Michal's two rings amidst the debris and body parts. Avner reported from Hadassah Mount Scopus

Hospital that she was not among the injured there. The circle of possibilities was beginning to close in on them like a dark vise.

Back at the emergency information center, where Sarah's description of Michal had been sent out to all the hospitals, word was received from Hadassah Ein Kerem Hospital that they should come there immediately. They were told to meet two social workers at the entrance to the hospital. Sarah's friend Penny, a nurse, who had been saying all along, "She's probably in shock and can't think to call home," offered no more reassurances. Avner, being driven by a neighbor to Ein Kerem, managed to locate Hadas Jungreis's father. He told them he was on his way to the Abu Kabir Forensic Institute to identify his daughter's body.

When Sarah and Penny arrived at Ein Kerem, two social workers met them at the door of the hospital and ushered them into a carpeted room furnished only with chairs. One of the social workers sat down close to Sarah, looked straight into her eyes, and said, "There is someone who fits your daughter's description, but she is dead."

The words were like a terrorist bomb exploding in Sarah's heart.

The unidentified body was on its way to Abu Kabir, but there was a photograph of the swollen, bloody face. In order to spare Sarah the horror, a social worker showed the photo to Penny. Penny looked, but was unable to identify Michal. Next they showed the photo to Avner, who had by that time arrived. He could not identify his beautiful, gentle Michal from the grotesque photograph.

After every terror attack, the Jerusalem Municipality, with too much experience in such matters, provides a car, a driver, and two social workers to take family members to Abu Kabir to identify the bodies of their loved ones. Sarah and Avner got into the car and rode three-quarters of an hour to Abu Kabir. There, while Sarah waited in a separate room, Avner was taken to the sheet-covered remains. An attendant uncovered half the victim's face, keeping the other half discreetly hidden. Avner stared down at the half visage before him, but he was not able to identify his firstborn daughter.

The only step left, the final clinch before the death's dark vise closed in on them for good, was DNA testing. A technician took blood samples from both Sarah and Avner, to match against blood from the corpse in the next room. The blood matched.

❦

The next morning, my husband returned from prayers weeping. In the 15 years we have been married, I had only once before seen him cry. "What's wrong?" I asked desperately. Between sobs he managed to wrench out the words, "The Franklins' daughter... was... in last night's terror attack."

I screamed in horror and fell into a chair. I held my head and wailed, "Not Sarah! Not Avner!" We had lived upstairs from the Franklins during our first year in the Jewish Quarter. And for years Avner had been the plumber of the neighborhood. Everyone knew him. Everyone loved him. Our kitchen filled with horror and anguished tears.

I had a 9 a.m. class on the weekly Torah portion. At 9:15, I managed to compose myself enough to leave my house. I walked through the Jewish Quarter's narrow lanes oblivious to the tears streaming down my face. When I opened the door to the living room where the class is held, a scene of utter desolation greeted me. The women students were all sitting or standing there crying, and the rabbi sat at the head of the table, his head in his hand.

Two days before, 19 people had been killed in a terrorist bombing of a bus at Pat Junction. The French Hill attack murdered seven more. Jerusalem's single civilian cemetery had a steady succession of funerals; the Franklins had to wait until late that afternoon for their turn to bury their child.

The Jewish Quarter, inside the walls of Old Jerusalem, is often compared to a village, because all the 500 families know each other. That day the whole Jewish Quarter became a scene of shock, devastation, and despair. The grocery store resembled a funeral parlor. People who usually smiled as they scurried past now trudged through the narrow lanes, their shoulders bent, holding back their tears. At the local girls' elementary school, where the Franklins' second daughter attends sixth grade, half of my daughter's eighth grade class voted to cancel their forthcoming graduation ceremony and the musical play they had been rehearsing for weeks. We were a community bereft, horrified, doleful, and frightened.

The unspoken fear in everyone's heart was: Whose child will be next?

At Michal's funeral, hundreds of people crowded outside the small hall at the edge of the cemetery. Our distinguished Rabbi Avigdor Nebenzahl cried throughout his eulogy, four or five times breaking down entirely.

As I stood there, surrounded by my sobbing neighbors, it struck me: Earlier in the day, and throughout the previous day, and hundreds of times in recent months, different communities had stood here and mourned their dead, some families burying two, three, four, or five members. Now it was our turn.

As I stood near young Michal's open grave, framed by the hills of Jerusalem, I saw a scene more wrenching than any other. Rachel Herczl, now 73 and widowed, stood next to her daughter Sarah, her arm on Sarah's back, either to support her grief-stricken daughter or to be supported by her. On the bereft grandmother's bare forearm, stretched across her daughter's hunched back, was a tattooed concentration camp number.

THE NECHMADS

Eliyahu and Rachel Shrem owned a jewelry store in the Syrian town of Halib, where their family had lived for centuries. After the State of Israel was declared in 1948, Syria's tens of thousands of Jews suddenly became identified with the "Zionist enemy." Anti-Jewish pogroms broke out all over Syria, burning ancient synagogues and murdering Jews. At the same time, emigration to the new Jewish state was declared a capital crime.

The rule of law no longer protected Syria's Jews. Arab customers would enter Eliyahu's jewelry store, try on expensive necklaces and bracelets, and then simply walk out with them. Eliyahu's desperate calls to the police were futile.

The pogroms were still raging in 1952 when, with Rachel nine months pregnant, the Shrems decided they could bear no more. They determined to escape to the Jewish homeland with their four children. One night the family surreptitiously left their ancestral home with whatever they could carry on their backs, and on foot crossed the mountains, heading toward Lebanon. When they reached the Lebanese coast, they bought a small boat and sailed it south, toward Israel. During the two-day boat journey, Rachel gave birth to their fifth child. They landed on the Israeli coast and settled in the town of Rishon L'Tzion.

A decade later, their daughter Sarah married Saul Cohen, a glassblower. In 1964, their daughter Daliah was born. While the family was religiously traditional, Daliah decided during high school that she wanted to become fully observant. After high school, she became a kindergarten teacher.

In 1984, Saul had a heart attack. While attending to her father in the hospital, Daliah met Ezra Nechmad, whose aunt was also in the coronary unit. Ezra's parents, Eliyahu and Hanna Nechmad, had made aliyah from Turkey in 1952. They came not to escape anti-Semitism, which was not a problem in Turkey, but rather, as Hanna would later explain, because of the holiness of the Land of Israel.

Daliah and Ezra married later that year and settled close to their families in Rishon L'Tzion. A year later their first child was born. They named him Eliyahu, the same name as the great-grandfather who had braved all to bring his family to the safety of Israel, and called him Eli for short. Ezra worked as a cab driver and Daliah stayed home with the children, who eventually numbered five.

Eli grew up to be an earnest, hard-working student. In yeshiva, the study of Talmud was difficult for him, so he tackled it with zeal and perseverance. At night when everyone else went to sleep, Eli stayed up to study. He strived for perfection; any mark less than 100 on a test left him dissatisfied.

On the first Shabbat in March 2002, the Nechmads came to Jerusalem to celebrate the bar mitzvah of Ezra's nephew. The sun had already set on Saturday night, and the family was congregated outside the synagogue at the conclusion of the evening service, when an Arab terrorist sprinted into the crowd and blew himself up. Daliah and Ezra's 15-year-old son Saul was killed immediately, along with his uncle, aunt, and four cousins. The bomb ripped off the hands of two other relatives.

Eli's left hand was blown off and he was critically injured. He was raced to Hadassah Hospital at Mount Scopus, where he was operated on, the first of seven operations. A week later, when a devastated Daliah and Ezra got up from sitting shiva, the seven-day mourning period, for Saul, they immediately went to Eli's bedside in the Intensive Care Unit. Eli, aged 16, was still unconscious. When the doctor apprised Ezra of the results of that day's operation, Ezra stood in the corridor and cried.

Eli remained in a coma for three and a half months. Every morning Daliah would make the hour and a half trip from Rishon L'Tzion to Jerusalem and stand the entire day by the bedside of her firstborn, talking to him, stroking his hair, massaging his three remaining limbs.

On the night of June 19, Eli died. It was the same night that Michal Franklin was killed.

Two families came to the fledging Jewish state, one escaping the blood-soaked continent of Europe, the other fleeing the Arab pogroms of the Middle East.

A half-century later, in the Land of Israel, they buried their murdered children on the same day.

As for us, the Jews of Israel:

Our hearts are broken, but not our resolve.

We are traumatized, but not daunted.

We fear for the survival of our children, but not for the survival of our people.

Before God, we submit and surrender.

Before our enemies, we are staunch and unyielding.

Ari Shavit, a prominent, left-wing Israeli columnist, describes the despair which has gripped Israel: "There is this feeling, 'We tried politics, we tried the army, we tried everything. What's left?' "

The Torah says that the Jews suffered slavery in Egypt for 210 years, but only when they cried out in anguish to God were they redeemed.

We can all still cry out to God.

Liba Pearson

At One in the Fire

*March 9, 2002 — 11 Israelis are killed and 54 injured
when a homicide bomber explodes in the crowded Moment
Café in the Rechavia neighborhood of Jerusalem. The terror proceeds with numbing frequency and intensity: In the
first nine days of March, 50 Israelis are murdered in 13
separate attacks.*

*I*can't work.
I have a job, and the way Israel's economy is these days, that
should be enough of a blessing.

I have a pile of things to do on my desk and the privilege of
working for an organization in whose mission I believe, and I believe that the work I do is important.

But I can't work.

On my office wall is a picture of my nephew in the United
States and a picture of my parents, smiling. My brother and his
wife sit near the Liberty Bell, happily sharing the moment.

But I barely see them in front of me.

All I see, in my mind's eye, is a woman shrieking as she turns to
see her two-year-old daughter, in her stroller, engulfed in flames.
She reaches to pull her daughter out of the fire — but can't because

For biography of LIBA PEARSON, see p. 51.

the explosion that has sheathed the carriage in flames has blown off her own arm below the elbow. She can't pull her daughter out of the burning carriage because she no longer has two hands.

Then it goes dark.

She awakens to her husband sitting beside her hospital bed, and sees immediately, from his jacket torn in mourning, what has happened.

It happened last Saturday night, when a demon blew himself up outside a synagogue here in Jerusalem.

I can't work.

My office mates are mostly Israeli and they know I don't always deal well with the *matzav* — "the situation," as it's called. When bombs go off and lives are blown apart, they come into my office to check on me.

"Are you okay?" they ask, concerned, their eyes searching mine to see if I am or am not responding.

Today I arrived late, shell-shocked, having woken up to the news of the mass slaughter at the Moment Café, just a few minutes' walk from my office in Jerusalem. At least I arrived. A secretary in my office is at home — she was at the café and narrowly missed the blast when she returned to her car to get something. Her friends weren't so lucky.

March is only 10 days old, but already it has assailed us with 13 separate murderous attacks, including restaurant shootings in Tel Aviv, a grenade attack on the beach in Netanya, and 10 Israelis picked off, one by one, by a sniper at a roadblock about 40 minutes north of Jerusalem.

And by a twisted miracle, only one Israeli — only one — killed by a bus explosion in Afula.

It's a blessing these days when "only" one life, one world, one family, is blown apart. Thank God, they only got one.

And so I walked in without my customary bright smile, blinking hard. The receptionist looked up and said, "You heard the news?" I nodded. A secretary put her arm around me and followed me to my office, saying gently, "You're too sensitive to live here, you know."

Sensitivity. It's something to be prized today.

We are all worn numb, worn raw, worn into rage.

My friends in the States ask me how I deal with it, how we — Israelis — deal with this constant killing that lurks around every corner, flaring up in periodic, spectacular displays of just how evil man can be.

There is no answer. No answer for how Israelis deal with it, or how we feel — because each of us responds differently. And there is no answer because I myself respond differently to each and every attack.

Last week when the lives of five 18-year-olds were cut suddenly and violently short, I felt that I couldn't breathe. It's as if my skin was covered in blisters of fury and grief, and each time I moved, they split open and bled.

Yet last night at the café, when another 11 lives were taken from those to whom they had belonged, and from their families and all who loved them, I felt deeply ashamed, because this time, after the initial shock, I felt nothing. It was as if my skin had been shellacked over. I was impenetrable.

My Canadian roommate gets silent and withdrawn. She is far more consistent than I, I who can sometimes pretend I am Israeli by birth and stoically lock away my thoughts, but who then at other times spend half a workday behind a closed door, weeping intermittently.

The radio used to play only soft, sad music after terror attacks, but they stopped doing that months ago. I suppose they had to change that policy because otherwise, we might have never heard happy music again.

Sometimes I wonder: If I allow myself to feel all the time — if I didn't work to bottle down what I'm feeling now — would I ever be able to feel happy again? I am so scared of both possibilities: Scared that if I let myself feel, I'll never stop crying. Scared that if I don't let myself feel, I might stop feeling altogether.

Another friend, also more consistent than I, reacts by raging: He rages at policies, at various sectors of Israeli society, at the sick irony of a "peace march" which took place at precisely the same moment that a suddenly one-armed mother couldn't snatch her child away from — the one time this cliché is actually appropriate — the fiery jaws of death.

But we all agree that to be scared would be granting victory to them, to those who blow themselves up setting two-year-olds on fire, and to those who celebrate them as heroes. But more so, I say, insistently, that they're doing us a sick, perverted, but necessary favor.

There is no difference to the people who blow themselves up. We are all the enemy, whether we wear uniforms or not. Whether we wear yarmulkes or not. Whether we vote left or right.

When this war began, the country was painfully divided along those lines. Public discourse was strident and painful; our divisions more clear to us than our unity.

But scores of Jewish lives later, our own vision has been cleared by the hatred of those who seek to drive us from here; we see that we are indeed, one.

The Jewish state was founded as a refuge, to provide a guardian entity that could use the powers of a state to protect Jews from those who seek to annihilate or otherwise harm us — wherever we are. Be it in Ethiopia or Entebbe, the armed forces and political power of the Jewish nation would be there to protect us.

The armies who oppose us are clear. Read their newspapers or watch their TV: they seek to destroy the Jewish nation not by conventional warfare, but by breaking it down slowly from the inside, by making mothers afraid to take their children out to play, by making young couples afraid to go to the movies, teenagers afraid to go out to get a slice of pizza.

Ultimately, what they seek to destroy is much more than our bodies: it is our spirit.

It is in this that they are most mistaken. Is there anything so indomitable as the Jewish spirit?

The Torah instructs: "Let not your heart become soft, do not fear, do not panic, and do not tremble before [your enemies]" (Deuteronomy 20:3).

The Torah is speaking to soldiers, but the aims of the "militants" have put the entire Jewish nation on the front line.

The more horror and hatred heaped upon us, the more resolute we become. The more clear we are about what we are facing. The more we understand our interconnectedness, the unity of the

Israeli nation and of the Jewish people that goes beyond its borders.

We may be a fractured people, but through all the blood and anguish and confusion, all of this makes one thing utterly clear: We are one. We may be battered practically into insentience, and we may simultaneously be hurting beyond what anyone could imagine. And I may not be able to work. But this we know: We are one people.

And we are not going anywhere.

Anna Yakobovitch

Survivors in Netanya

March 27, 2002 — Per capita population, no Israeli city has been hit harder than Netanya, which has suffered five suicide attacks. The carnage reaches an apex as 30 Jews are killed and 140 injured in a homicide bombing at the Park Hotel, in the midst of the Passover Seder.

The Ben Aroya family had gathered at the Park Hotel to enjoy the Passover Seder. Their family table was in the middle of the room. It took the brunt of the explosion. Shimon Ben Aroya was killed outright. His wife, Corinne, was blown off her feet as a shower of nails and ball bearings punctured her body. One piece entered to the right of her nose, and today remains lodged in the back of her head. Another entered her chest and is embedded in her back. A third broke her ribs. Others peppered her arm and body.

Their nine-year-old son, Elad, needed plastic surgery on his back. Their 13-year-old daughter, Hilla, suffered shrapnel entries to her neck and colon. As for their eldest daughter, 20-year-old Sherry, a nail entered her right eye and exited through the left side of her brain. She is struggling to regain her speech faculties and the use of her legs and lower body.

ANNA YAKOBOVITCH made aliyah at age 70 to be closer to her grandchildren.

The grandparents (Corinne's parents) were also seriously injured. The grandfather has undergone three eye operations. The grandmother was blasted with shrapnel which left her with a damaged colon.

And the list goes on. Corinne's brother had a metal piece break his jaw. His seven-year-old daughter, Ravid, suffered back injuries. His five-year-old son, Gavriel, is still in the hospital with serious injuries to his head and main arteries.

The life of this extended family now revolves around trips to doctors, hospitals, physical therapists, psychologists — and to the fresh grave of their beloved father, Shimon.

⨯

Anna is a pretty, 24-year-old recent immigrant from the Ukraine. She is married and has two small children. Things were always tough financially for this young family since their arrival in Israel. Anna's husband worked in a poorly paid menial job, and she traveled daily to Ra'anana to work in a supermarket storeroom. Though the wages were low, Anna enjoyed her work and the atmosphere.

To supplement their income, Anna also found work as a part-time waitress. She was pleased to have been given a job for Passover in the Park Hotel in Netanya.

As she prepared to serve the guests at the Seder that night, another waitress remarked that a strange-looking man had entered the hall. Anna looked up just as the man detonated his explosive belt.

Anna was unconscious for three days. Surgeons removed three shards of glass from her stomach, and another from her chest. They reconstructed her nose and removed nails from her body, including her right eye.

Anna, now with a glass eye, is determined to get on with her life. Despite her disabilities, she continues to care for her family and is holding her job in Ra'anana on a part-time basis. But Anna is uncertain whether her children will be allowed back into their kindergarten next month; she still owes for all the months when she was hospitalized from the terror attack.

❦

Victoria immigrated to Israel with her husband, Arkady, and their one-year-old daughter, Shulamit, from the Ukraine 12 years ago. They looked forward to establishing a fresh life in the Jewish state. Arkady's parents joined them a year later. Now age 13, Shulamit has a six-year-old sister, Rinat. Victoria works as a nurse.

Arkady worked as a chef in the Park Hotel and escaped with his life from the Passover massacre that hit that fateful Seder night.

But a few weeks later, the angel of death was waiting again for Arkady when another homicide bomber carried out his mission in the local market. Arkady, while buying groceries for his family, was blown up by a member of Hamas.

The family — together with Arkady's parents — lives in a cramped two-bedroom apartment in a poor section of Netanya. They made the best of their lives — until the terrible events of May 19, 2002. Victoria stoically tries to get on with her life, mainly for the sake of her two young girls.

Arkady's parents, however, are mourning their son — and blaming his death on Victoria, who had asked Arkady to go to the market. So she, in the grieving minds of her in-laws, has replaced the bomber as the source of blame for their son's death.

The tension in the small household has become unbearable. Victoria has been forced to find a place where she and her daughters can find some peace of mind. But she cannot afford to move. She is stuck.

❦

May 18, 2002, was a special day for Liliane — her 64th birthday. She decided to head for Netanya's Kanion Shopping Mall to buy herself a bunch of flowers. At the entrance to the mall she came face-to-face with a terrorist. She instantly had a feeling of dread and fear. It lasted for one moment, milliseconds before the huge explosion.

Over 70 pieces of shrapnel, and parts of the terrorist's bones, ripped through Liliane's body. Someone dragged her to the sidewalk and wrapped her burning body. That probably saved her life.

She screamed all the way to hospital and wanted to die. Instead, a team of surgeons removed the pieces of bone and metal from her body and, in a series of operations, brought her back to her family.

Now Liliane must walk with a heavy metal walking stick. She needs additional operations, more than a year after the bombing.

Each May 18, Liliane celebrates a double birthday. One for the day she was born, and one for the day she escaped death.

Stories from the Netanya Terror Victims Fund (www.ntvf.8m.com).

Tova Lebovits

Shiri, My Song

June 18, 2002 — 19 people are killed and 74 injured when a homicide bomber destroys Egged bus #32A traveling from Gilo to the center of Jerusalem.

We arrived at Har HaMenuchot (Mountain of Rest) cemetery, our hearts heavy with grief. *Our beloved Shiri!* our thoughts screamed.

Nestled in the majestic hills of Jerusalem, we saw neat rows of rectangular headstones stretching endlessly below. They looked like a miniature city made of stone. In the distance stood a group of apartment buildings, made of the same beige Jerusalem stone. For a moment it looked as if the headstones were a mirrored reflection of those tall buildings. An eerie city of the dead below, reflecting the city of the living above.

The past few days, we kept hearing warnings of a suicide bomber that had entered the city. Jerusalem was on high alert, leaving each of us to deal with our feelings of dread and apprehension. *Whose time was up now?* we wondered. "Keep safe," we told each other as we went about our daily lives.

In the morning, when I learned that the bus of death had

TOVA LEBOVITS was born in Israel, grew up in the United States, and now lives in Jerusalem. She studied communications and journalism at Hebrew University in Jerusalem.

started out from Gilo, the first thought that came to mind was Shiri. I calmed myself, reasoning that it was highly unlikely that the only person I knew from Gilo would be on that bus. What were the odds?

As news came in of the terrible carnage, I grew restless and called my daughter Sarah, Shiri's friend. There was no answer. Around noon, I heard Sarah's choked voice on the phone. "No!" I cried out. "Not Shiri! Please tell me it isn't Shiri!"

We both sobbed in piercing pain and disbelief.

The first thing anyone noticed about Shiri was her long, thick, blond braid reaching her waist, adorning her beautiful, lively face. Her disarming smile, her kind and intelligent eyes, and her delicate, lovely frame belied her inner strength.

Over a year ago, after serving in the army as a teacher who prepared soldiers for their high school matriculation exams, she told her family and friends that she was going on a trip to South America for a year on her own. The reaction was one of misgiving. How would such an innocent girl fare in the big wide world on her own? Who would watch over her? Though she had shown maturity, responsibility, and caring beyond her years, she was still Shiri, the beautiful girl with the longest hair, who looked more like a teenager than a young woman of 20.

Shiri proved these concerns misplaced. She visited far-flung places, absorbing the culture, and lovingly connecting with those around her. She sent home exciting, insightful e-mails, keeping people breathless for more, and signing them, "Shiri, world traveler."

When the year was up, realizing how Shiri was blossoming, her mother told her there was no rush in coming back home. After all, times were stressful in Israel, and a little more enjoyment couldn't hurt. But Shiri missed home. She returned right before Passover and fell right into shouldering the pre-holiday chores without skipping a beat. She reunited with her friends, tended the garden, painted her room, and planned to go to dental school — all with the enthusiasm, joy, and love that so characterized her.

Sarah, my daughter, met up with Shiri several weeks ago and was so happy to reconnect with her. Just this past Shabbat, Sarah spoke about Shiri with such warmth. "Of all the girls from our high school, there's no one as special as Shiri," she said. "Her goodness, her caring, her intelligence, and her sense of humor is unmatched. I'm so lucky to be her friend."

I'm told that Shiri once playfully contemplated her slight "obsession" about her refusal to cut her hair since birth. It was a curious anomaly in this day and age. She wondered what this meant about herself, and what it symbolized, if anything.

Some years back, when she visited a concentration camp in Poland with her high school class, one of the exhibits had a display of human hair. One of the girls pointed to a long, blond, thick braid, just like Shiri's. They always thought of her as the girl with the longest hair... yet here in the concentration camp she had met her match.

A strange thought struck Shiri. Perhaps her obsession was somehow connected to the terrible tragedy that befell her people and family in the Holocaust? Maybe in some strange, symbolic way, she was connecting with those innocent girls with the long braids, whose young lives were cut down so brutally.

Yesterday, as hundreds of weeping people followed "Shiri, world traveler" on her last journey, to her eternal resting place in the Jerusalem hills, we asked how this could have happened to one so pure and young.

It was, it seems, the same question Shiri had asked when she visited Poland.

Dr. Avraham Rivkind

Awaiting the Wounded

June 19, 2002 — eight Jews are killed and 50 injured when
a homicide bomber blows himself up at a crowded bus stop
at the French Hill intersection in Jerusalem.

When a human bomb goes off in Jerusalem, I know within seconds. I wear two beepers and a cell phone, even to bed. Driving my own car, I can nearly always beat the first ambulances to the hospital, even if I'm asleep when the first call comes.

The sirens blare as ambulance after ambulance pulls up in front of the main square of Hadassah Hospital. I wait outside, with dread in my heart. As the doors swing open, my greatest fear is that one of my own four children or my next-door neighbor's will be lying there among the terror victims, so many of whom are only kids.

Our enemies choose their targets to maim our youngsters. They strike at pizza parlors, school buses, frozen-yogurt kiosks. The medics make their own quick decisions in the field: The worst patients are brought to Hadassah Hospital, the only level-one trauma center from the Jordan Valley to Beersheba. I'm in charge of that unit.

PROF. AVRAHAM RIVKIND, M.D., is head of the Department of Surgery at Hadassah (Ein Kerem) Hospital in Jerusalem.

My first job is triage, instantly evaluating which treatment each patient is to receive: being hurried onto the trauma table with a dozen top medical experts surrounding him, wheeled away to surgery, or brought to the regular emergency room for care.

I listen to the reports of medics, I look at the patients, and I touch them.

My medical training in Israel and the United States, years of experience, intuition, and help from the Almighty — something we're not embarrassed to talk about in Jerusalem — help me make these life and death decisions.

The medical challenges are daunting. Victims with blast injuries can seem perfect on the outside but may be burning up inside. A few days ago, I kneeled over a beautiful young woman named Shiri Nagari in the hospital parking lot. I asked her how she was feeling, and she answered that she was okay. But I sensed that something was wrong.

She was slowing down. I ordered immediate intubation to create an airway. Some of my colleagues thought we needed to spend time on the patients with more visible wounds. But her chest X ray confirmed my hunch: a white butterfly on the black background.

Shiri's lungs had exploded.

The same loud wave of air that smashes your eardrums can compress the air in your lungs and send it to destroy the organs in your abdominal cavity. Three concussive waves do lethal damage when a bomb explodes in an enclosed area.

We rushed Shiri to our trauma operating room, always left empty for emergencies, and opened her up: blood in her chest and abdomen, a liver torn apart. No matter how much blood we pumped in, she couldn't survive.

I'm 52, and like most Israelis I serve in the army, too. I have seen my share of tank injuries, unrelenting cancers, and traffic accidents.

Shiri's death was the first time I ever cried at losing a patient.

I dread telling the patient's parents, but that is also part of my job. Even less dire pronouncements are tough. Recently, after a terrorist attack in the open-air market in Jerusalem, I had to inform a victim's wife that we had amputated his leg. His wife flew into a rage. That's an anger I'm familiar with. I'm always coping with my own anger that we can't pull off a miracle for each patient.

Concussive injuries are only part of the damage caused by urban bombings. We have been treating damage to the brain, lungs, bones, and heart caused by nails, bolts, and ball bearings packed into the high-velocity bombs.

Adi Hudja, only 14, had more than 40 metal objects in her legs from the suicide bombings on Ben Yehudah Street last December. She was bleeding uncontrollably from her wounds. On the spot, we came up with the idea of trying a coagulant for hemophiliacs still not approved by the U.S. Food and Drug Administration, certainly not approved for trauma. It costs $10,000 for a small bottle, but it worked.

Six months later, she's coming for therapy three times a week in Hadassah's Mount Scopus Rehab Center, and she's learning to walk. Next year, maybe she'll be able to go back to school. She's the same age as one of my daughters.

⎛⎝∞⎠⎞

No matter the sophistication of medical care, speed counts. Most of the thousands of procedures we surgeons in my department do each year are elective, but trauma is different. Our chief trauma nurse, Etti Ben Yaakov, always talks about the "golden hour" we have to save our patients' lives.

The clock is ticking from the obscene sound of the blast. In the trauma center, I am assisted by a remarkable team of doctors, nurses, and technicians. Suicide-blast victims almost all need multidisciplinary care.

We need to figure out who's going first: the neurosurgeon, the vascular surgeon, the general surgeon, the orthopedic surgeon, the facial surgeon? Even in the middle of the night, doctors and nurses and technicians and cleaning staff arrive at the hospital without even being called.

Who will do the anesthesia? Hands fly up: Our entire operating room staff is ready for an unscheduled shift.

Every decision I make is informed by my core belief that every patient wants to live. Sometimes this credo forces me to try so-called heroic surgery when everything seems lost.

In October 2000, Shimon Ohana, an 18-year-old border police officer, was declared dead in the field. But I asked the ambulance driver to bring him to the hospital. Some decisions are hard to make in the field. I uncovered him, we opened his chest cavity and began to work. He came back to life but remained in a coma for 17 days.

At last, he woke up.

Today, he is a fully functioning young man who trains dogs and loves computers. He lives in Beersheba, but he often comes to Hadassah Hospital for follow-up care or to encourage our other patients. I can't resist hugging him: He's my continued reminder that we can't give up hope.

The lines of ambulances, inevitably, bring a fair percentage of Arab patients. We can't tell whether they are perpetrators or victims. Even if we could, it wouldn't matter: Everyone who enters the Hadassah Hospital courtyard is treated equally.

And yes, I have operated on terrorists. Once, I was awakened at 2 a.m. on Shabbat to do emergency surgery on a terrorist who had been injured while he was being apprehended. I had seen the grisly results of his bus bombings.

More than any other question, friends and visitors and even patients want to know how I feel using my medical training to save the lives of these mass murderers.

Because I'm a doctor, a believing Jew, a human being, I would never allow a patient to die whom I could save. But this saving of life is more than my medical requirements: It's a mission. By fixing the holes in their chests and bellies, I'm making a statement that I'm not like those forces of darkness that want to engulf this country in blood.

Do they understand? I haven't the slightest doubt that they do. They thank me. They look at me differently. My people and I are no longer the demons of their ugly propaganda. And they suddenly comprehend what the American women of Hadassah who established our hospital and most of the hospitals and clinics in this land with no regard for race or creed understood 90 years ago.

The Hadassah motto is taken from the prophet Jeremiah who cried for the "healing of my people." Indeed, the healing of all peoples is the only way to rescue the future of our troubled region.

Liba Pearson

Why I Am Not Afraid

July 31, 2002 — Nine people are killed, including five Americans, and 85 injured when a bomb explodes in the Frank Sinatra student center cafeteria on Hebrew University's Mount Scopus campus.

I am standing in line in a grocery store in Jerusalem when my cell phone rings. I look at the display and answer when I see that it is a call from overseas.

It is my former roommate, married just about a month, calling from her honeymoon in Canada. She is sobbing.

And I immediately know why.

The Hebrew University bombing.

The terrorist worked as a painter for a contractor employed by the university. He chose the cafeteria, apparently because it is a favorite of foreign students and not generally by Arab students. And he knew that lunchtime is its busiest hour, when it is stuffed full.

On the day of the attack, the terrorist hid the bomb in the building where he was working. At lunchtime, he casually wandered into the bustling cafeteria, chose a central table, left his package covered with a newspaper, and left the building. Then he detonated the bomb with a cell phone.

For biography of LIBA PEARSON, see p. 51.

During the three weeks it took to arrest him, the terrorist returned to the campus several times. He even painted the building he bombed. In Israel, we clean up the mayhem as soon as we can — it helps us return to normal life. Such as it is.

What on earth, I cannot help but wonder, was he thinking when he returned? Did he smile as he soothed the scorched surface with the antiseptic white paint? Did he have to stifle a laugh? Did anyone notice?

While he painted, the injured were in the hospital fighting for their lives.

I listen to my friend's crying, aware that the people around me are listening, aware that they are — somehow — hoping that I will have something to say to her, to comfort her, because they also need to hear it. We all do.

Through her tears, she tells me that a friend of hers (also a newlywed) who survived the blast has just learned that she will have to wear a special — painful — bodysuit day and night for the next year or two. The pressurized suit will help her skin heal from the massive burns and other trauma she suffered. This woman is fighting bravely to recover — a luxury not afforded to two friends with whom she was sitting, who were killed.

And I think of the others at home recovering from shock, the others who are beginning to face life without an arm or a leg or both, injuries that will vastly affect every day of the rest of their lives. All of them will carry on their bodies the physical scars that the terrorists are trying to inflict on an entire nation.

And that is why I refuse to be scared.

Earlier in the day, a colleague of mine had expressed dismay that I still go to the *shuk*, the Ben Yehudah open-air market — the site of several terrorist attacks. My concerned colleague was expressing a certain reality we all face: There are people — a lot of them — who are quite good at killing and maiming Jews in Israel. And they like to find places — such as an open-air market, such as a university's dining hall — that are crowded with civilians. More blood for their bang, in essence.

The Israeli security forces, and average Israelis, have brought about miracle after miracle. They have stopped attackers in their tracks through elaborate intelligence operations, or by simply snatching wires out of bombs that are about to explode. But even if we thwart 90 percent of the would-be killers, it only takes one bomber to slip through and inflict mass carnage.

This is what we live with.

But we also live with this: that the actual deaths and maimings are merely a means to end.

Yes, the streets in Nablus and Ramallah predictably fill with dancing after each attack, and today, Hizbullah's leader, Sheik Nasrallah, called for the "rivers of blood" to continue. (Ironic, isn't it, that *hizbullah* means "party of God." God must find that really irritating.)

But I don't think they rejoice over spilling our blood nearly as much as they rejoice over the fear they put in our hearts.

Do they want us dead? Yes, undoubtedly. But they know they're not going to kill all 5 million of us. What they can do, in the space of a year or two, is to traumatize our entire nation by slaughtering hundreds of us, and by mutilating thousands more. That's why it's called "terror." The killing is secondary: They want us to feel fear.

They want to make us prisoners in our own home. (And by "home," I mean not just our houses or apartments, but Israel: our Home.)

They want our American relatives and friends to be afraid to visit.

When my roommate got married, in addition to picking out her wedding dress and the menu, she had to consider which wedding hall offered the best security. After all, they've been targeting bat mitzvahs and bachelorette parties.

Do we recognize the world we live in?

But weeping and mourning do not have to make me fearful; weeping and mourning don't have to make me want to leave my home. If anything, it makes me more resolute than ever. I may loathe Israel's semisocialist infrastructure, knotted with bureaucracy and waste, and the economy may be in shambles. (The terrorists did that, too, by knocking out the tourism industry and much hi-tech investment.) Furthermore, I am a proud American —

proud to come from the nation I believe to be the most free, the most efficient, and perhaps the most just country in the world.

But Israel is my country.

Every time a bomb goes off and I remain, I feel an increasing pride — the privilege of being here.

I am reminded of the words of Marla Bennet, a 24-year-old American killed in the Hebrew University blast. I knew her barely, only in passing. But her grace and gentle smile had left an impression on me. A few months before her murder, this is what she wrote to friends and family back in San Diego:

> Here in Jerusalem I've found a community of seekers: people who, like me, want to try living in another country, who want to know more about Judaism; people who are trying to figure out exactly what they want their lives to look like. The air is charged with our debates and discussions as we try to assimilate into our lives all that we've learned. Life here is magical.
>
> But I also feel energized by the opportunity to support Israel during a difficult period. This is undoubtedly an important historic moment for both Israel and for the Jewish people. I have the privilege of reporting to my friends and family in the United States about the realities of living in Israel at this time, and I also have the honor of being an American choosing to remain in Israel, and assist, however minimally, in Israel's triumph.
>
> My friends and family in San Diego are right when they call and ask me to come home, since it is dangerous here. I appreciate their concern. But there is nowhere else in the world I would rather be right now. I have a front-row seat for the history of the Jewish people. I am a part of the struggle for Israel's survival.

We all know what Marla meant.

I used to work in Jerusalem's Old City. My commute included walking alongside those famous walls through Jaffa Gate. And many mornings, the commute moved me to tears. "What on earth did I do to deserve this?" I would marvel silently. For 100 generations, Jews have longed for Zion and yearned to glimpse Jerusalem. Some of the greatest Jews who ever lived only dreamed of the privilege of being buried in the Land of Israel! And me? I get to live here. And live I will.

Today, I got an e-mail from an Israeli friend saying that he is organizing a "sit-in" of sorts. In the nearly abandoned restaurant districts, large numbers of people are going to go sit in coffee houses.

This is the pioneering spirit reimagined for the new millennium. Where brave souls once drained swamps and cleared fields, we now sit in cafés. And in the war of terror, cafés are the front lines.

I realize this is nothing new. The Haggadah tells us: "In every age, they have risen against us to annihilate us. But in every generation God saves us from their hands."

"Do you really want to go to the *shuk*?" my colleague had asked me.

As I walk out of the grocery store, I think of a passage from Psalms: "O God, fight my adversaries, battle those who do battle with me. Take hold of shield and armor and rise up in my defense. And draw the spear, and bar the way before my pursuers; say to my soul, 'I am your salvation.' "

And I think of Marla Bennett's words.

In the meantime, yes, I'm going to the *shuk*.

Marla Bennett quotes used with kind permission of her family.

Vadim Sirotnikov

Tears on Gray Cement

March 5, 2003 — Two months of relative calm is shattered by a gruesome homicide bombing on a Haifa bus.

Elizabeth Katzman was born in the USSR 17 years ago. She immigrated to Israel at age five. Her Hebrew was fluent, her accent untraceable. She had snow white skin, pink cheeks, and coal black hair. Liz, as her friends called her, was affectionately known as Snow White.

I didn't know Liz very well, but there was hardly anyone in our high school in Haifa who didn't know her name or didn't recognize her face. Always well mannered and hospitable, when passing me by, she would smile, say hi, and call me by my first name even though we were hardly acquainted.

Liz studied theater and media and was known for her talents. She hosted and coedited the school's show on local television. In three weeks, she was scheduled to star in the school's theatrical production, "Best of Friends." Rehearsals were going well.

Last Wednesday, after school, Liz and her best friend went downtown to do some shopping and check on costumes for the

VADIM SIROTNIKOV was born in Ukraine, made aliyah at age six, and has lived in Haifa ever since. He was the editor, designer, and founder of his school's student paper, and for the last several years has been participating in online forums trying to improve Israel's image.

play. After that the girls took a bus to the upper town center, and from there boarded a bus home.

On the same day, a 21-year-old Palestinian, a student in the Hebron Poly-Technical university, arrived to the upper town center of Haifa. He had been out of touch with his family for three days. His body carried more than 50 kg of explosives packed with nails, nuts, and metal specks. Plus a suicide note proclaiming the victory of Islam over America and Israel on September 11.

At about 2 p.m., he boarded an Israeli bus. Previous suicide bombers have been tense and excited, fearing they will be caught, and exploded within seconds of boarding the bus. This time, the terrorist was sure of himself. He wore nice clothes, and blended well into this upper-middle class neighborhood.

Bus #37 headed toward Haifa University, a university with a high number of Arab students, with an active Arab Student Union and representation. Haifa is a "stronghold" of Jewish-Arab coexistence in Israel. It is the third largest city in Israel and has a large Arab population, with Arabs in key positions in the local government.

The terrorist stayed cool. The bus was half empty, so he waited for several minutes, passing a few stops, so that more people would come on. He slowly approached the middle of the bus, toward a group of children and teenagers. He wanted them all to die.

❧

Wednesday, 2 p.m. My physics class has just ended and my dad is supposed to pick me up and drive me to a dentist appointment. It was rescheduled several times, and by now I have a rather large cavity.

Many schoolchildren are on their way home. I watch the cars pass by. A police car suddenly speeds up.

Then the school guard (we have armed guards on every entry to school, as required by law, since terrorists have targeted schools) approaches me.

"What are you waiting for?" he asks.

I think I might look suspicious with my heavy coat and large schoolbag.

"My dad is about to pick me up," I answer.

"There has just been a suicide bomb," he informs me. "Just uptown, here in Haifa."

Haifa is a northern city, relatively far from the "green line." Yet we have seen many deadly terror attacks, and several others have been prevented by the police. It's been almost a year since the last attack here, in a co-owned Israeli-Arab restaurant near the largest shopping mall in the Mideast. My math teacher lost her entire close family and was very seriously injured. She never returned to teach.

Yet people here think we're safe. Especially since we're a mixed city. There have been Arabs among the victims here, and Arabs among the medical staff. People try not to break the already fragile coexistence here.

But now I'm in shock. Most of my school friends either live uptown or take buses there. They should be on their way home just about now.

"I don't know much," the guard says. "I have a small radio, but I'm officially not allowed to listen to it on the job. If you come, I can turn it on for you, and I'll listen in." We go to his small shack, and he turns on the radio.

"This just in: A terror attack in Haifa, on Moriah Street.... Bus has exploded.... The roof has flown off.... It's on fire.... Rescue teams are struggling through high-noon traffic...."

I try to call my family to tell them I'm fine. The network is dead. There's a cellular antenna on every street corner, but the networks overload easily.

Also, the cellular networks initiate a cut-off when there is an attack. Several times terrorists have used cell phones as triggers for second-wave blasts. They'd leave a bomb connected to a cell phone, and then five minutes after the first blast, when rescue forces arrived, they'd call the cell phone and detonate another powerful bomb, killing the survivors and rescue teams.

Suddenly, a car pulls up and my classmate's father gets out. "Where's my son?" he demands. "When did he finish school? Does anybody know?"

We don't know. Another classmate passes by. "Eric went home

much earlier," she calms down the worried father. "He ought to be home already."

I decline an offer for a ride. I hope my father will pick me up — as he does minutes later. "I couldn't reach you, so I just came to take you home," he says.

I think about all the people I know who could be hurt. Eli went home an hour early, since a water pipe in his house burst. He could have somehow ended up on that bus, though it's unlikely. Can't reach him now.

David could be on that bus. Could have had business at the university or uptown. I call him as soon as I get home. His mother answers in a frightened voice.

"Is David there?" I ask.

"No, he isn't home. Who is this?" She hopes I know something about his whereabouts.

"A friend of his. I'll call again," I say, thinking that it's better to keep the line free for him to call home.

My friend calls. She's gone for IDF training for the week. It's a mental preparation for boot camp that people can take while in school, to prepare you for real service.

"Are you okay?" she asks. "They let us watch TV and use phones since we're from Haifa."

"I'm okay. My family, too. How are you?"

"I'm fine. Lucky my brother is in the IDF and my mother is on a vacation in Eilat."

My grandma returns home. She is shocked to hear the news. "I took that bus route an hour before it blew up! And your seven-year-old twin cousins took it half an hour before that, from school."

I watch the news. The explosive charge was huge this time. The bus is in ruins. I keep posting news to on-line forums, keeping in touch with my friends. Manage to reach Eli and David, they're safe.

I connect to the internet. The ICQ messaging system is filled with people demanding information. Chain letters pass with the speed of light. "Amit has not been seen or heard since the attack. If anyone has seen him, please contact his home. His parents are worried sick."

After a while, a message comes through: "Amit is safe. Pass on." Whew.

But alas, this is the only good message.

Several friends from other schools inform me that their friends are missing. I never knew well how to comfort people, but now I'm needed.

"My best friend Liz has not come home," my friend Roni writes.

"Liz?" I ask. I have a bad memory for names.

"You know, the pale girl with long black hair."

"Couldn't she just be injured?" I suggest, knowing it's a false hope.

"No. Her parents called all the hospitals. She's either missing or dead. I don't know what to do. My best friend is gone."

How can I reply to that?

Our school walls are gray cement. It was popular for some reason when the school was built, but now it's considered ugly, and rightfully so. But paint won't catch on the naked cement walls.

Today the walls are grayer than ever.

When I arrive at school, only half our class is there. The 17-year-olds are sitting in absolute silence. It's very dark and gloomy, while outside the sun is shining. I see the shock in people's eyes, even when they're closed.

A TV breaks the silence. Someone hands out the morning paper. People begin telling their experiences. Someone knows several people who were killed. Another was near the blast. Another ran and began rescuing people. The unspeakable horrors make him burst into tears... again.

The principal announces that he has spoken to Liz's parents. She is confirmed among the dead. Soon we will convene for a ceremony. Those who knew Liz well stay outside and cry. The others try to avoid talking about it directly and return to their classrooms.

The ceremony starts with texts being read by Liz's teachers and friends. Liz's picture is hanging on the wall. A picture taken three years ago when she was admitted to school. Alongside is her name in black bold square print — the kind used in obituary notices. And candles. (One gets used to memorial candles in Israel.)

The speakers talk about Liz. Say goodbye. Say prayers for her soul. Say prayers for peace. Someone sings a song he has just written and composed for her. It's difficult to see students cry. It's even more difficult to see your teachers and school board weep.

I manage to avoid breaking out into tears. I'm not sure why. I feel perhaps that I have no right to cry, since I didn't know Liz that well.

The perfect weather outside quickly becomes a perfect raging storm. I want to go to the place of the suicide bombing, but I can't get a ride. And it rains terribly. I catch a ride home and sleep for most of the day.

I watch the late night news to see Liz's picture among the victims. They misspelled her name, got her age wrong, and chose a really bad picture, for such a pretty girl. I go back to sleep.

⁓

The next day, we try to resume our studies. No teacher dares to demand discipline or keep records of students coming and going. How can you make a person torn up inside sit down in a classroom? In a classroom with Liz's chair, now forever empty.

We board the buses to Liz's funeral. I still can't believe she is dead. The whole school attends. And students from other schools. Former pupils leave their army posts. Representatives of the government arrive. Why don't they ever come to share joy? Only anguish.

Then Liz's family arrives. I can't face their pain. I turn around, then walk away. It's awful to see parents mourn over a child.

Liz's sister reads a eulogy. Then her drama teacher. Then her best friend. Their words tear one's heart like sharp razors, and you feel you're about to cry blood onto your shirt. Of all people, the most lively, innocent, and talented girl, was taken from this world by a cruel murderer.

As the rabbi chants songs of mourning, Liz's casket is moved to a special area of the cemetery dedicated to terror victims. Usually, a dead body is wrapped in a shroud and buried that way. Not Liz. Her body, hardly recognizable, with no more human-like contours, is not in a condition to be wrapped this way. This time, they use a casket.

A crowd of several hundred, trembling from grief, stand in absolute silence. The prayers are said and then, orderly, one by one, people pass by her grave, and place a flower, a picture, or a rock where her body was lowered just minutes ago. We stand quietly under a burning sun, in silence, waiting patiently for our turn.

As I near the grave, it still feels like I'm dreaming. I look at Liz's picture and it seems like a weird parade. I just knew her name and image. I came because I wish I'd gotten to know her better. I came to return a favor, for the time she smiled at me and called my name, and made me feel great for that split second.

I place a rock on her grave, and it falls somewhere behind the flowers. As I begin to walk away, I stumble onto a grave with a familiar name. It is the daughter of my math teacher, killed one year ago. I sigh and put another stone on her grave.

So many victims. So many freshly dug holes.

As I exit, I suddenly feel a wet drop. It rains, but not aggressively like the day before. The sun hid its tearing eyes behind a cloud. The rain caresses our heads, gently, lovingly, in sympathy.

As I step in the wet mud, with the skies crying over my head, I think of the girl we left behind, all alone in the cold earth, in a casket and a body bag. I think I left more than a stone with her. I still expect this whole event to end, and then she will appear again. She's so real and so alive. And her smile is so wide and so healing.

But I hardly knew Liz Katzman. And alas, I never will.

Sara Yoheved Rigler

Laughter in a Time of War

*March 10, 2003 — As war with Iraq looms, months of
diplomatic start-and-stops leave Israelis teetering on edge.*

*I*t had been a harrowing week.

On Wednesday, a suicide bomber on a crowded Haifa bus
killed 15 Jews, most of them teenagers on their way home from
school.

On Friday night, two Arab terrorists infiltrated the security
fence around Kiryat Arba. First they sprayed bullets on a family
walking on the street, injuring five. Then they forcibly entered an
apartment where Rabbi Eli Horowitz and his wife, Dena, were enjoying a quiet Shabbat dinner. They murdered the middle-aged
couple.

On Saturday night, Anatoly Brikov, aged 20, died of his
wounds from the Haifa bombing.

On Sunday night, I went to a show.

It was no ordinary show. My daughter and I and most of the
audience had to travel there in a bulletproof bus. The production
was being staged in Gush Etzion, an archipelago of 23 communities south of Jerusalem. Although Efrat, the largest of the communities with a population of 7,000, is a mere 20-minute drive from

For biography of SARA YOHEVED RIGLER, see p. 94.

Jerusalem, the road, winding between Arab villages, was so treacherous that the Israeli government built a bypass road, cutting tunnels through two hills.

They needn't have bothered. From the very beginning of the wave of violence, the "tunnels road" became a popular target for Arab snipers. Eight Jews driving from the bedroom communities of Gush Etzion to Jerusalem were murdered in their cars. Residents of Gush Etzion adapted by installing shatter-proof glass on their car windows (bullet-proof glass and armoring the car doors were prohibitively expensive and too heavy for most private cars) and staying home at night. Gush Etzion became an area under siege.

It wasn't the first time. Gush Etzion, perhaps more than any other place in Israel, embodies the tragedy and resilience of the Jewish people.

Between 1928 and 1943, three contingents of Jewish pioneers tried to settle the barren, rocky, waterless hills between Jerusalem and Hebron. Plagued by recurrent outbreaks of Arab violence, they all failed.

In 1934, a Jew named Shmuel Holtzman bought the bloc of land which would become known as Gush Etzion. (The prefix *Gush* means "bloc." *Holtz* in Yiddish and *etz* in Hebrew both mean "wood." And the suffix *Zion* rounds out the name.) In 1943, the religious kibbutz of Kfar Etzion was established. With much sacrifice and hard work, it thrived. By the autumn of 1947, the bloc comprised four villages with a total population of 450 Jews, including 142 women and 69 children.

The United Nations vote, in November 1947, to partition the Land of Israel into a Jewish and an Arab state, was furiously rejected by the Arabs, who launched a fierce war to drive out the Jews. On December 10, 1947, Arab militias attacked a convoy bringing food and water to Gush Etzion and killed 10 Jews. After that, Gush Etzion was effectively under siege. Only convoys escorted by British forces managed to safely reach the bloc of settlements.

On January 5, 1948, the mothers and children of Gush Etzion were evacuated to the safety of Jerusalem. The men, and women with vital skills such as nurses and radio operators, stayed behind to protect their settlements and to defend the southern approach to the holy city. They were too few, with too few guns and too little ammunition.

On May 12, two days before the State of Israel was declared, Gush Etzion was attacked by the full strength of the Jordanian army, known as the Arab Legion. The defenders fought — and died — until they ran out of ammunition.

The surviving fighters surrendered to the Arab Legion. Leaving behind their precious, now empty, guns, they came out waving white flags and assembled in an empty lot next to the school building. A photographer wearing a keffiyeh came and photographed them. Then the Arab forces massacred all the survivors, except three who managed to escape thanks to the aid of humane Arab individuals.

In the two-day battle, 240 Jews fell, including 21 women.

The Six Day War in 1967 liberated the area of Gush Etzion. Immediately after the war, the orphaned children of Gush Etzion, now grown, approached the government of Israel and asked to be allowed to start again on the land that their fathers had died for. Although the Labor government was averse to any Jewish settlements in the newly liberated territories, Prime Minister Levi Eshkol could not resist the entreaties of the children of Gush Etzion. He gave them his consent with the words, "Children, you may return home."

Three months later, the new generation was ready to carry on the vision of their parents. They visited their fathers' graves in Jerusalem, and directly from the cemetery, a line of cars set out for Gush Etzion. The same armored car which had evacuated the children in 1948 led the cavalcade home.

Our bulletproof bus traced the same route through the hills of Gush Etzion on our way to the performance of "Esther and the Secrets in the King's Court." The show itself had been born out of a similar phoenix-like spirit.

After two Efrat residents were murdered on the tunnels road in May 2001, a stifling depression gripped the community. Even after the month-long mourning period for 20-year-old Esther Alvan and 53-year-old Sara Blaustein (who had made aliyah from New York less than a year before) had expired, the residents of Efrat found that they could not banish their tears and sense of hopelessness.

The terror was ongoing. An Arab construction worker who had been building a house in Efrat entered the local supermarket on a crowded Friday morning with an explosives belt under his coat. An alert shopper took out his gun and managed to shoot the terrorist before he could detonate his bomb. A short time later, another suicide bomber was caught making his way through the town.

Sharon Katz, an Efrat resident who had made aliyah from New York nine years before, decided that something had to be done to lift the morale of the local residents. She understood that redemption issues from prayer and repentance, but prayer and repentance cannot issue from depressed hearts. As the Talmud asserts: "The Divine Presence can dwell only in an atmosphere of joy." Sharon sent an e-mail out to the Efrat list announcing, "We're putting on a show."

The result was the Efrat/Gush Etzion Raise Your Spirits Summer Stock Company.

Their first production was "Joseph and the Amazing Technicolor Dreamcoat." Since most of the Gush Etzion communities are religious, they adhere to the principle of *kol ishah* (women do not sing in front of men). Therefore, the entire cast and production crew, as well as the audiences, were women. The once-a-week show (because most of the cast were busy mothers and working women) played 11 performances, plus a presentation for the Women's Caucus of the Knesset.

During the period that "Joseph" played, Israel experienced a terror attack almost every day. The cast would literally race from funeral to stage. "We would cry our eyes out," Sharon recalls. "Everyone back stage would be crying and reciting Psalms, then we'd have to go on stage and make the audience laugh."

The show's director, Toby Klein Greenwald, made aliyah from Cleveland 37 years ago. Toby's experience with theater as a response to terrorism dates back to 1975, when she worked with teenagers who survived the PLO attack on a school in the northern town of Ma'alot in which 16 classmates were slaughtered. "It's frightening to think," reflects Toby, "how that was more than 25 years ago, and the necessity still exists to use drama to help people overcome the stress of living in terror."

❦

A year later, the terror had not abated. The "Raise Your Spirits Company" decided to create their own original show. They chose as their theme the Book of Esther, because it is a true story of the Jewish people being in dire straits and being redeemed.

The Jews of the Persian Empire in 357 BCE were a comfortable and complacent minority. King Achashverosh's edict of extermination of every Jewish man, woman, and child filled them with shock, fear, and despondency. "In each and every land, wherever the king's word and decree reached," records the Megillah, "there was great mourning among the Jews, with fasting, weeping, and wailing."

While summoning the Jews to pray and repent, Mordechai sent secret messages to his niece Esther. Five years before, Esther had won a sordid "beauty contest," and had become the queen of Persia, not revealing to anyone her Jewish identity. Now Mordechai entreated her to go to the king and plead for the lives of her people.

Esther balked. To appear before the king unsolicited was courting death.

Mordechai's reply reveals an often-overlooked key to redemption: "If you remain silent now, relief and salvation will come to the Jews from another place."

Mordechai believed absolutely that the Jewish people would not be eradicated. If Esther would not act to save them, God would use a different avenue. Belief in redemption is the prerequisite for redemption; despair breeds defeat.

This is why the central Jewish prayer, the Amidah, is preceded by the blessing, "Blessed are You, God, Who redeemed Israel." The

Talmud asserts that prayer for the future redemption must follow a reminder that God has redeemed us in the past.

That is the essence of the "Esther" show: a vivid reminder that God has redeemed us in the past in order to galvanize our faith that He will redeem us this time as well.

The women of Gush Etzion conceived, wrote, and choreographed "Esther"; they also composed, arranged, and play the 34 musical numbers which constitute the show. The cast of over 100 ranges in age from 6 to 60. Everyone who wanted to participate was given a job: from the onstage pianist to the women who sewed the capricious costumes, from the little girls who do cartwheels to the comics who act out the hilarious "beauty contest."

The two shows have raised over $60,000. All profits from "Esther" are donated to the nonprofit, tax-deductible Gush Etzion Foundation (TheEstherShow.com), which distributes the money to the families of terror victims and to local community projects to counteract the effects of the ongoing terrorism.

On Sunday night, the show starts late. The funeral procession of Rabbi Eli and Dena Horowitz that afternoon wended its way through Gush Etzion en route to Jerusalem, tying up traffic. We wait for the latecomers.

The show is introduced by the director, Toby Klein Greenwald, whose daughter is a close friend of the daughter of Dena Horowitz. Lest any of the audience are wondering how to justify a musical comedy on a day when four terror victims are buried, Toby asserts: "At the very beginning, we decided that we would not cancel rehearsals nor performances because of terror attacks or funerals. We are not politicians. We are not soldiers. This is our way of fighting back."

I am dubious. I understand theater as catharsis, and theater as diversion, but theater as fighting back?

The musical unfolds: the gaily-clad citizens of Shushan, the bombastic King Achashverosh, the sassy Queen Vashti, the eunuchs in tunics, the sage Mordechai, the ethereal Esther, the villain

Haman in black leather portrayed like a West Side Story gang leader.

The dramatic climax is Esther's moment of truth, when she summons the courage to risk her life for her people. Rachel Abelow, who plays Esther, made aliyah from New York at the height of last year's worst wave of terror. She sings plaintively:

> Give me the courage, O Lord, I pray.
> Give me the strength, show me the way.
> Though my heart trembles, I'll overcome my fear;
> For I know You are always near.

Then the denouement proceeds topsy-turvy. Haman is exposed and hanged. Mordechai is elevated in his place. Messengers are dispatched with new edicts. The Jews of Shushan celebrate.

The production's most emphatic statement comes with the final scene. The full cast pours onto the stage singing:

> They'll come down from the mountains,
> They'll come from the skies,
> They'll come up from the valleys,
> With music and with sighs.
> They'll walk across the desert
> With laughter and with prayer,
> Their sisters and their brothers
> Will be waiting there.

The scenery has shifted from the palace of Shushan to the hills of Gush Etzion, those fought-for, died-for, returned-to hills of Gush Etzion. And when the ensemble repeats the lilting refrain, they change the final two lines to:

> Our sisters and our brothers
> Will be waiting here.

Suddenly the performers are playing themselves: women who have faced off with terrorism and death and their own fears, and who have remained steadfast for the sake of their ideals. Every one of them has lost a friend or a neighbor or the child of her friend or the friend of her child. Yet instead of giving in to despair and depression, every one of them is standing on the stage, hands uplifted, belting out the finale culled from the Prophets and fulfilled in recent history. These women are not performers playing heroes. These women are heroes themselves.

The whole audience is clapping and crying. Because it's a true story. Just as God redeemed us in the past, He will redeem us in the not so distant future. In fact, it's happening right before our eyes.

Sarah Shapiro

Preparing for War

*March 20, 2003 — As the American invasion of Iraq be-
gins, Israelis anticipate a possible repeat of the 1991 Gulf
War, when Saddam Hussein attacked Israel with Scud
missiles.*

By the time Kol Israel Radio reported, on a rainy, windy night
last week, that the invasion of Iraq was finally underway, we
were supposed to have prepared ourselves for war. But like
millions of others around the world, in those hours edging up close
to the unknown, I had no idea if we'd gotten ready.

I had been obsessed, in the preceding days, with the flowers on
our porch, which was as good a preparation as any. I bought two
bags of fresh dirt, transplanted some white nasturtiums into new
clay flowerpots, threw out the petunias that hadn't weathered the
recent snow, and spent hours pruning, meticulously plucking off
winter's dry leaves.

In the 1950s, Americans who were optimistic enough to build
fallout shelters were criticized scornfully by their compatriots.
How could a concrete bunker, naively fitted out with air filter and a
two-week supply of bottled water, protect you from a nuclear fire-

SARAH SHAPIRO lives with her family in Jerusalem. She has written and
edited many books on the themes of women and Judaism, including the
Our Lives anthologies and, most recently, *A Gift Passed Along.*

storm equal to a hundred Hiroshimas? Even assuming you and your family did somehow make it into the shelter in time and shut the hatch successfully against your neighbors, what kind of landscape would eventually greet you if you survived — if you hadn't melted down into the concrete of the underground chamber? What would you dine upon when your supplies ran out? No way, anymore, to pick up a quart of milk at the supermarket. Busses would not be running. And what would you plan on breathing in the brave new world, once the dust settled and you emerged into the radioactive light, or darkness, of day?

Today it's duct tape and plastic sheeting that stand between us and death. Several months ago, a local hardware store ran an irresistible sale on attractive, ready-to-use Family Survival Packages. "It has everything you'll need," the salesman persuaded me. Two rolls of tape (an extra in case of nuclear attack?), six feet of plastic sheeting, a transistor radio, an emergency lamp, a big flashlight (already fitted out with batteries), and an appealing little first-aid kit complete with syringes. Did I ask if the syringes were filled with atropine? I thought: needles, but was curiously lacking in curiosity. It didn't occur to me to wonder how many injections we were getting, and whether the antidotes would be effective for both smallpox and anthrax.

Survival for 250 shekels — around $50. It seemed a bargain. But when it came time to prepare our sealed room, for the life of me I couldn't remember where I'd stashed the Package. Just as was the case during the first Gulf War in 1991 — when it was not only the nifty gas masks themselves which proved to be obsolete, but also my suburban American brain — my mind balked dumbly, stubbornly at the seriousness of our situation. Every time, back then, when the sirens would start wailing, what came to my mind in our sealed room was the Beatles' line, "You have only waited for this moment to arrive." Gazing at our petrified little children, all in a row, as they sat staring back at us for reassurance from behind their long-nosed masks, wondering if we were going to die, what else was I reminded of? The indefinable rubbery odor inside my stuffy gas mask evoked nothing other than the chlorine-saturated swimming goggles of my Connecticut childhood, excellent for high-diving into the country club pool.

Today, Jewish immigrants from Ethiopia, Russia, Iran, South Africa, Argentina — and Iraq — surely have their own memories to ponder as we again await the possibility of attack, but in one respect we Israelis seem remarkably of one mind, these days. We are possessed, as a nation, by an uncanny calm, a remarkable bravery. The ongoing terrorism, especially that which has taken place during this last period, seems to have wiped out any vestigial notion that there is such a thing as safety measures. To live one's life has become synonymous with risking one's life. It seems we love, more than ever, the simple phenomenon of being alive, alive here, in our land, and have gotten to the point of not wanting to relinquish that love to any fear.

I am surprised at myself, surprised at everyone. I am proud of us.

The windows of one room in our apartment have now been taped shut with plastic sheeting — a task carried out by the same child who in 1991 forgot, one never-to-be-forgotten night, to drag in his dear, frayed security blanket when we entered the sealed room. Back then, in our innocence, we wouldn't open up, even for that. We were believers, still, in plastic sheeting, and gas masks, and bleach-soaked towels placed under the door. Today, who among us trusts that salvation would arise from our sealed rooms, were Saddam, feeling cornered, ever to fulfill his declared ambition of becoming the modern Nebuchadnezzar, going down in history as the one who finally came up with a Final Solution?

I asked a Palestinian taxi driver a few weeks ago if he thought Saddam would attack Israel if America attacked Iraq. He said, "Yes, I think so." I asked if he thought Jerusalem, in such a case, would be safer than other cities, given its large Arab population. He shook his head. "No. Saddam doesn't care," he said. "Look what he did to his own people. Look what he did to his sons-in-law." (He had them executed.)

I asked, "What about Arafat? Do you think he cares about your people?"

The driver's eyes shifted uncomfortably in the rearview mirror. He replied, reluctantly, "No."

"Is there any Arab leader who does care?"

Silence. Then: "No. None."

This is the open secret that the Palestinian taxi driver and I share. It's not Saddam's unconventional weapons which constitute the unparalleled danger to his own people, and to all of us here on Earth, but rather, his conventional weapon, the ancient one: cruelty. That, and the indoctrinated hatred which serves as its fuel, are the supremely low-tech factors which can turn a bus into an inferno, a plane into a missile, and a young man or woman into a bomb aflame.

In a war such as this, security measures are as effective as security blankets, and antidotes deliverable by syringe only as effective as those delivered by the flowers on our porch.

For a sealed room is no protection against a sealed heart. Such deliverance is delivered within.

Rabbi Nechemia Coopersmith

On the Bus with Mayor Bloomberg

August 19, 2003 — A suicide bomber strikes a bus full of families on their way home from prayers at the Western Wall, killing 23 people and wounding 135, many of them children and babies.

This war has wrought many tragedies, too numerous to re-count. But the bombing of Jerusalem bus #2 set a new low, sinking to even more unfathomable depths of evil. How could a summertime family excursion to Judaism's holiest site turn into such devastating, horrific carnage?

In the aftermath, New York City Mayor Michael Bloomberg came to Jerusalem on a nine-hour lightning solidarity trip that included visiting survivors of the bus — and lighting a candle at the spot where the attack occurred.

He also visited the Western Wall and then took a ride on bus #2, the route on which the bomber struck. It happens to be the same bus I take home every day from work at Aish.com's offices

RABBI NECHEMIA COOPERSMITH is the co-editor of Aish.com. He is the author of *Shmooze: A Guide to Thought-Provoking Discussion on Essential Jewish Issues.*

near the Western Wall. I didn't plan it, but I found myself on the same bus as Mayor Bloomberg — along with Jerusalem Mayor Uri Lupolianski, former NYC Mayor Ed Koch, 30 security guards, 40 reporters — and 10 other regular passengers like me crammed in the middle. (And I had to pay for this ride?)

I told the *Associated Press* reporter who interviewed me that I thought it was terrific that the mayor came to show his support, and that everyone should do the same. I would have told Mayor Bloomberg directly, but the cameraman's elbow pressing down on my chest — not to mention those 30 security guards — prevented me from doing so.

When I got home late and told my wife, who has pleaded with me to stop taking buses, about my surreal bus ride, she was relieved. "I was hoping you would end up taking that bus home. It's the only one I knew for sure wouldn't be bombed."

She had a point. With all those mayors on the bus — not to mention the 30 security guards — we were totally safe.

Then it hit me: Why am I or my neighbor or some guy named Mayer any less worthy of a safe ride than Mayor Bloomberg? Is Israeli blood so cheap? Shouldn't we all be able to feel safe and secure riding the bus home?

Part of the problem is how we define victory over the terrorists. I hear it all the time: if you're afraid to go out for dinner, to ride the bus, or to send your kids on an outing, then you're giving in to terror and letting the terrorists win.

Mayor Bloomberg's ride on the #2 bus was meant to send a message to Arab killers. "You cannot let terrorists win," he said.

I said the same thing to the AP reporter who asked how I felt traveling on the bus. "You have to carry on living, otherwise you're giving in to terror."

On further thought, perhaps the truth is exactly the opposite. Carrying on with normal life as if nothing really happened is giving in to terror. Just imagine if after this horrific suicide bombing, 500,000 Israeli citizens said, "Enough! We are no longer taking the bus. We are no longer going downtown. We are no longer sending our kids to school — until we can feel as safe as Michael Bloomberg."

That would be a powerful statement of our unwillingness to accept the terror — and our government's reaction would be very different from what it is now.

Israelis refer to this relentless onslaught as the *matzav*, which means "the situation" in Hebrew. Caroline Glick of the *Jerusalem Post* points out the danger in this label. A situation is something we learn to tolerate; we get used to it. After a bombing or a drive-by shooting, we're shaken for a few hours, at most for a few days. [The daily failed attempts at murdering our people no longer even register.] Yes, it's terrible, but we need to move on and live with it.

By accepting the "situation," we are giving in to terror. We need to start labeling this for what it really is: a war. At stake is not our willingness to take the bus; at stake is our very survival in our ancient homeland.

Wars need to be fought and won with the conviction that victory is the only option. They are not "tolerated."

As Jews, we recognize that our response to this ongoing war of terror needs to be not only in the physical realm; the underlying spiritual causes need to be addressed as well. The physical world reflects the spiritual realm and can be used as a window to understand the specific areas of growth we need to work on.

After a terrorist attack, we frequently fall into a similar trap vis-à-vis our spiritual growth, by viewing our personal shortcomings as a *matzav*, a situation that yes, we need to deal with, but all too often learn to tolerate. Perhaps we feel a fleeting sense of urgency to work on genuine change — a brief insight, a moment of inspiration to take on an area of growth and become truly different — but then it fades and we slip back to the same negative habits. We remain the same and get accustomed to our personal situation, no matter how ineffective it may be.

As a response to this gruesome bombing, let's start calling the need to tackle our personal shortcomings a "war" — a war against our yetzer hara, our lower selves, that must be fought with the conviction and dedication to win. No more tolerance.

Let's not allow ourselves to go back to "normal life" and the way things were before the bombing. It's time to say, "Enough! I'm going to work on being different." With the merit of this collective spiritual growth, may the Almighty bring true peace to the region and to our own inner lives. And may there be no need for those 30 security guards on Mayor Bloomberg's next visit to Israel.

Jon Medved

Our Heroes and Theirs

September 9, 2003 — Eight Israelis are killed and 30 wounded in a suicide bombing near the Tzrifin army base. A few hours later, seven people are killed and over 50 wounded when a suicide bomber blew himself up at the Cafe Hillel in Jerusalem.

*L*ast night's terror struck close to home. The boom of the blast at Cafe Hillel shook the windows of our house and left no doubt that we were hit again — this time in our own neighborhood.

Our son, Yossi, was on the phone with his brother, Momo, asking when he would be back so they could watch another episode on DVD of "24," the addictive United States series about terrorism.

Momo was crossing Emek Refa'im Street, which is two blocks from our house, and they both heard the blast. Momo, 16, is a trained paramedic with Magen David Adom. He took out his plastic gloves, which he keeps in his school backpack, and ran to the cafe to help the injured. Yossi ran out the door with my wife, Jane, to get Momo.

Momo was one of the first to arrive at the scene. As he described it later, it was a scene straight out of Dante or Eli Wiesel.

JON MEDVED is a venture capitalist and a partner in Israel Seed who lives in Jerusalem.

Victims were screaming and strewn about. A group of bystanders was attempting to put out a fire that was consuming a man. Amputated legs and arms were lying in pools of blood. A man's head was in the middle of the street.

Momo acted according to the training he received this summer, in a course designed to teach him how to handle these kinds of events. As soon as the lead ambulance arrived, he was told who to evacuate and helped carry the injured on stretchers. Within 10 minutes it was over, and the amazing Israeli emergency medical teams had again acted with alacrity and professionalism.

Momo's mother and brother found him covered with victims' blood and walked him home.

I was in my office when the blast hit and was frantic with worry because I could not reach anyone at home by phone. Finally I got a call from my son, Yossi, telling me that our family was okay and that we would meet at home.

Getting home and seeing your son's clothes splattered with the blood of a terror attack is a parental experience I will not forget — the relief of seeing him unhurt, mixed together with the pain, outrage, and grief of an attack so close to home.

After Momo showered, we together watched on TV the surreal scenes of our beautiful neighborhood hit, hurt and bleeding. Momo was curled up with his dog, Lucy, hugging her and trying to regain some semblance of normalcy. A 16-year-old boy, having done his heroic work and having seen scenes that one should never see, trying to return to what's left of his adolescence.

We watched the scenes of jubilation in Gaza, with crowds of Palestinians taking to the streets in spontaneous celebration, delirious with joy at the "quality" attacks. Sheikh Ahmed Yassin praised the "bravery" of the suicide bombers and extolled the "great" Abu Shnab, the "engineer" of dozens of Israeli deaths whose death was now "avenged."

I was struck by the contrast between the two societies. Our heroes were out on Emek Refaim fighting to save lives, to practice emergency medicine, to reduce casualties. Their heroes were sowing death and destruction; their engineering was the science of terror.

This morning as the bright Jerusalem sun came up again over our neighborhood, most of the outward signs of destruction had been washed away and cleaned up. Despite the continued terror alerts and torrent of news about yesterday's attacks, the children need to go to school, to get on with our lives. But the news contained more bitter tidings that literally took my breath away. Among the dead in last night's blast were Dr. David Appelbaum and his 20-year-old daughter, Nava.

Nava was due to be married tonight in a joyous wedding of 500 guests. Instead of escorting her to the *chuppah*, they escorted her to a grave on a rocky Jerusalem hillside. Nava's fiancé tenderly placed the wedding band into her open grave.

David was a doctor of emergency medicine who was a fixture in Jerusalem's medical scene, having treated hundreds of terror victims as the head of the emergency department in Shaare Zedek Hospital. He was the founder of Terem, Jerusalem's 24-hour private emergency medical clinic, and my best friend's partner. He was a learned man, a kind man, a tzaddik — a righteous person. He was a true hero of Jerusalem.

I am letting Momo sleep in this morning. I tried to wake him, but he said he needed some more sleep. His teacher from school just called to say that he heard from Momo's friends that he had a "tough night" and was among the first on the terror scene. He suggested that after today's funerals, I take him to school, so he could be with his friends and talk out what has happened. My son and his friends — true heroes of Jerusalem.

ISRAEL PERSPEC- TIVES

Rabbi Noah Weinberg

To Restore Our Destiny

For 2,000 years, the Jewish people were wanderers. Exiled to every corner of the world, we were oppressed, beaten, and gassed. Yet in the process, something incredible happened: We defined the moral makeup of humanity. Values that the civilized world takes for granted — monotheism, love your neighbor, peace on earth, justice for all, universal education, all men are created equal, dignity of the individual, the sanctity of life — are all from the Torah. This is an enormous impact and we accomplished it under the most adverse conditions.

When the State of Israel was proclaimed, the world watched with great anticipation. Everyone knew that the Jewish state had the potential to change the course of human history. If the Jews had such an awesome impact despite the great difficulties of exile, then reunited in their ancient homeland they would surely transform the world!

Indeed, the first 50-plus years have been miraculous. The first generations of immigrants knew this was a historic opportunity and they were infused with a tremendous sense of idealism. Jews were willing to dig ditches in return for peanuts! The result? We've succeeded in building the finest hospitals, roads, schools, and in-

RABBI NOAH WEINBERG is the dean and founder of Aish HaTorah International. Over the last 40 years, his visionary educational programs have helped bring hundreds of thousands of Jews closer to their heritage.

dustry — even amidst hardship, terror, and wars.

But along the way something got lost. We got so caught up in building an infrastructure that in the process we forgot what we really came home to accomplish. The Jewish dream of a utopian society somehow became muddled in a hodgepodge of Western ideals. For example:

The Jewish system of jurisprudence is the basis for every great legal system in the world. The Romans derived their judicial system from the Torah, as did the Magna Carta and the United States Constitution. So you would think that in setting up the modern Israeli legal system, we would look directly to the Torah for guidance, framework, and principles. But instead — we adopted Ottoman law!

The result is devastating. Not only do we have a less effective legal system, but on a much deeper level, we have communicated a message to Israeli youth that "the Jewish way" is archaic, to be replaced by a more progressive, "non-Jewish" approach.

This is just one example of how, in the process of building a state, we have too often made tactical decisions that have devalued fundamental principles of Jewish life.

In Israel today, much of the idealism is gone because we're not really sure we want to be Jewish. What respect is there for the words of the Prophets, the Talmudic Sages, or the rabbinic giants of today? One million Israelis are now living in the Diaspora because if life is all about McDonalds and MTV, then frankly there's a better version available in Los Angeles.

So what do we do now?

We have to recapture our destiny, our sense of purpose. And that begins with a recognition that *tikkun olam* (rectification of the world) is the basis of what drives the Jewish people to greatness. It all started back with Abraham. His business was to go out and teach what it means to be "created in the image of God." He demonstrated how a human being has to take responsibility for the world. Abraham's undertaking was the first progressive, liberal movement the world had ever seen. And look how it succeeded!

In looking back at the first 3,000 years of Jewish history, we don't recall the names of great entertainers or athletes or corporate executives. Rather we recall the great teachers of the Jewish message: Moses, King David, Maimonides, the Vilna Gaon. That is the essential Jewish legacy. The message was ingrained in our souls at Mount Sinai and it is the single defining characteristic of our people. To ignore it is to commit national spiritual suicide.

Whether you say our message is God-given or whether you say it was written by man is a separate issue. The fact is that humanity is thirsting for Jewish ideals.

And the world needs that message now more than ever. Consider, for example, the institution of marriage. In Western society, the divorce rate is over 50 percent. That's a crisis of immense proportion. Family structure is crumbling, and dysfunction in relationships is at an all-time high. It seems that nobody has a clue how to stem the tide.

Not long ago, *morality* was a dirty word. It implied an imposition of conscience and a curtailment of personal freedom. But today, the leaders of Western society realize that morality is the key to human survival. The great civilizations of Greece and Rome fell due to moral decay. That's why the great universities — Columbia, Harvard, Hebrew University — are investing hundreds of millions of dollars to develop curriculum for teaching "morality" to primary and high school students. They're scouring centuries of philosophical texts to try to find an effective approach.

Yet the answer is right before our eyes! Our very own Torah has time-tested tools for personal and communal success: How to give and how to receive; when to be strict and when to be compassionate; individual rights versus communal responsibility; how to show appreciation and respect; when to lead and when to follow; balancing family and career; the boundaries of modesty in actions and in dress; how to listen and converse effectively....

Torah methodology is universal — for Jews and non-Jews, religious and secular, Israel and the Diaspora, left and right. The Torah is alive and relevant for today. And for the Jewish people, the ability to effectively communicate this message is our single most important undertaking.

Now as our globe becomes increasingly complex, we need solid moral direction to navigate the maze. The world needs to know... and we need to teach.

In its essence, morality is a "Jewish" movement. It's the natural self-expression of a Jew. I've seen it time and time again: When a Jew is turned on to Torah, it sparks enthusiasm, energy, and unbridled passion. Imagine an entire nation of Jews empowered to carry forth the Jewish message!

The Jewish people are experts in this field and we have an obligation to share. Not by yelling, nor by condemning. But by offering rational, relevant wisdom for living. This is precisely Isaiah's vision of "Light Unto the Nations."

With technology, the world is far more reachable today than ever before. The message can go forth rapidly and effectively. As Isaiah said, "*Ki miTzion teitzei Torah* — For out of Zion shall come Torah, and the word of God from Jerusalem." How beautiful this would be.

Ultimately, the solution may come in some far different form. But one thing is certain: We must do something to turn this ship around. The State of Israel is hemorrhaging in terms of enthusiasm, idealism, and commitment. Our challenge is to instill in each Jew a pride in our heritage, a confidence in our future, and an appreciation of how precious his involvement with the Jewish people can be for himself, his children, his grandchildren, and all humanity.

Otherwise, the State of Israel will have squandered its single greatest opportunity: to fulfill our destiny of *tikkun olam*.

We've succeeded before. And with the Almighty's help, we can do it again.

Elie Wiesel

Murdering Our Hopes

Elie Wiesel spoke at an Israel Solidarity Rally on October 12, 2000, in New York City, two weeks after Palestinians launched their war of terror.

We have gathered here to affirm our solidarity with Israel. We are outraged by the hypocritical vote in the Security Council, which did not condemn Palestinian excessive reactions but condemned Israel's response to them. We stand by Israel whose present struggle was imposed upon her by the intransigence of the Chairman of the Palestinian Authority.

Those of us who reject hatred and fanaticism as options and who consider peace as the noblest of efforts finally recognize Yasser Arafat for what he is: ignorant, devious, and unworthy of trust.

We had hoped for a genuine peace between Israel and her Arab neighbors, including the Palestinians. We had dreams of Israeli and Palestinian children playing together, studying together, laughing together, and discovering each other's worlds. The pain, the agony, the death of any child, Palestinian or Jewish, is a torment to us. But why does Chairman Arafat not protect them but instead uses them as shields for adults throwing stones and worse?

Yes, it is with a heavy heart that we say that our dreams of peace have gone up in the smoke of ransacked synagogues, in the

ELIE WIESEL is a Holocaust survivor and Nobel Peace Prize laureate.

lynching of Israeli prisoners, and in the bloodthirsty mobs shouting their version of a Jerusalem without Jews and a Middle East without Israel. And I blame the supreme leader of the Palestinians, Yasser Arafat.

By rejecting Israel's unprecedented generous territorial concessions, he is burying the peace process; in so doing, he has betrayed the confidence not only of his negotiating partners but of President Clinton and other Western leaders, just as he has betrayed [the Nobel Peace Prize,] the highest honor society can bestow upon a person. How can a leader, any leader in Israel, renew discussions with him before all the kidnapped soldiers are returned to their families?

By unleashing mob violence and bloodshed in the streets, rather than guiding his frustrated people toward coexistence and peace, he renounced their legitimate aspirations for a future free of suffering and hatred.

I hold him responsible for the murder of Rabbi Hillel Lieberman and the lynching of two young reservists. All his promises were lies; all his commitments were false. Indeed many peace activists here and in Israel are now reassessing the Oslo accords.

Under Israel sovereignty, Christians, Jews, and Muslims alike could pray without fear in Jerusalem, our capital, which is at the center of Jewish history. A Jew may be Jewish far from Jerusalem; but not without Jerusalem. Though a Jew may not live in Jerusalem, Jerusalem lives inside him.

No other nation's memory is as identified with its memory as ours. No people have been as faithful to its name or have celebrated its past with as much fervor. None of our prayers are as passionate as those that speak of Jerusalem.

Jerusalem is the dream of our dreams, the light that illuminates our hopeless moments. Its legitimacy lies in its sovereignty. To oppose one is to deny the other. Israel will never give up either. I accuse him of being morally weak, politically shortsighted, and an obstacle to peace.

I accuse him of murdering the hopes of an entire generation. His and ours.

Rabbi Shraga Simmons

Ramon's Legacy

February 1, 2003 — 16 minutes before touchdown, the space shuttle Columbia *disintegrates in midair, killing Israeli astronaut Ilan Ramon and his six American crewmates.*

The image is seared in our national consciousness: deadly white streaks across the blue Texas sky. Not since the assassination of Yitzhak Rabin has one death so shaken the State of Israel. For Ilan Ramon was more than Israel's first man in space. He was a composite of the Jewish nation — child of a Holocaust survivor, decorated air force pilot, galvanizer of American-Israel ties, and self-declared representative of all Jewry.

For 16 days, Ilan Ramon defied gravity by lifting his country from the morass of incessant terror, a battered economy, and vilification in world political and media circles.

For 16 days, Ilan Ramon embodied the age-old Jewish yearning to soar beyond the heavens.

And for 16 days, Ilan Ramon made every individual Jew feel connected and proud.

RABBI SHRAGA SIMMONS, originally from Buffalo, New York, holds a degree in journalism from the University of Texas. He is now coeditor of Aish.com and lives in the Modi'in region of Israel with his amazing wife and children.

And that makes his death so gut-wrenching for us all.

It has been said that three main themes define contemporary Jewish life: Torah, Israel, and the Holocaust. Nearly every Jew will cite one of these as the primary source of his Jewish identity.

Ramon had impeccable Israeli credentials. As a combat pilot in the Israeli Air Force, he arguably held the country's most prestigious job. He was a member of Israel's first F-16 squadron, fought in two wars, and survived a collision where he ejected from his jet.

"I'm not afraid," Ramon stated flatly when I asked him about his upcoming shuttle mission. He even bemoaned the fact that it was more dangerous to drive on a highway than to fly in the shuttle.

Although he was not afraid, he knew the risks involved — just as he knew the risks in 1981, when he and seven other pilots flew a daring raid to bomb the Iraqi nuclear reactor at Osirak. They flew over enemy Arab territory for hours, avoiding detection by flying mere meters from the ground, and in a tight formation that emitted a radar signal resembling a commercial airliner. Ilan volunteered to fly at the vulnerable rear position, since he was the only pilot not married.

Yet as Israel celebrated the successful raid, condemnation was near-universal. One prominent United States senator called it "one of the most provocative, ill-timed, and internationally illegal actions taken in that nation's history."

In this light, Ramon and his colleagues underscored the deep Jewish principle of doing the right thing, even when it means going against the grain. It's a trait bequeathed by the first Jew, Abraham, whose moniker *Avraham Ha'Ivri* (the Hebrew) literally translates as "the one who stands on the other side." As the entire idol-worshipping world stood on one side, Abraham and his monotheism stood firmly on the other.

And, as with Abraham, those who bombed the Iraqi reactor were vindicated with time. Two decades later, as Washington prepared to oust Saddam Hussein, the international community was ever grateful for Israel's strike at Osirak. At a memorial service in Houston, President Bush told Ramon's family: "Ilan bombed the Iraqi reactor, and I will finish the job."

The Holocaust is another primary theme in contemporary Jewish life.

It was widely publicized that Ramon's space luggage included a mezuzah adorned with barbed wire symbolizing the concentration camps, as well as a copy of the drawing "Moon Landscape," a celestial view of Earth created by a 14-year-old boy killed in the Nazi inferno.

Yet for Ramon, the Holocaust was more than mere symbol. His mother survived Auschwitz, and his grandfather was murdered there. As such, Ramon saw his shuttle flight as testament to the invincibility of the Jewish people.

"The look in their eyes is very powerful," Ilan told me of his meeting with concentration camp survivors. "They see their hopes that died in the Holocaust as living on through me. They see that despite the horrors we have endured, we are going forward."

It is difficult for outsiders to understand how deeply the Holocaust is embedded in Jewish consciousness. The State of Israel arose from the ashes of Hitler's ovens, with the promise of "Never again," and the Holocaust plays a central role in the Israeli obsession with survival.

In June 1967, as Arab armies amassed on Israel's borders, Martin Luther King, Jr., was asked on American television if Israel has justification for launching a preemptive strike.

"Yes," said King. "They have 6 million good reasons."

Incredibly, Ramon viewed his 1981 Iraqi mission in this context. "If I can prevent a second Holocaust," he was quoted as saying then, "I'm ready to sacrifice my life for this."

Between his air force heroics, his Holocaust ancestry, and his seat on the space shuttle, there was surely enough for the Israeli media to confer hero status on Ramon.

But for Ilan, there was something more central to achieve. He knew that Jewish destiny cannot survive without Judaism.

That is why, when Ramon spoke with Prime Minister Ariel Sharon during a televised news conference from outer space, he pulled out a Torah scroll. Yes, this special wallet-sized scroll symbolized the Holocaust, having survived Bergen-Belsen. And yes, this scroll — whose owner is a physicist at Tel Aviv University who oversaw one of Ilan's space shuttle experiments — symbolized Israeli achievement in technology.

Yet most importantly, as millions of Israelis sat glued to their TV screens, Ramon held aloft this Torah scroll and declared that "it is very, very important to preserve our historical tradition, and I mean our historical and religious traditions."

Ramon was reaffirming the centrality of a Torah that neither Hitler's Hell, nor a long list of oppressors before him, could extinguish.

For Israel — a country that could not agree to include God's Name in the Declaration of Independence — this was an enormous step forward.

Ramon added other important Jewish elements to his flight. He sanctified the Shabbat with the first intergalactic Kiddush. He ate vacuum-packed kosher food. And as he passed over Jerusalem, he recited the age-old declaration of Jewish faith: "*Shema Yisrael* — Hear O Israel, the Lord our God, the Lord is One."

By placing Torah tradition in such a highly visible role, Ramon broke from the norm of Israeli public figures. This makes his actions all the more praiseworthy, and his reward all the more great.

After the *Columbia* tragedy, I saw an editorial cartoon that depicted a father and son, gazing at the night sky. Seven stars dotted the heavens — six regular stars, and one Star of David. The father placed his arm around the boy's shoulder, pointed to the Star of David, and explained: "That one is Ilan Ramon."

For 16 days, Ilan Ramon occupied the world stage, and everyone knew that the Star of David on his shirtsleeve meant he was a Jew. And the entire world looked at him and wondered: What is a Jew?

They saw someone eating kosher food, holding a Torah scroll, and unafraid to give the ultimate sacrifice for his people.

That is a *kiddush Hashem*, a sanctification of God's Name, the single highest level that a Jew can achieve.

Many people dream of unity for our fractured nation. Of those who dream, some try to do something about it. Of those who try to do something, only a select few actually succeed.

For 16 days, there was no right-left, religious-secular, or Israeli-Diaspora rifts among our people.

For 16 days, we felt what it means to be a unified nation, a rare glimpse of what we hope for our future.

To have that image so suddenly and brutally smashed was a visceral shock to our collective system.

If one word could describe Ilan's death, it is the Hebrew word *challal*, which has three separate meanings: Outer space. A human corpse. And a vast, crushing emptiness.

But as Ilan taught us, Jewish destiny means to pick up the pieces, gather our inspiration, and move on.

The Talmud tells the story of a man who came upon a tree — in Hebrew, *ilan* — and enjoyed its sweet fruits and pleasant shade. Before departing, the man wanted to bless the tree. But its fruits were already sweet and its shade was already pleasant. So what more could he wish for that *ilan?*

The man said: "May it be God's will that all which derives from you will be like you."

Ilan Ramon gave each of us so much, and now it is time for us to give back, to continue his legacy, so his death should not be in vain.

Perhaps we can try to feel more connected, to care about those who are different from us, knowing that every Jew is holy, and has the potential to create a *kiddush Hashem*.

And we can, like Ilan, try to sanctify Shabbat, eat kosher food, and keep the Torah close by our side.

And we can, like Ilan, put Jewish tradition at the forefront of

Israeli public life — not out of coercion, but through a recognition that Torah is the foundation from which all else flows.

And we can, like Ilan, pursue the dream that despite the tension and enmity, underneath it all we are united as one family.

"We have to find a way to bring our people closer together, to show more patience and understanding," Ramon told me with urgency in his voice.

In 16 days, Ilan Ramon reached the heights of this world. In one shattering moment, he took his place in the next world.

May his memory be for a blessing.

Rabbi Ahron Lopiansky

Home for the Soul

D iscussions over the future of Temple Mount have aroused intense feelings among Jews the world over.

For some, the issue is incredulity that Islam's third holiest site should be considered more significant than Judaism's holiest site. For others, it is the challenge to Judaism's most profound historical memory. For still others, the issue is the violation of an archaeological site that possibly contains the most vivid authentication of Jewish history. And for almost everyone else, it is just an intuitive feeling that there is something extremely special about this place.

But then there is another side, which uncomfortably nags us as well. Are a few old rocks worth a war? Do we not look askance at the Serbs and Bosnians that can't stop slaughtering each other on account of centuries-old "historical" and "hallowed" sites? We see them blindly trapped in history, rather than surging forward to a beautiful, unencumbered future.

Even at the theological level, we begin to hear some contrary voices: "Judaism is about people, not about things." Or, "Pagans believe in holy rocks and earth; Jews believe in a transubstantial Divine." Indeed, if Judaism believes in an incorporeal God, shun-

RABBI AHRON LOPIANSKY is *rosh yeshivah* of Yeshiva of Greater Washington. He is the author of *Timepieces* (Targum Press) and a number of scholarly works in Hebrew.

ning icons, paintings, and graven images, then why do we cherish
this heap of stones?

At the time of the encounter with God at Mount Sinai, the Jewish people were commanded to make a *mikdash*, "sanctuary," so
that God could dwell among them (Exodus 25:8). This portable
structure (containing the Ark of the Covenant) traveled with the
Jewish people throughout 40 years in the wilderness and while
they were settling the Land of Israel. Then, some 3,000 years ago,
King David built an altar on Mount Moriah in Jerusalem (the site of
Isaac's binding and Jacob's dream). And on this spot, David's son
Solomon built the first Temple — making the portable *mikdash* permanent.

The Temple was called Beit HaMikdash, "the Holy House." The
"house" aspect was reinforced in many ways:

- The furnishings of the Temple itself were a table and a lamp
  (together with an incense altar).

- The inner sanctum was called *chadar mitot*, "bedroom" (2
  Kings 11:2).

- The outer courtyard served the function of courtyards in
  those days, such as food preparation, washing, and so on.

- The Talmud expresses the Divine bereavement as "Woe, My
  house is destroyed."

What does the concept of "house" mean in relationship to
God?

Imagine two separate individuals, A and B. Each has his own
circle, A and B respectively. Each has an area that intersects and
overlaps with the other. The area where they overlap is the
"house." It is the area where two distinct entities find their common denominator. *Bet* is the Hebrew letter whose numerical value
is two. Its literal meaning is "house" — for a house brings together
two elements and includes within itself their commonality.

Thus, a home of marriage includes two people of distinct nature and personality. Those character traits that the spouse finds
unbearable are left on the outside, and those elements that are
common to both are included and accentuated in the home. As the

marriage progresses, both sides divest themselves of offensive behavior, and learn more and more to enjoy their common dreams
and goals.

How does this relate to God, man, and the Beit HaMikdash?

God and man are as distinct elements as could be. God is the
ultimate spiritual essence, devoid of materiality. Man is (at least su-
perficially) physical material, with a seeming lack of much spirituality.

To solve the problem of the gulf between spirituality and materiality, God created a place in the material world that would serve
as a house, where Israel and God could unite their commonality,
the Divine soul.

This in essence was Jacob's dream. While running away from
his brother Esau, Jacob fell asleep on a mountaintop, which tradition says was Mount Moriah. He dreamt of a ladder reaching from
the heavens down to the very spot where he was sleeping, as angels
ascended and descended upon it. He woke up, awestruck, and exclaimed:

> How awe-inspiring this spot is! This must be God's abode. It
> is the gate to Heaven.
>
> *(Genesis 28:17)*

The Malbim, a 19th century commentator, remarks on this
passage:

> Jacob understood that this place was the site of the future
> Temple... for the Temple is the ladder, whereby Heaven and
> Earth kiss each other. Man's worship ascends upward, and
> the Divine providence descends thereby.

How was the Divine presence manifest in the Temple?

The Talmud (Avot 5:7) states that there were 10 ongoing miracles at the Temple: "No meat rotted, no fly was seen there... the
rain did not extinguish the Divine fire, etc." Maimonides states
that, in general, miracles are not meant to persist over time. Yet
here was a steady, ongoing set of miracles.

Besides the steady stream of miracles, something about the
number of the miracles strikes us as significant. The number 10, as

used in Jewish text, represents the totality of a system, much as the number 10 represents the totality of the unit integers.

Indeed, the Talmud lists the 10 miracles at the Temple in the same series as the 10 utterances with which the world was created. Just as the world in its completeness encompasses 10 utterances of God, so does the Temple consist of 10 elements, which compose an entire world.

In other words, the Temple is a "parallel" world, physical in substance, but more refined and God-like. It is a world of meat, but the meat does not rot. It is a world of dampness and rain, which does not extinguish the flame of the altar. As the most physical manifestation of Divine spirit, it is as if God has moved into this "house."

Man, on the other hand, must elevate himself in order to enter this house. He must either dedicate himself to Divine service, as do the *kohanim* (priests), or must be temporarily on an elevated level of spirituality, as the Jewish people achieved during the festivals through purification and offerings. Thus, man enters the Divine house after bringing out in himself the spark of Godliness, the Divine soul.

The Temple is where the human and the Divine include their points of commonality, and where the two can embrace and unify — if only for a moment.

This is our collective memory of this awesome place.

And we await longingly for the day when both God and man are ready for that communion again.

Looking at the rocks and ruins from this perspective, we see that their value is not merely historical. Nor, however, are these rocks imbued with magical powers. Rather, they remind us of the time when this place brought out the best and most beautiful in man, and the most fathomable and concrete of God.

The Temple Mount is far above politics of the right or the left. It is a place where God came closest to revealing himself to humanity in a permanent and tangible manner. And it is a place where man reached the peak of his awesome potential. When these two occurred simultaneously, "Heaven and Earth kissed." Man and Creator, so to speak, embraced.

The essence of Judaism is that we are a nation tied to God, enacting His moral designs, and thereby seeking to bond with Him.

For reasons known only to Him, one tiny plot of land is where God chooses to reveal as much of the Divine as possible and to elevate man to the highest peak of spirituality humanly possible. As we pray three times a day, we face this point, knowing that this is the spiritual pole of planet earth.

We are not dealing with mere history and remembrances. We are dealing with our most essential present and our profoundest hope for the future. This is who we are — our most important place, the very soul of the nation.

Our remembrance of what the Temple Mount once was should evoke in us a pang of yearning and an elevation of self. Yes, the day will come when we will be beckoned "home" again, when God will again be willing to set up a "home for Divine embrace."

And there will be no bloodshed on that day. For on that day, the world will recognize truth and embrace it.

Sara Yoheved Rigler

What Are We Dying For?

Nineteen-year-old Jason Aguilar was sitting in an Israeli tank on the Syrian border with nothing to do but think. Born in the United States, Jason had come to Israel the year before and joined the Israeli army because he considered it an "exciting, macho thing to do." Now, enclosed in the tomb-like confines of the tank, it suddenly hit him that he could get killed.

"I started to think," recounts Jason, "that if I died, what would I be dying for? I couldn't really articulate an answer."

Jason, who was raised with a minimal Jewish education, vaguely intuited that his putting his life on the line as an Israeli soldier had something to do with Judaism. His search to define an answer led him, after he was discharged, to a Jerusalem yeshiva.

There, in a lecture by Rabbi Noah Weinberg, Jason heard his own question used as a springboard to confront an even greater issue. Rabbi Weinberg told the room full of young people: "If you want a meaningful life, you have to ask yourself, 'What am I willing to die for?' Then go live for it."

With hundreds of Israeli civilians killed by terrorists, Jews here are increasingly asking this question, in the most practical terms.

For biography of SARA YOHEVED RIGLER, see p. 28.

"Am I willing to die to go to work in downtown Jerusalem?" "Am I willing to risk my life to go sit in a café?" "Should I put my life on the line by taking a bus?"

Even before the establishment of the State of Israel, arguments raged about the purpose of the Jewish people's return to its ancient homeland.

Theodore Herzl (1860–1904), the founder of political Zionism, was quite clear about his goal: to provide Jews a safe haven from anti-Semitism, which (four decades before the Holocaust) he predicted would sweep Europe yet again. Herzl himself was a university-educated, totally assimilated Viennese Jew married to a non-Jew, an aficionado of European culture.

As to the nature of the Jewish State which Herzl proposed, it would be a state like any other, a nation among the nations, distinguished only by its particular Jewish population. Its form of government would be "an aristocratic republic." Its language, in lieu of a common language ("We cannot converse with one another in Hebrew," wrote Herzl. "Such a thing cannot be done.") would be "a federation of tongues" on the Swiss model. In *The Jewish State*, Herzl proclaimed: "We shall remain in the new country what we now are here, and we shall never cease to cherish with sadness the memory of the native land out of which we have been driven."

Not all secular Zionists shared Herzl's thinking. In Russia, the poet Ahad Ha'am (Asher Zvi Ginzberg, 1856–1927) claimed that the primary problem facing the Jewish people was not anti-Semitism but assimilation. Thus, the goal of Zionism, proclaimed Ahad Ha'am, was not to save the Jews, but rather to save Judaism: "The Land of Israel must become a Hebrew-speaking spiritual center in which the process of assimilation will come to a halt." The Judaism envisioned by Ahad Ha'am, who was also intermarried, was not the traditional religion of Torah and mitzvot, but a new Jewish culture, an amalgam of Jewish ethics and values with the intellectual concepts of the European Enlightenment.

Two significant pre-Herzl movements of Jews returning to Palestine were the Lovers of Zion movement and the B.I.L.U. movement, a combination of religious and secular idealists who championed working the land. By 1896, the year Herzl launched his Zionist movement, these immigrants of what later became known as "the First Aliyah" had established 16 agricultural settlements, including the wine-producing villages of Rishon L'Tzion and Hadera. As B.I.L.U. member Ze'ev Dubnow wrote in 1882: "The ultimate aim... is to take possession of the Land of Israel and to give back to the Jews the political independence of which they have been deprived for 2,000 years."

Thus, the self-proclaimed purpose of the Jews who returned to Zion can be classified as: 1) a refuge from anti-Semitism; 2) a locus for Jewish cultural revival; 3) political independence and nationalism. Something happened in 1903, however, which hints at a goal and a vision deeper than what most "Zionists" themselves could define.

∞

On Easter 1903, the first and most notorious pogrom of the 20th century took place in Kishinev, in Czarist Russia. For two whole days, while the police did nothing, rampaging locals attacked the city's Jews. They threw children out of upper-story windows, gouged out their victims' eyes, and drove nails into their heads. By the time the order came from St. Petersburg to stop the pogrom, 60 Jews had been murdered and many more were maimed for life.

Four months later, Theodore Herzl convened the Sixth Zionist Congress with the words, "I have a great surprise for you: His Majesty, Sovereign of the British Empire, is sending you a gift — a gift called Uganda!"

Indeed, the British government had offered Dr. Herzl an entire country in Africa, what the British Colonial Secretary Joseph Chamberlain described as a land with a comfortable climate and the possibility of raising cotton and sugar. "When I first saw Uganda," Chamberlain declared, "I said to myself: 'This is a land for Dr. Herzl.' "

In the wake of the Kishinev pogrom, Herzl felt gratified that he had procured for the Jews of Europe an immediate, safe haven. Raised with virtually no Jewish background, Herzl was totally unprepared for the reaction of the delegates at the Zionist Congress. "We don't want it!" they shouted. "We don't want it!"

Salome Levite, a Swiss delegate to the Congress, described Herzl's reaction: "He just couldn't digest what had happened here, how it was that such an unfortunate nation, suffering pogroms and denied all rights and privileges, could be offered an entire country and say, 'No.' The Russian Zionists began to explain: 'We don't want just any country! We are Zionists. We want to return to our ancient, ancestral homeland.' "

Herzl was particularly amazed that even the delegates from Kishinev rejected Uganda, claiming that they would go nowhere but the Land of Israel.

What had happened? If the purpose of Zionism was to provide a refuge from anti-Semitism or political independence, why wouldn't Uganda do? Max Nurock, a secular British Jew who served as Lieutenant-Governor of Uganda during the 1940s, years later explained: "Uganda wouldn't do. You know, it hadn't got the spark of divinity in it."

Almost a century before the birth of either Herzl or Ahad Ha'am, the two leading religious figures of European Jewry had issued clarion calls to their disciples to return to the Land of Israel. Both the Baal Shem Tov and the Vilna Gaon had, in the latter half of the 18th century, sent their disciples to live in Jerusalem, Tzfat, Hebron, and Tiberias. By 1896, the year Herzl launched political Zionism, there was already a Jewish majority of 28,112 Jews living in Jerusalem (compared to 8,560 Muslims).

The goal of this religious influx was simple: As the Torah makes eminently clear, it is the will of God for Jews to live in the Land of Israel. According to Judaism, exile from Israel is considered a particularly harsh punishment because outside of Israel the Jewish nation is incapable of fulfilling its potential.

The mission or function of the Jewish people can be compared to the function of a bodily organ, say the heart. The heart performs a unique function in the body. This is not to claim that its function is more important than the lungs or the brain. Yet if an organ is not in its proper place, it cannot perform its function properly. The Jewish people transplanted to Uganda or New York would be like a heart transplanted to the head or the lower abdomen. It simply would not work.

When Rabbi Nachman Kahane of Jerusalem's Old City was recently asked, "What are we dying for?" he replied by quoting Psalm 118: "I will live and not die, and proclaim the glory of God." He explained: "The purpose of the Jewish people is to proclaim to the world the greatness of God. That's what we live for and that's what we die for."

A recent *Newsweek* cover story on the future of Israel quotes a prominent Israeli journalist suggesting that it is time to find new narratives.

The idea came to him when he happened on the scene of a bloody suicide attack at the Moment Café a few weeks ago. The coffee house had been, for Shavit, a kind of sanctuary of civilization and normality. Now he saw a horrific scene. Bodies were torn apart.... "Twenty minutes after I saw the bodies, I understood what this narrative is about," he said. "It's about the freedom to have my croissant and coffee in the morning. And the right to drink a beer at night. It's about a quiet heroism in trying to live a Jewish life, flirting, taking your kids to school in an almost unbearable situation...."

Doesn't a Jew have the freedom to have a croissant and coffee in Los Angeles or a beer in Miami? The banality of this "new narrative" against the backdrop of blown-apart bodies is dismal. Jews can live a normal, even a Jewish, life in New York or Houston... or Uganda of 1903. Why fight — and die — for the right to live in Israel?

Israeli Air Force Major S. Ghelber, 37, a secular Jew born in the Tel Aviv area, calls the Israeli journalist's narrative of being free to have his croissant and coffee "very superficial."

To live as Jews, with our heritage and tradition, in our homeland — this we cannot have in any other country. America could never be our homeland, because a homeland is a place where you have your roots. In every mile of Israel you see a historical place where Jews lived 2,000 years ago.

A couple of years ago the Air Force sent me to do a course in California. My wife and I were traveling in Colorado and Arizona, and we saw many Indian historical places. They were very interesting, but I never felt a connection to those sites. Here in Israel, wherever you go, you come upon the connection to our Jewish roots, our history, our heritage.

We secular Israelis may not be able to articulate what we feel, but the most powerful sign of our strong identification with this land is the unbelievable response to the call-up of reservists [during the Jenin operation]. Not only did 95 percent of those called show up, but even men who were not called up due to their age or state of health showed up, begging to be allowed to fight. People feel they are fighting for their homes. They feel there is a threat, a real threat, all over Israel. We want to make it safe for our children.

What is significant about Major Ghelber's statement, "We want to make it safe for our children," is that Major Ghelber has no children (yet). When he says, "our children," he means my children and the children of his next door neighbor. In his identification with the Jewish people as a whole, both in the present and the past, he has hit upon the crux of Zionism.

It is significant that the pivotal battle of Jenin began on the holiday of Passover. After all the terrorist slaughters at discotheques, pizza parlors, and cafés, the people of Israel could not stand the specter of Jews sitting down to a Passover Seder, commemorating the birth of our nation, being blown apart by our enemies.

The Talmud says that the Jews in ancient Egypt had sunk to the lowest level of impurity. They were engaged in Egyptian idolatry and depravity. In what merit, then, were they saved? The Talmud answers: "They did not change their names, their dress, and their language."

By continuing to identify as Jews — even while committing grievous sins — our ancestors made themselves worthy of redemption. In fact, the singular act required of them on the awesome night of the Exodus was to slaughter a lamb and smear its blood on the doorposts — the inside of the doorposts. It was a sign not for God, or for the Angel of Death, but for themselves.

That is what the current war — the seventh war in the short history of the Zionist State — is about. This is what Zionism is about. Do I identify as a Jew, with the Jews of history, with my fellow Jews of today? At a time when assimilation in the Diaspora has topped 60 percent, do I define myself as Jew? If so, then this is my land, the land that God gave us to perform our particular sacred mission.

According to Maimonides, any Jew who is killed because he or she is a Jew is *kadosh*, holy. Their place in the Next World is among the holy of our nation, even if they died drinking an espresso while chatting about the latest movie in a café. And as for the soldiers who die defending the lives of other Jews, the Talmud says that their place in the Next World is on the very highest level, with the patriarchs Abraham, Isaac, and Jacob.

Make no mistake: God wants Jews to keep all the mitzvot. But a Jew who makes that essential act of identification — smearing the blood on the doorposts — is worthy to be redeemed. In the years of terror atrocities, we have seen much blood smeared on doorposts, floors, walls, and buses. And although no one chooses such a gruesome death, every Jew who stays in Israel during these traumatic times is making a de facto decision to be part of the Jewish people, even at the risk of his or her life. Our blood-splattered bus stops are no less holy than the doorposts of Egypt.

In this merit, may we witness the Final Redemption.

Natan Sharansky

The Power of Freedom

April 2003

Year after year, generation after generation, Jews spend Passover night retelling the story of their Exodus from Egypt. We try to instill in our children a sense of our ancient journey from slavery to freedom and try to provoke discussion over its meaning. In fact, our need to recall the past is so strong that each of us is obligated to imagine that he or she personally went forth from Egyptian bondage.

Mankind easily forgets the meaning of the great events that have transformed it. We must constantly struggle to remind ourselves of the forces that have truly shaped our destiny. For most of us, appreciating one of those forces — the power of freedom — requires nothing less than a Herculean effort.

In 1974, at the age of 26, I participated in my first Seder with a group of Jewish activists in the Soviet Union. Though we knew little about that night's rituals, identifying with the seminal story of freedom's triumph was not particularly difficult for us — especially with KGB agents waiting in a car downstairs.

The 10th plague, the slaying of the firstborn which challenged each Jew to decide whether to smear the blood of the false Egyp-

NATAN SHARANSKY, a former prisoner of Zion, serves in the Israeli cabinet as Minister for Jerusalem and Diaspora affairs.

tian god on his doorpost, was another idea to which every refuse-nik could relate. By publicly declaring our desire to emigrate to Israel, each of us had chosen to challenge the Soviet god and stand up against tyranny. The same yearning for freedom that once drove our people felt as if it was literally pulsing through our veins.

Some years later, I would have the opportunity to lead a Seder for the first time. In truth, my memory of the text of the Haggadah was by then rather sketchy, and the Seder itself had none of the traditional trappings. There was no unleavened bread to eat, no bitter herbs to taste, no Haggadah to read, and I was the only Jew present. In fact, I was the only person in the room. But my outside "guests" didn't seem to mind. As I retold the story of Passover through the small window of my punishment cell to two fellow inmates, they too could immediately identify with its universal message.

The reason was simple. This isolated group of dissidents in the Soviet Union had already experienced the power of freedom to transform an individual and understood its power to transform a society. They needed no reminders. The idea that a nation of slaves could win its freedom and defeat the most powerful empire in the world was to us not an ancient legend, but an eternal truth.

We knew that missiles, planes, and tanks were in the end no match for the inner strength of people willing to resist tyranny. We also understood the undeniable logic in one of our fellow dissidents' prediction that the arms of a state that always had to point a gun at its own subjects would eventually tire. To us, the collapse of the Soviet Union was as inevitable as freedom's march was inexorable.

More than a decade later, after hundreds of millions have been liberated, many have again forgotten the power of freedom to change the world. Promoting democracy among the Arabs, as a few have boldly called for, is again cast as naive adventurism. The Arabs, we are told, have never lived under democracy. Their culture and religion, we are assured, are inimical to the idea of liberty.

The realists dangle the "pragmatic" alternatives before us: Cut a deal with "friendly" dictators. They will fight terror. They will preserve order. They will make peace.

For the past 10 years, Israelis have witnessed the horrific consequences of this type of realism. Rather than place its faith in the power of Palestinian democracy, Oslo placed its faith in the power of Yasser Arafat's dictatorship. Arafat, we were told, was a man with whom we could do business. We would give him unlimited power and in turn he would protect us from terror and make peace with the Jewish state.

Even today, after Arafat's 30-month terror war against Israel and 10-year reign of terror over the Palestinians, the lessons have not been learned. Again, the rush to create a Palestinian state with "a man we can deal with" before Palestinian democracy has a chance to take root is in full swing. And again, it is being sold as the product of hard-headed realism.

In sharp contrast to this latest turn of events, last summer the power of freedom was remembered. In his historic speech, President Bush articulated a vision that Andrei Sakharov always championed: Only a country that respects the rights of its citizens will respect the rights of its neighbors. If the Palestinians were to build a society that protected individual freedom, President Bush promised that America would support the Palestinians' legitimate yearning for self-determination. It was not only the most noble vision of peace this region has ever heard, but also the first realistic one.

But predictably, the president's ideas were received as "naive" and "impractical" by those who have forgotten the power of freedom. Democracy, the critics argued, is nice in theory, but pragmatism demanded a different course be pursued. In London, in Paris, in Moscow, and even in most quarters in Washington and Jerusalem, the skepticism took a familiar form: nice dream, but let's get back to reality.

Alas, if the fall of the evil empire couldn't change these skeptical minds, it is doubtful that the celebrations erupting in Baghdad will. There will be more excuses, more cynicism, and more hesitation.

But now it's the turn of Iraqis to experience the overwhelming power of freedom. Men and women who have lived for decades under tyranny will soon know, perhaps for the first time, what it is like to live without fear. The challenge for America and its allies will be to convince them that they need not live in fear again.

More importantly, the leaders of the free world will have to convince themselves that tyranny is no more inherent to the Arab condition than it is to the human condition. To ensure that the institutions needed to preserve and protect liberty in Iraq are given the chance to develop, these leaders must once again believe in the power of freedom.

The effect this freedom will have on the region is sure to be breathtaking. It will prove as contagious in the Middle East as it was in the Soviet Union. Soon, Iranians, Saudis, Syrians, Egyptians, Palestinians, and all who live in fear will envy those who no longer do. And they will increasingly find the courage to stand up and say so.

And I will know in my heart that the dream for peace and stability in the Middle East will only be realized when we stop believing that the power of freedom is only a legend.

Originally published in the Jerusalem Post.

Rabbi Noson Weisz

Land of Spiritual Acquisition

The Midrash says that God gave the Jewish people three presents which were also desired by the nations, and which can only be acquired through suffering: 1) Torah, 2) the Land of Israel, and 3) the World to Come (*Sifri*, Deuteronomy 32).

The fact that the Midrash groups these Divine gifts together indicates that they share a common unifying factor. As Torah and the World to Come are clearly spiritual gifts, the Land of Israel must have a spiritual aspect as well. In fact, the proper appreciation of this spiritual quality is the key to unlocking the mystery behind the current Mideast conflict.

Why should acquiring Israel be any different than acquiring Uganda?

There is no way to understand this if we conceive of Israel as being just another country, much like the United States or Canada in quality, although considerably smaller. Such countries do not need to be "acquired through suffering"; they have no intrinsic spiritual aspect. God designed them as suitable habitats for people who possess their spiritual reach at the moment of creation. There is no need for them to "grow into" these lands.

But Israel was not designed to be user-friendly. Just as the

RABBI NOSON WEISZ is a Toronto native with degrees in microbiology, international relations, and law. He lives in Jerusalem with his family and teaches Talmud and Jewish thought at Aish HaTorah and Yeshivat Beit Yisrael.

World to Come is only open to the spiritually deserving, the Land of Israel was designated as the earthly habitat of the one who strives to perfect himself and reaches out to God. In the unperfected form in which they were created, humans cannot live in Israel.

∞

Humans are unique because they are a mixture of physical and spiritual. We have a body which is similar to all other life forms, but we also have a soul. Body and soul jointly participate in most human activities. When a person eats, for example, the taste of the food, the setting, the cutlery, and the background ambience are almost as important as the nutritional value of the meal. Nevertheless, it is the need of the body for nourishment that provides the impetus for the meal.

Mitzvot are different. While many of them do involve both body and soul — eating matzah, wearing tefillin, blowing a shofar, and so on — in the case of mitzvot it is the needs of the soul that provide the impetus for engaging in the activity.

To appreciate the subtle flavor of mitzvot, one must look at human activities that are purely spiritual. Deep meditation, for example, is an attempt to leave the confines of the body and express oneself as a pure soul. Because the impetus for mitzvot is, likewise, always a spiritual one, their performance is existentially equivalent to a purely spiritual experience.

But man is not pure soul. The body gets in the way when we engage in a "pure soul" activity. Removing the obstacle of the body necessarily involves tearing away and discarding a piece of oneself, a process that is invariably painful.

Living in Israel has all the distinguishing marks of a spiritual experience. The same process of divesting one's physicality is a necessary step in its acquisition. You can only get a grip on Israel as a soul.

We need only look at the history of Israel to be convinced of this truth.

There is no other territory on Earth over which so much human blood has been spilled. The secular theory attributes this strife to the strategic importance of this tiny patch of land, located at the junction of the trade routes connecting the lands of the north and east to Egypt.

An examination of the historical conflicts themselves points to Israel's importance as another sort of junction: its status as the Holy Land. In the minds of believers, Israel is located at the crossroads between the physical and the spiritual, where the mundane can cross over to the holy.

It is here that Cain and Abel brought the offerings to God that served as the background to civilization's first homicide. It is here that Noah offered his sacrifice when he emerged from the Ark. It is the locale where Abraham was tested and told to sacrifice Isaac. Jacob's ladder was planted here, and King David later designated this site for the Holy Temple.

Christians and Muslims revere the land as well. As all the monotheistic religions subscribe to the "Old Testament," they must necessarily regard Israel as holy ground. For monotheists, the Land of Israel lies at the entrance to Heaven. Whoever holds it is already partially through the gate.

Christians and Muslims fought bitterly over Israel's possession as a holy resource in the Crusades, and today Arabs are fighting Jews for much the same reason. The terrorist acts from which Jews suffer are the work of suicide bombers and gunmen who believe they are earning eternal reward by sacrificing their lives in a religious crusade to drive the infidel out of the Holy Land.

The Western mind may find it difficult to comprehend how a portion of earth that seems no different from any other can be designated as the habitat of the soul. But it is impossible to explain how Israel could have engendered so much conflict through history — or become the major focus of world media and the United Nations — without relating to it as a spiritual, rather than physical, place.

Settling land physically translates into clearing the soil and taming the landscape. All the labor involved is focused on the outside environment; there is no particular need to work on one's character.

To conquer a spiritual land, this is not enough. Besides taming the soil, whoever wants to settle in such a land must also do heavy work on his soul. To live in a spiritual land, you have to grow into a spiritual person.

All spiritual growth is painful. "With much wisdom comes much grief," said King Solomon, "and he who increases knowledge increases pain" (Ecclesiastes 1:18).

The pain of spiritual growth is the suffering associated with the acquisition of Israel. The land punishes anyone who thinks of living in it as you would in any other country.

How ironic. The early Zionists, who organized the return of the Jewish people to their ancestral homeland, did so with the intention of creating a secular democratic state. They intended to solve the problem of anti-Semitism once and for all, imagining that once the Jews were living in their own land — once they were indistinguishable from Canadians or Americans or Englishmen — the "Jewish Problem" would finally disappear.

Through Divinely ordained history, there are now 5 million Jews in Israel — the majority nonreligious — in a land that demands soul-based behavior in order to acquire it.

The actualization of the secular Zionist scenario — the successful establishment of a Westernized Jewish welfare state in Israel — would effectively bring the history of the Jewish people to an end. True, there would be hi-tech and Gucci and even Nobel Peace Prizes. But there would be no more "from Zion shall go forth the Torah, and the word of God from Jerusalem" (Isaiah 2:3).

Is it any wonder that Divine Providence cannot allow Jewish history to end this way? Through 2,000 years of exile, Jews have clung to a messianic vision with astonishing stubbornness. We bled rivers of blood in our determination to lead humanity to recognize God and accept His rule.

Is it reasonable to believe that God could allow the loyalty and self-sacrifice of several thousand years to just fade away?

Which brings us to the Mideast conflict. God is demonstrating to the Jewish people that you cannot live in Israel as you would in New York. After all, this is the land of Abraham, Isaac, and Jacob, who were promised it as an inheritance so that they could worship God at the holiest place on Earth.

Many Israelis are not presently living with this commitment to Judaism, through no fault of their own. But this doesn't alter the fact that you can only live in Israel as a spiritual country. Somehow everyone needs to consider what it means to be Jewish.

How can God accomplish this? One way is by allowing Jews to be terrorized simply for being Jewish, until they reach the stage of hopelessness. Eventually, this intense pressure will compel Jews to start asking some very pointed questions. "What's going on here? Why are we so different than other people? What value is being defended here that makes it worth all this blood and sacrifice?"

When an individual Jew reaches this point of soul-searching, he will either leave Israel or set out to discover the meaning of Judaism. If he chooses the latter course, he will find answers in the Torah, and in so doing, move the Mideast problem one step closer to its true resolution.

God is not out to destroy the remnant of the Jewish people or to drive us out of our ancestral home — certainly not after allowing us to miraculously regain it after a 2,000-year hiatus. God is just applying some pressure. He is teaching us that it is impossible to live in His Holy Land without thinking about the significance of being Jewish.

The greatest weapon the Arabs possess is the will to sacrifice their lives for their beliefs. The focal point of Jewish vulnerability is that we no longer believe in any higher power and can only rely on the might of our hands. We have absorbed the skepticism of the Western intelligentsia. For many Jews, the highest value is social justice and democracy, and we are seriously weakened by the fact that many of us question the justice of our cause. Torah values and promises are no longer useful to many as a means of justifying sovereignty over our ancestral homeland.

Our immense military power has not led to a speedy resolution. No matter what solution we attempt, we seem helpless to stop the carnage. Our national frustration and pain is aggravated by the fact that a large part of the civilized world regards Jews as the perpetrators of the violence from which we suffer, instead of perceiving us as its victims.

It is essential to have a stubborn belief in the justice of our cause to provide us with the necessary stamina to face the long haul.

Yet many of us come up empty.

What is the solution? For the Jewish people to succeed in our quest of reacquiring this junction between Heaven and Earth, we must regain our faith and the belief in our cause. We must recognize our current suffering as spiritual growing pains. Because in the end, that is the only means by which the Land of Israel will be acquired.

Lawrence Kelemen

Learning from Sadism

November 10, 2002 — Revital Ohayon, 34, was reading her sons, Matan, five, and Noam, four, a bedtime story when a Fatah terrorist burst into their home on Kibbutz Metzer. She jumped in front of the children to protect them, but he shot all three dead.

A few months ago, on a Shabbat morning, Palestinian terrorists burst into the bedroom of Shiri Shefi, took aim, and sprayed her and her three children with bullets using M-16 assault rifles. Shefi, her four-year-old son Uriel, and two-year-old son Eliad were wounded. Five-year-old Danielle, shot in the head, was killed.

About a year ago, a Palestinian sniper trained his high-powered rifle on 10-month-old Shalhevet Pass, killing the baby girl in her father's arms.

About six months before that, Vadim Novesche and Yosef Avrahami, two Israeli reserve officers abducted by Palestinian police, had their heads beaten into unrecognizable pulp and were then disemboweled by a waiting crowd outside the Palestinian Authority's Ramallah headquarters, who then danced, entrails in hand, through the city's streets.

LAWRENCE KELEMEN is professor of education at Neve Yerushalayim College of Jewish Studies for Women in Jerusalem. He is the author of *Permission to Believe, Permission to Receive,* and the recent, *To Kindle a Soul: Ancient Wisdom for Modern Parents and Teachers.* For more about Rabbi Kelemen, see his website, www.LawrenceKelemen. com.

Cases like these stand out among the hundreds of murders of Israelis and foreign visitors in recent months, not because of their evil but because of their inhumanity. They reveal a terrifying angle of the story of this war.

Beneath the strata of Islamic unity, Pan-Arabism, and Palestinian national aspiration — at the root of this great campaign engineered by Arab leaders — is pure, unbridled sadism, a delight in cruelty that boggles the Western mind. And even if this lust for savagery is slightly less evident in the "ordinary" shootings and suicide bombings that people suffer in Israel on a daily basis, there is a growing suspicion that much of this violence flows from a visceral, Palestinian truculence — a craving for Jewish pain, for blood.

Those of conscience ask not only what practical steps we can take to escape this nightmare, but also how it could ever have been conceived. What great power have Palestinian leaders tapped into? How do they draw forth so much human energy and direct it for evil? And can we learn from them how to harness the same energy and use it for good?

"The sword and the book descended intertwined" (*Midrash Rabba*).

The Palestinian leadership takes education very seriously. On the Palestinian National Authority website (www.pna.org), the first three listings are the ministries of Higher Education, Information, and Education — before the ministries of Planning, Labor, and Health.

Since September 2000, the PA composed and introduced into its elementary and high schools a series of new textbooks, replacing Egyptian and Jordanian texts on four grade levels.

These books obliterate the State of Israel from history and maps, showing instead a greater Palestine that stretches from the Jordan River to the Mediterranean Sea — with Jerusalem as the capital of the Palestinian state.

These texts present the liberation of Palestine as a struggle against Jewish occupation, describe the waves of aliyah as "infiltration," and glorify jihad and martyrdom. (See examples at www.edume.org.)

Beyond its local educational products, the PA also imports a wealth of materials from its neighbors. A 30-part series, produced by Arab Radio and Television, featuring a cast of 400, and aired during the second half of Ramadan 2002, "dramatized" *The Protocols of the Elders of Zion*. Arab viewers were also treated to a popular political satire showing Ariel Sharon drinking the blood of Palestinian children. The myth that Jews sprinkle the blood of Arab children into their matzah is graphically described in *The Matzah of Zion*, published in 1983 by the current Syrian minister of defense, Mustafa Tlas. The Egyptian mass circulation daily *al-Ahram* also recently reported "many cases of the bodies of [Palestinian] children who had disappeared, being found, torn to pieces, without a single drop of blood. The most reasonable explanation is that the blood was taken to be kneaded into the dough of extremist Jews."

One can only imagine the effect that academic and media presentations such as these have on the Palestinian soul.

⚬⚬

However frightening this propaganda and its effects might be, we must confront the possibility that an even more hideous engine drives the terrorists' cruelty. Relative to the West, life in Arab countries has always been harsh. Corporal punishment of children is thoroughly embedded in the culture. No mainstream Islamic authority has yet spoken out against slapping children's faces, dragging them by the hair, or any of the other disciplinary approaches that shock Western onlookers.

Survival in such a culture necessitates some numbing. But this psychological component might be insignificant relative to the neurobiological effects of being beaten and tortured in childhood. It was Harvard researchers who first revealed that stress hormones released when children experience physical and sexual abuse actually impede development of that part of the brain responsible for empathy and conscience.

Brain scans of those who suffered through events common in the childhood of Palestinian children reveal an underdeveloped hippocampus and vermis. Among the behaviors associated with this sort of brain damage: impulsivity, sadism, and suicide. It is almost too frightening to consider that Israel today faces a population with many members hardwired for the sort of violence we have been witnessing.

More terrifying is the long-term prognosis for Palestinian society. Martin Teicher, a lead researcher in the Harvard study, reports that sadistic parents neurobiologically infect their children with the same trait: Society reaps what it sows in the way it nurtures its children. Whether it comes in the form of physical, emotional, or sexual trauma, or through exposure to warfare, famine, or pestilence, stress can set off a ripple of hormonal changes that permanently wire a child's brain to cope with a malevolent world. Through this chain of events, violence and abuse pass from generation to generation as well as from one society to the next.

Our stark conclusion is that we see the need to do much more to ensure that child abuse does not happen in the first place, because once the key brain alterations occur, there may be no going back (*Scientific American*, March 2002).

❧

In the short term it is unlikely that Israel will do much to stem the flow of anti-Semitic propaganda or reduce the violence that Palestinians commit against their own children. We must accept that Israel is locked in a battle with a population with many members programmed for inconceivable callousness and hatred.

Ironically, we can learn from our neighbor's example: Islam is a powerful force. If given a chance, Judaism can be, too — but in a very different way. If Palestinians use the Koran to teach hatred, we can use the Torah to teach sensitivity, altruism, and righteousness.

But this would require teaching our tradition as passionately as the Palestinians teach theirs. Just as Palestinian parents speak to their children about the need to sacrifice for the Palestinian national dream, so too we can speak to our children about giving of themselves to achieve real *tikkun olam* (repairing the world).

To date, we are failing at this mission. The percentage of Jewish charitable funds directed to teaching Torah to Jews is minuscule.

Too often, Israeli leaders and heads of major Jewish organizations in the Diaspora downplay or outright deny the value of an immersion in Judaism.

The solution might also require changing our parenting habits. Just as the harshness of Palestinian parenthood might be wiring children for hatred and violence, so too might attentive, loving parenting wire our children for goodness.

Perhaps the moment has arrived to rethink the amount of time we spend (or don't spend) with our children; the way we discipline them; and the media we expose them to.

Perhaps, ironically, we can be inspired by the horrors of this war to commit ourselves to raising a different sort of child.

Perhaps those of us who survive the current crisis can emerge different, better, for the horrors we have seen.

Sara Yoheved Rigler

When Humanism Becomes Fundamentalism

January 23, 2003
one year after the abduction and murder of Daniel Pearl

Just after 7 p.m. on January 23, 2002, *Wall Street Journal* reporter Daniel Pearl got into a car outside the Village Restaurant in downtown Karachi. According to friends, Danny was feeling good. He had lined up a scoop: an interview with Islamic radical Ahmed Omar Sheikh, whom Danny suspected held the key to the case of Richard C. Reid, the al Qaeda recruit who tried to blow up a trans-Atlantic jetliner with plastic explosives in his shoes.

Fazal Karim, one of the men in the car with Danny that night, was arrested last May. He told police that Daniel Pearl appeared calm as he was driven around Karachi for several hours, even when he was made to change vehicles.

After all, Danny must have thought, a militant in hiding has to cover his tracks, lest the reporter lead the police to his hideout. The long, circuitous drive, the change of vehicles, was all standard cloak-and-dagger fare for a veteran journalist like Daniel Pearl.

Finally, late in the night, the car drove down a dirt road to a

For biography of SARA YOHEVED RIGLER, see p. 28.

nursery situated in the middle of a vast field. Danny was told to get out and was taken into a cinderblock storehouse.

At what point did Danny realize that he was no longer a journalist in pursuit of a story, but a Jew in a trap set by Islamic terrorists? When his "escorts" locked the metal door behind him? When he surveyed the 10-by-15-foot room and realized that his prize interviewee was not there? When they tied him to a chair? When, six days later, three Arabs from Yemen arrived with a satchel filled with assorted knives?

It appears from Fazal Karim's testimony that Danny was optimistic until the end. One of the Arabs spoke to Danny in a language Mr. Karim did not understand, but Danny's face seemed to light up. According to a Western official privy to Mr. Karim's account, "Danny seemed to get some sort of encouragement that he was near release."

Immediately after that, Danny was videotaped saying: "My father is Jewish.... My mother is Jewish.... I am a Jew." He read a statement criticizing the United States. Then, rather than releasing him, his executioners put a blindfold over Danny's head and decapitated him. Afterward, the Arabs ordered Mr. Karim and the other guards to cut Danny's body into pieces.

❦

The place was Pakistan. The year was 2002. The murderers were Arabs. But something about the tragedy of Daniel Pearl reminds me of another place and time, another set of villains....

In his memoirs, Elie Wiesel writes of the period before the Holocaust spread to his Transylvanian hometown:

> We were told of arbitrary arrests, systematic humiliation, collective persecution, and even of pogroms and massacres. And yet. The truth is that, in spite of everything we knew about Nazi Germany, we had an inexplicable confidence in German culture and humanism. We kept telling ourselves that this was, after all, a civilized people, that we must not give credence to exaggerated rumors about its army's behavior.

Mr. Wiesel goes on to describe how, after the Jews of his town were prohibited from conducting business, were made to wear the yellow star, were ghettoized, and had their valuables confiscated, and even after the deportations began, his family still did not suspect the murderous intentions of the Germans.

Their loyal Catholic maid Maria offered them a hiding place: a remote cabin in the mountains far from the Germans and their Hungarian accomplices. Maria begged them to come with her. She promised to feed and take care of them. The Wiesel family, after a hasty meeting at their kitchen table, refused Maria's offer. "We surely would have accepted her offer had we known that 'destination unknown' meant Birkenau."

Two days later, the family was deported to the death camp, where Elie's parents, grandmother, and little sister were killed in the gas chambers.

Citing how kindly the advancing German troops had treated the Jews during World War I, Mr. Wiesel writes: "We all fell into the trap history had set for us."

The trap was not of history. History, if objectively observed, would have warned that in Europe both educated and uneducated, religious and secular, left-wing and right-wing peoples have murdered, maimed, raped, and savaged Jews for the last two millennia. Jews at the advent of the Holocaust, no less than Daniel Pearl, fell into the trap not of history, but of humanism.

Humanism is the philosophy that emphasizes the dignity and worth of the individual, with the basic premise that people are rational beings who possess the capacity for truth and goodness.

Jews believe that human beings are created in the image of God, which many take to mean that all human beings are essentially good. Peel away the misguided notions of this or that system, and you have a good, decent, kind human being who would not deliberately choose evil.

But it is precisely the ability to choose evil that is the uniqueness of human beings. "Created in the image of God," the Sages inform us, means that human beings were created, like God, with free choice. Animals act from instinct. Humans have the unique ability to choose between good and evil.

The starting point of each human being's free choice varies, according mostly to his or her upbringing. Thus, I suspect that nobody reading this would murder for money — even a lot of money. It is simply beyond our choice box, given the values our parents inculcated in us. But many of us would cheat on our income tax; others of us would not bother to report a bank error in our favor; while some of us would gladly pocket the extra change a supermarket cashier mistakenly gives us. Each of these scenarios poses a choice to the average, ethical human being. "Choice" implies it could go either way.

We are created by our choices. The person who chooses not to report a bank error in his favor will go on to choose to cheat in small ways, which will grow to bigger, more egregious deceptions. Enron executives were not born swindlers; they got there by a myriad of graduated choices.

But once they are there, do not trust them with your money! A person or a nation who has chosen perversity becomes perverse. "The capacity for truth and goodness" which humanism credits to all people can be deactivated by consistently choosing evil. The result is evil people, evil groups, evil nations.

When President Bush speaks about the "axis of evil," humanists shift uncomfortably in their seats. The word *evil* to a humanist is like the word *God* to an atheist. It is simply not part of his or her belief system.

Evil is a reality, not a matter of taste or relative values. "One person's terrorist is another person's freedom fighter" is a repudiation of any meaningful values. Such mesmerizing of our moral capacities is the ultimate legerdemain of evil; if you can't see it, you can't fight it.

Humanists, who usually inhabit the liberal end of the political spectrum, are quick to array themselves against those they call "fundamentalists." Such "fundamentalists" are usually painted as Bible-thumping, religious fanatics. But "fundamentalism" also refers to "a point of view characterized by rigid adherence to fundamental or basic principles." What could be more rigid than adhering to the belief in the essential goodness of man after the Holocaust? After the Ramallah lynching? After the beheading of Daniel Pearl?

Professor Judea Pearl of UCLA marked the yahrtzeit of his son by publishing an article in the *Wall Street Journal*:

> The murder weapon in Danny's case was aimed not at a face-less enemy or institution, but at a gentle human being — one whose face is now familiar to millions of people around the world. Danny's murderers spent a week with him; they must have seen his radiating humanity. Killing him so brutally, and in front of a video camera, marked a new low in man's inhumanity to man. People of all faiths were thus shocked to realize that mankind can still be dragged to such depths by certain myths and ideologies.

Should we really be "shocked to realize that mankind can still be dragged to such depths"? In Jewish history, there are no "new lows in man's inhumanity to man," only old lows, repeated and re-cycled. In fact, the way Danny was murdered, by decapitation, was the murder mode of choice during the Chmielnicki massacres of 1648–49, when nearly 100,000 Jews were slaughtered.

In his grief, Professor Pearl finds it hard to comprehend why, after spending a week with his gentle son, seeing "his radiating humanity," his captors did not repent of their hatred. After knowing him for a week at close range, how could they have killed him?

The Jewish tendency to trust in the humanity of those who hate us is as old as Jew-hatred itself. In the Hebron Massacre of 1929, 67 Jews were tortured and brutally murdered by their Arab neighbors who had lived next door to them for decades. The story of Ben Zion Gershon was typical.

Ben Zion, who had worked for years as a pharmacist in the Hadassah clinic in Hebron, was known for his acts of kindness to his Arab neighbors. He was so sure of their gratitude, so compassionate for their plight, that he opened his door to an Arab woman feigning labor pains on the first night of the rampage. The mob, hiding in the shadows, rushed in, tied up Ben Zion, and gang-raped his wife. When he pleaded with them, calling them by their names to stop, they replied, "If you don't want to see it, you don't have to," and proceeded to poke out his eyes. In front of the Gershons' two daughters, their neighbors dismembered both Ben Zion and his wife. The story was testified to by one of the daughters, who lived for a week before dying of her wounds. The other daughter spent the rest of her life in a mental institution.

Danny Pearl's captors knew him for six days. Ben Zion Gershon's murderers had known him — had benefited from his kindnesses — for decades. The assumption that "if they only know how good, how humane we are, they wouldn't hate us" is a tenet of humanistic fundamentalist that its proponents hold despite all the historical evidence to the contrary.

Trusting the compassion and essential goodness of our enemies is a naiveté Jews cannot afford. In today's Israel, surrounded by Arabs committed to eradicating the only non-Muslim state in the Middle East, trusting in humane intentions is worse than naiveté; it is sheer madness.

⧜

There is no more patent example of this refusal to recognize evil than the worldwide opposition to America's effort to dethrone Saddam Hussein. How many thousands of his own citizens does he have to gas to death, how many millions does he have to kill and maim in aggressive wars, how many weapons of mass destruction does he have to amass before he will deserve the appellation of evil in the eyes of the demonstrators in Paris, Berlin, and Moscow?

Here in Israel, the country most likely to be targeted by Iraqi missiles carrying chemical warheads, drills were held in every school to rehearse the students for what to do in the event of an Iraqi attack. (We had 39 such missile attacks during the first Gulf War.) When the siren sounds, everyone is supposed to dash to a designated sealed space.

My eight-year-old son studies at a small religious boys' school on Mount Zion, some 10 minutes away from our home in Jerusalem's Old City. Mount Zion has three principal buildings: a giant cathedral called the Church of the Ascension, an ancient Crusader complex which houses my son's school, and the "Chamber of the Holocaust."

This last structure, put together by survivors in the early 1950s, was the very first museum in the world to commemorate the Holocaust. Unlike the large, well-endowed Holocaust museums at Yad Vashem, Washington, and Los Angeles, this one has a single stark room of exhibits: a lamp shade and shoe insole cut out from a Torah scroll, soap purportedly made from Jewish fat, and photographs of piles of naked corpses, their ribs protruding under their starvation-stretched skin. The rest of the Chamber of the Holocaust consists of walls covered with memorial plaques, each one commemorating not an individual, but an entire Jewish community.

The evening after the civil defense drill in the schools, I asked my son where the children from his school were supposed to go when the siren sounds. He answered: "The Chamber of the Holocaust."

I was taken aback. Then I realized that the partly subterranean chamber is no doubt the only sealable space on Mount Zion. A good choice from a tactical point of view.

I am haunted, however, by the image of my son and his young classmates, wearing their juvenile-sized gas masks during an Iraqi attack, sitting amidst the artifacts of the genocide of European Jewry.

And I realize that only the circumstances of time and place distinguish the evil of the Holocaust from the evil of Arab jihad. Essentially there is no difference between Elie Wiesel's family and Daniel Pearl. They both walked unsuspectingly into the clutches of evil. If we don't learn from the tragedies of history, will humanistic fundamentalism be our final folly?

Rabbi Emanuel Feldman

Israel Independence Day: Pain and Blessings

April 2002

*I*am not looking forward to Yom HaAtzma'ut this year. It will be rather painful, especially for those of us fortunate enough to live in Israel.

It is not only that celebrations in the midst of a bloody battle against terrorism will make the day so difficult. Rather, it is the persistence of delusion, the continuing inability of those who urged Israel to give arms and land to the enemy at our gates, to admit their mistake. And they are still at it: still blaming Israel for the present situation, still expressing understanding for Palestinian brutality, still urging Israel to give away more territory in order to appease the hungry lion, still pointing fingers at everyone — the "settlers," the right-wing, the Orthodox — everyone but themselves.

And there is a second source of distress, related to the first. The

RABBI EMANUEL FELDMAN was rabbi of Atlanta's Congregation Beth Jacob for almost 40 years. The former editor of *Tradition Magazine*, he holds a Ph.D. from Emory University, is the author of seven books, and now lives in Jerusalem, where he heads a project to translate Bible commentaries into English.

collapse of Oslo has been marked by intensified incitement against Jews around the world. Beyond the immediate threat to Jewish security, this, too, marks the collapse of one of the major ideological underpinnings of secular Zionism; that once we have our own homeland, flag, and army, we will become a normalized people; that anti-Semitism will cease, because we will then be no different from anyone else.

The Yom HaAtzma'ut speeches will ignore the new reality of our times and will gloss over the bankruptcy of the modern Zionist ideology. The new reality is that the State of Israel has become the contemporary counterpart of the old European Jewish shtetl. In Europe, the thugs of the region, in complicity with the authorities, would incite pogroms against the Jews; and today, so-called civilized nations, with the complicity of world authorities like the United Nations and the European Union, vilify and demonize the Jewish state and stand idly by as bombings and murders are committed upon its people by the neighborhood thugs.

(Interesting how the world clucks its mild disapproval of suicide bombers who kill innocent Jews at random, but then mobilizes all its wrath against the Israelis who move into the areas which house those terrorists.)

Nothing much has changed. Once upon a time the world wished there were no Jews; today it wishes there were no Jewish state. The rallying cry used to be "Jews, go to Palestine"; now it is "Jews, out of Palestine." How ironic that Western Jewish youth groups will visit Auschwitz this spring in perfect safety, but will avoid Israel because of the supposed security risks.

But why should we point fingers at the delusions of others when we ourselves, both in and out of Israel, religious and nonreligious, also find it so difficult to change our ways — not our political ways, but our spiritual ways? We are quick to point at others, but perhaps we share some blame for our current situation.

Even Jews who like to call themselves religious, who observe the mitzvot, are not yet fully aware that the present Jewish predicament is a wakeup call to all of us — a reminder that it is time to begin to reach out to God in a much more serious fashion. If we continue blithely along our normal routine; if we maintain our status quo with the One Above; if our prayers to Him are as perfunctory and mechanical as they always have been; if our consciousness as Jews has not intensified; if our relationship to our Torah has remained static; if we have not once said an urgent personal prayer or passionately read a chapter of Psalms — if, in a word, this crisis has not affected our Jewishness, then in what way are we better than the supporters of Arafat who also find it difficult to change their ways?

The ability to change course, to acknowledge errors, is the true sign of a mature person. What better time for this than now, when the Jewish people are in crisis, not only in the State but throughout the world? Beyond the current difficulties in Israel, we face alarming rates of assimilation and intermarriage throughout the world, plus abysmal levels of Jewish ignorance and illiteracy, coupled with the recrudescence of anti-Semitism.

We cannot simply sit idly by, but yet are not sure what we can do to help. Of course, we can continue to support Israel in the various lands in which we live; we can resolutely visit the State; we can help her financially and emotionally; we can support intensive Jewish education for young and old.

But one vital aspect of our Jewishness must not be overlooked: the need for a bit of personal introspection. God is tapping us on the shoulder and reminding us that He is still our Creator. There are a number of things we can do:

- Reach out with sincerity to our fellow human beings by increasing our *tzedakah*-giving and our acts of kindness.
- Reach out to God through genuine, heartfelt prayer.
- Intensify our devotion to Torah study and practice.
- Begin working on ourselves to become better Jews and better human beings.

Change is never easy, but a small beginning can be made.

I began by saying that we are fortunate to be living in Israel right now. At a time when daily security is an issue, when few people are visiting Israel, when even pro-Jewish groups are canceling scheduled trips for themselves and their young people, it must seem strange to consider oneself fortunate to be here during such times.

But in a profound sense this is so. For one does not always have a chance to be an eyewitness to history as it unfolds before our very eyes. Yes, we ache when we hear the almost daily reports of bombings and murders, and we listen anxiously to every newscast. Yes, we worry when our youngsters leave for school in the morning. And we choose carefully the places where we shop, or eat, or travel, lest we encounter a murderer whose religion teaches him that the quickest ticket to his heaven lies in his ability to murder as many children of Abraham as possible.

But we are fortunate to suffer with the Land of Israel within the Land of Israel and not from the outside. Living here in these times, one feels connected with the people Israel horizontally — across the world today, and vertically — through Jewish history past, present, and future. Jewish suffering is not just an abstraction; it becomes our suffering. Jewish triumph becomes our triumph. Jewish destiny becomes our destiny.

The Talmud reminds us that "Whoever mourns for Jerusalem will be worthy to witness her jubilation" (*Baba Batra* 60b; *Taanit* 30b). We are, then, in a deeply spiritual sense, the fortunate ones: living in the Holy Land during her time of travail, we are assured that we will also be found worthy enough to witness her jubilation. And this is no delusion.

This thought makes it possible to bear the painful aspects of this Yom HaAtzma'ut.

Rebbetzin Tziporah Heller

Feeling the Loss

Mourning is never easy, nor is it meant to be. Recognizing the empty space that can't be filled with distraction or replacement is one of life's most profound experiences. There are losses so devastating that words, no matter how carefully selected, are cheap and banal at best and patronizing at worst. When there is nothing to say, nothing is more eloquent than silence.

There are losses that not only defy any lexicon, but they are so enormous that even our minds cannot grasp them, and we find ourselves in emotional denial. When we realize that the life of any Holocaust survivor has chapters that can never be digested, let alone expressed, we can begin to understand the awesome silence of loss.

When we have no words, there is no way to transmit information. A tragic result is that often the most profound losses are also the least understood, and most often forgotten. To our great-grandchildren, the horror of the Holocaust may become a dusty relic of antique memory, much as the Spanish Inquisition is to us.

No one today can begin to understand the enormity of the loss of the Holy Temple in Jerusalem, the Beit HaMikdash. When it

REBBETZIN TZIPORAH HELLER lives in Jerusalem and is a popular international lecturer on topics of Jewish spirituality. She is the author of *More Precious than Pearls*, *This Way Up*, and *Our Bodies, Our Souls*.

stood, the Temple let us experience spirituality directly. God's presence could be felt in every stone, in every corner — no external catalyst needed.

We have been mourning the loss of this connection for thousands of years, and we no longer have the words to convey its meaning. We go through the motions of mourning, but we need words to make it real.

Let us focus on what the loss of the Temple 2,000 years ago means to us in the new millennia.

The words *Beit HaMikdash* literally means "Holy House." A house is by definition a place to find shelter and comfort and express our identity.

Without a house to call our own, Jews experience discomfort in the world. Physically, we are not comfortable in the face of ceaseless persecution. Nor are we psychologically comfortable unless we have spiritual means of being ourselves. Without it, our collective life is painful and gray.

The need to express our most genuine selves manifests at times in pursuit of justice. This is reflected in social activism. Our collective need to give has been reflected in our caring and generosity. We are an extraordinarily interactive people, but we are still restless. The inner serenity that we seek eludes us; we are not quite at home.

The material world that fulfills us also distracts us from searching for our deepest sense of identity, and at times corrupts us. In recognition, other religions have idealized "rising above" worldly desire. Jews recognize the power and beauty of the world as a catalyst for our capacity to live meaningfully, and we embrace it. But our two worlds, the outer one and the inner one, sometimes remain separate realms.

In the Beit HaMikdash, the spiritual world was not obscured by the physical. The two worlds existed perfectly together through the grace of God's presence.

God Himself is referred to as HaMakom, "The Place." He is the place in which the world exists. The engaging nature of the world conceals God from us, and we drown in the endless pursuit of what the world cannot give us. The exception to this was intense realization of God in the Temple, where the physical stones revealed more holiness than they concealed. It was a place of intense joy. There, we were truly home. We were ourselves, at our best.

The Beit HaMikdash was the glue that held us together as a people. Not only were we "at home," but we also developed a collective identity — one family with common goals, while retaining our individual roles. In such a setting, the external differences between individuals fades, leaving only our yearning for goodness.

Yet when our ability to see the common bond of goodness fades, our focal point changes. Inexorably we focus on the limitations that separate us. Our sense of justice is degraded into ceaseless negativism and biting criticism. This eventually leads to senseless hatred.

Hatred is senseless when there is no desire to improve the relationship between oneself and another person. The fact that "they" are not you is enough of a threat to fear them at first, and then hate them. The more different they are, the greater the threat.

The Temple's destruction was caused by senseless hatred. The factionalism and xenophobic fear of others catapulted a 2,000-year journey toward rectification. Now, the physical return to Israel has given us, for the first time in centuries, a physical means of redefining our nationhood. And though there are signs in the right direction, we are not yet at home.

Will we ever be truly home? Is there a way out?

Maimonides offers a formula that has often been referred to as "senseless love." We must reach out to each other without agendas that corrupt into another form of acquisition. The process is transformative in the way that it changes our focus:

- We are obligated to speak well of other people, sharing our joy at having glimpsed his/her inner beauty. The act of speaking positively allies us to each other. It makes us aware that we are on one team.

- We are obligated to care for each other's material needs. By being aware of how frail and needy our bodies make us, we become more forgiving and tolerant.

- We are obligated to seek out situations that bring honor to others. By doing so, we give them the precious gift of self-esteem and simultaneously remove ourselves from the ego-tistical traps of center stage.

This three-step process is deceptively simple. Yet it can change us dramatically. It can change not only our relationship to others, but can lead us to rediscover ourselves. In doing so, the endless mourning for our lost selves, and for our national tragedies, will cease.

Tisha B'Av, the day we lost the First and Second Temples, is also the day in which the Inquisition edicts were signed over 500 years ago. It is also the fateful day in 1914 that started the World War One, which inevitably led to the worst atrocity mankind has ever experienced, the Holocaust.

For two millennia, the Jewish people have been targeted again and again by hatred and persecution. It seems that we are held to-gether by the world's hatred rather than by love for each other. Yet things can change. We only need to take the steps from hatred to love, from criticism to appreciation.

God Himself has promised that once we achieve this transfor-mation, we will merit to truly come home.

Sara Yoheved Rigler

A Zionist Manifesto

"**R**ead this if your stomach can take it," was the e-mail my cousin Phil sent, along with John Derbyshire's *National Review* article, "Israel's Future," on the odds of the continued existence of the State of Israel.

Sitting here in the Old City of Jerusalem, my stomach barely took it. Mr. Derbyshire presents a compelling case for Israel's inevitable extinction. He quotes Norman Podhoretz in *Commentary* declaring that there is "no glimmer of light at the end of this dark and gloomy tunnel," and counseling Israeli Jews to hunker down and wait for the Arab world to someday make its peace with the existence of a Jewish state in its midst. (Does he expect me to restrain my daughter from venturing into downtown Jerusalem not for weeks, but for decades?!)

Mr. Derbyshire counters this point of view with an even more pessimistic stance, that of policy intellectual Ron Unz, who wrote in a letter to *Commentary*: "I expect Israel's trajectory to follow that of the temporary Crusader kingdoms, surviving for 70 or 80 years following its 1948 establishment, then collapsing under continual Muslim pressure and flagging ideological commitment."

Mr. Derbyshire, who is British, bases his contention that "Israel will go down" on the experience of Northern Ireland. There the

For biography of SARA YOHEVED RIGLER, see p. 28.

terrorist IRA emerged victorious, even enjoying their own offices in the House of Commons, proving, according to Mr. Derbyshire, "that democracy is no match for terrorism":

> Dedicated irredentist terrorists with a single clear goal — Unite Ireland! Destroy Israel! — will get what they want in the end. They have too many things going for them that their opponents, the modern constitutional democracies, do not have. They have stamina — the iron determination to press on for decades, for generations, brushing aside all reverses, weathering all storms, expelling all doubters... They have the luxury of perfect ruthlessness as regards method...
>
> While their enemies debate the morality of this weapon or that, and the best way to avoid "collateral" casualties, and whether their terrorist prisoners should have air conditioning, the terrorists themselves are planting bombs in busy shopping streets, shooting up 12-year-old girls at a bat mitzvah, or leading away the single mother of 10 children to be executed for the "crime" of comforting a dying enemy soldier.

Mr. Derbyshire's logic is infallible and his conclusions would be irrefutable — if there were no God who had promised otherwise. But there is a God. And although He did not promise Northern Ireland to the Protestants, He did — repeatedly and emphatically — promise the Land of Israel to the Jews. And although logic and historical experience usually carry the day, God's will always carries the century.

This does not mean that the knots in my stomach can relax. God's promise of the Land of Israel to the Jews has its unconditional clause and its conditional clause.

God's unconditional promise to Abraham, Isaac, and Jacob is that their children will inherit the Land of Israel as an eternal inheritance. That means that it will always belong to us and will never belong to any other nation, even if they conquer it, claim it, and rule it. Much has already been written about how, during the

2,000-year Jewish absence, the land flowing with milk and honey became a barren wasteland, as if unwilling to yield her fruits to strangers.

But God never promised us a rose garden. The specific quality of the Land of Israel is that God is palpably, constantly present. The inescapable, meticulous Divine providence which is evident in Israel — what the Torah describes, "God's eyes are on the Land of Israel from the beginning of the year to the end of the year" — lends itself to spiritual growth, not to soporifics; to confrontations with self, not to comfort.

The Jewish people has a purpose: to come close to God and reveal His light. The essential nature of the Land of Israel — the goading presence of God here — facilitates this purpose. Thus, only in Israel can the Jewish people be who we were meant to be. The people of Israel and the Land of Israel are united in a marriage which is destined, made in Heaven, for which there can be no divorce. This bond is indissoluble and unconditional.

When the Jewish people is not engaged in its purpose — to come close to God and reveal His light — they do not need to live in the land whose whole raison d'être is to accommodate that purpose. The result is exile. Thus, although the people of Israel and the Land of Israel can never be divorced, they can be separated, as witness two millennia of exile.

Thus, God's promise of the Land of Israel to the Jews has two parts:

1. The promise that we will inherit the land is unconditional.

2. The promise that we will actually reside in the land is conditional.

In the Torah, God clearly and repeatedly lays out the singular condition for living in the land: the fulfillment of the mitzvot. As it says in the second paragraph of the Shema: "If you continually obey My commandments which I am prescribing to you today, and if you love God your Lord, and serve Him with all your heart and with all your soul, then I will [enable you to remain in the Land, but if not]... you will swiftly be banished from the good land which God gives you" (Deuteronomy 11:13–17).

However determined, wily, and brutal the Arab terrorists are, our remaining in Israel depends on one factor only: whether or not we Jews are fulfilling our end of the Covenant.

∞

When we Jews act according to God's will, no enemy succeeds against us. Even the short history of the modern State of Israel testifies to a supernatural providence which defies logic and numbers, confounding the experts' analyses and the pundits' predictions. What would Mr. Derbyshire and Mr. Unz have said on May 14, 1948, as five Arab armies mobilized to devour the Jewish state about to be born, which was so lacking in armaments and training that it sent newly arrived immigrants, mere days in the country, into battle without weapons? How did the universally accepted prediction of a Jewish bloodbath on the eve of the Six Day War turn into Israel's most stunning victory? During the Gulf War, what were the odds that of 39 Scud missiles launched by Saddam Hussein at densely populated Israeli towns, not one would score a direct hit on the Israeli families huddling in their plastic-wrapped rooms?

Anyone who reads Israeli newspapers knows that something other than the laws of physics applies here: "Bomb Explodes in Central Bus Station. No Injuries." "Powerful Car Bomb Guts Store in Mea Shearim. No Injuries." "Five Mortar Shells Fall on Nitzanim. No Injuries."

Walking down Jaffa Road in downtown Jerusalem, amidst construction crews rebuilding a swatch of six stores (!) decimated by a suicide bomber the week before, my logic goes limp trying to fathom how the bomb could have wreaked such damage on a crowded street and caused only one fatality.

Looking back into Jewish history, we see that the explicit promises of God have always been borne out, despite the odds. God promised that the Jews will be "an eternal nation" (Genesis 17:7). The mind-boggling mystery of Jewish survival, despite exile, dispersion, and persecution, was brought by Pascal as proof of the supernatural.

God promised that, after exile, the Jewish people would return to its land (Deuteronomy 30:5). The return of an exiled people to its land after 19 centuries (let alone even three!) is unprecedented in history.

That in the 21st century, Mr. Unz, a living and breathing Jew, is writing about an extant Jewish state is in itself a double miracle.

The annals of the Jewish people have always conformed to the spiritual causality of the Torah rather than to the laws of history. As David Ben Gurion, the first Prime Minister of the State of Israel, declared: "A Jew who does not believe in miracles is not a realist."

God's hand, however, does not always act to save us, as history and current events painfully attest. Historians assert that the First and Second Temples, and the ensuing exiles, were the result of the superior military might of the Babylonians and the Romans, respectively. The Sages of the Talmud contend that the first destruction was caused by three sins: bloodshed, idolatry, and adultery. The second destruction was caused by the even more grievous sin of Jews hating each other.

The shortsighted human propensity to blame tragedy on its immediate physical cause is compared by the Sages to a man beating a dog with a stick. The dog will try to save himself by biting the stick rather than the man.

According to Israel's leading contemporary rabbis, the Arabs are the stick which God is using to beat us. When we Jews turn around and start fulfilling the mitzvot, including, especially, the mitzvah to love one another, the Arab threat will dissipate as surely as the mighty Assyrian army which laid siege to Jerusalem in the eighth century B.C.E. On the brink of despair and defeat, the Jews woke up one morning and found the Assyrian forces gone, decimated by a mysterious plague which had struck their encampment during the night, sending the terrified survivors fleeing in panic.

Nor was this the only time that the Jews were saved by an unexpected reversal of fortune. The holiday of Purim celebrates an equally dramatic salvation from certain extinction. An arch-anti-

Semite (Haman) rises to political power in ancient Persia and convinces the emperor to exterminate every Jewish man, woman, and child. The decree of annihilation is already signed, sealed, and delivered throughout the Persian Empire, in which all of world Jewry resides. Faced with impending doom, the Jews, at Mordechai's urging, do *teshuva* (spiritual return). Three days later, the Queen of Persia (Esther) suddenly reveals to her husband of five years (Achashverosh) that she herself is a Jew. The Jews are saved and their would-be exterminator is hanged, leaving the Mr. Derbyshires of the day scratching their heads.

The prototype for Israel's current impasse should be 4th century B.C.E. Persia, not 20th century Northern Ireland.

❦

Mr. Derbyshire prognosticates that the State of Israel will collapse because the best of its citizens will be worn down by terrorism and leave: "Sick of terror, longing for a normal bourgeois life, those who can — those who have education, talents, marketable skills — will slip away. The dumbed-down remainder, outnumbered and outwitted, will sink into a defeatist lassitude..." He cites a recent poll of Israeli Jews aged 25 to 34: A third want to leave the country.

Here Mr. Derbyshire has hit on the raw nerve of post-Zionism. To the extent that "longing for a normal bourgeois life" defines the motives of modern Israelis (and defined the motive for their parents' and grandparents' aliyah), to that extent will his prophecy prove accurate. Israelis who came to Palestine as a refuge from anti-Semitism or in order to be a nation like all other nations have reached the end of the Zionist road. Today the most dangerous place for Jews to live is Israel, and the other nations of the world have shown, whether by active anti-Zionism of the Durban variety or by the all-pervading European refusal to allow Israel to defend its citizens, that Israel will never be accepted as a normal member of the "family of nations." In this impasse, one version of the Zionist dream has turned into a nightmare from which its erstwhile dreamers long to awake.

For other Jews, however, the Zionist agenda was different from the start. Rather than seeking safety or normalcy, they were seeking their destiny: to be a holy people in the holy land. No amount of Arab-inflicted suffering or loss can deter people for whom the service of God in the land He has chosen is the very purpose of life. Not only was a "normal bourgeois life" never their aim, but most of them accepted the Talmudic maxim: "The Land of Israel is acquired only through suffering."

Mr. Derbyshire, meet:

- Oksana Chelnokov, 32, who immigrated to Israel from Uzbekistan just four months ago and was seriously injured in a recent Jaffa Road homicide bombing. Having lost most of her intestines and her hearing in one ear, Oksana affirmed from her hospital bed that she does not at all regret coming to Israel. "Now I have two birthdays," she asserts, "August 12, the day I was born, and January 27, the day my life was miraculously saved from a terrorist bomber."

- The residents of Israel's northernmost city, Kiryat Shemona, who, after every barrage of Ketusha rockets from Hizbullah across the Lebanese border, emerge from their bomb shelters and proclaim: "This is our home, and even if we have to live in bomb shelters for days on end, we are not leaving our city."

- Ariella Feinstein, 20, from the United States, who came to Israel to study for two years at a Jewish seminary and was injured in the 2001 Ben Yehudah bombing. In the wake of the attack, Ariella — and her American family — decided to make aliyah. "Spiritually, it makes sense to live in Israel," Ariella declared. "I'm a better person in Israel. Besides," she added, referring to the terrorists, "I'm not going to let them win."

- Leonid Kagen, 42, who, one year after he emigrated from the Ukraine to a Jordan Valley moshav, was the victim of a terrorist auto attack. The car Leonid was driving was so badly mangled that an army helicopter had to pull it open for Leonid's crushed body to be extracted. After the army helicopter sped Leonid to Jerusalem's Hadassah Hospital, in the intensive care unit Leonid asserted: "Of course I'm not sorry I came to Israel! Do you think that in Russia they would have called out the army to save a Jew's life?"

- Ellen Fine, who left behind a prosperous medical practice and a luxurious house in California to move, with her family, to a rented apartment in Jerusalem. When the first intifada hit, her friends asked Ellen if she would be returning to the United States. "I was appalled by the question," Ellen recalls. "We came to Israel to build something. America was about getting. Israel is about giving."

- Deena Berlin, 57, born on a religious kibbutz. Recognizing the direct connection between mitzvot and getting to keep the land, Deena adopted two Down-syndrome babies who had been abandoned by their parents at birth, what she calls a "24-hour-a-day mitzvah," as a merit for Jews to keep the holy city of the Patriarchs, Hebron.

If we Jews — each of us individually — choose to love and serve God, then the State of Israel will survive, and our enemies will disappear, as the Psalmist says, "like chaff before the wind." If we choose not to (and the choice is up to us, not the terrorists), then it may well be that the State of Israel "will go down."

But it will not go down as Mr. Derbyshire predicts, with the best of our citizens giving up and moving to the lands of bigger malls and better jobs, safer and more salubrious sites. The Jewish people never willingly went into exile. The Babylonian and Roman victors had to drag us off in chains. No, Mr. Derbyshire, we will go down with our blood and the blood of our children washing over the land, knee-deep, as when the Romans wrested Jerusalem from us. In life or in death, we will not be sundered from our holy land.

When it comes to "stamina," the quality Mr. Derbyshire ascribes to the terrorists, "the iron determination to press on for decades, for generations," nobody has it over the eternal Jews.

Yossi Klein Halevi

Why Israel Fights

April 2002

D espite the blur created by the routinization of terrorism, when one atrocity supplants the next with such rapidity that we lose even the ability to mourn, several clarifying moments have emerged from the last 18 months of war. First was the lynching, in October 2000, of two Israeli reservists inside a Ramallah police station, which erased the distinction between Arafat's Palestinian Authority and "the extremists."

Then there was the bombing, last June, of a discotheque filled with Russian teenagers on a Friday night in Tel Aviv, which erased the distinction between settlements and secular Israel. And last week there was the Seder massacre, which merged mass murder with myth. "In every generation, they rise up against us to destroy us," read one newspaper headline about the massacre, borrowing the Hagaddah's rendition of Jewish history.

Even those of us who despise the far right's comparison of Israel's predicament to the Holocaust recognized this moment: The Nazis, after all, selected Seder night to begin the liquidation of the Warsaw Ghetto. Pragmatic Israelis, who usually avoid the grandiose language of good versus evil, have been forced by the Seder

YOSSI KLEIN HALEVI is a contributing editor at the *New Republic*, where this article first appeared.

massacre to concede that our conflict with the Palestinians isn't just a local squabble between competing nationalisms, but part of a global war against extremist Islamism — the latest totalitarian movement, after Nazism and Soviet communism — to "rise up against us" and target the Jews as its frontline enemy in a war for global domination.

The attack on the festival of freedom was a taunt — a reminder that we are no longer free in our land. Instead, we are being reghettoized through a gradually constricting siege that has taken from us a precious expression of our sovereignty — our ability to roam freely, to engage in possessing the land through tactile exploration. The first intifada denied us freedom of movement in the territories and the Arab neighborhoods of eastern Jerusalem. This intifada has done that for the country as a whole.

We are in danger of becoming a nation of agoraphobes. I know Israelis who don't leave their homes except for work and quick forays for groceries. My four-year-old son's baby-sitter won't take the half-dozen children in her care to the park downstairs. The fear undermines even the refuge of one's own home: One friend, who lives in a Jerusalem neighborhood where a car bomb was recently discovered in the underground garage of an apartment building, lies awake at night worrying that his building is about to explode.

During the 1991 Gulf War, Shlomo Lahat, the former mayor of Tel Aviv, denounced his city's residents as cowards for fleeing missile attacks; now he has called on Israelis to stay in their homes and avoid public places.

And the fear has not only forced us into our homes; it has locked us out of our national, communal space. In our dread of public places, notes Israeli journalist Ari Shavit, lies a threat to our collective identity. Striking at a Seder — which celebrates the founding of the Jewish people — is an unbearable symbol of the war against the Jewish collective. We are in the grip of an experiment testing how long a society can endure under relentless terrorism before it begins to disintegrate. If the experiment continues unchecked, we will become a completely atomized society — or no longer a society at all. A state founded on the survival instinct of the Jewish people risks devolving into the survival instinct of the individual Jew.

Rather than see Israel as the answer to Jewish survival, we are beginning to see it as a threat. Before I moved to Israel 20 years ago, Israeli relatives and friends would ask me when I was planning to settle here, convinced that this was the obvious place for a Jew to live. Now they ask me when I'm planning to return to New York. Our withdrawal from collective Israeli space could lead many here to withdraw from Israel altogether. And mass emigration of Israelis is precisely the goal of this Palestinian war.

And so, this time, the absence of a comprehensible government plan didn't matter. This time, we understood that striking at the Palestinian Authority — a collective response to the assault on our collective being — was itself the plan. On Seder night we knew that the Israeli restraint of the last two weeks, intended to accommodate the Zinni mission, was over. We had to hit back — not just against those attacking us, but also against our own paralysis. That's why — for all the talk of draft resistance — almost all of the 20,000 reservists mobilized for the invasion of Palestinian territories showed up, without the usual attempts to evade reserve duty by pleading sick or citing family or work-related emergencies.

In one sense, it hardly matters that this military operation won't stop the suicide bombers. (Indeed, nothing short of destroying the terrorist infrastructure known as the Palestinian Authority is likely to contain the terrorist assault.) In this war for the survival of our public spaces, reaffirmation of our collective identity is itself a victory. The Zionist revolution has long since forfeited its ideal of the Jewish worker and the Jewish farmer; now, it is the Jewish fighter whose existence is in the balance.

⚭

After the Holocaust, the only enemy with a chance of defeating the Jews was one that could hide behind its own weakness. The Palestinians presented us with an unbearable dilemma, forcing us to choose between the two nonnegotiable demands of Jewish history: not to be oppressors and not to be naive about our enemy's intentions. The very weakness of the Palestinians has been their strength: Precisely because of their vulnerability, we minimized their malevolence, going so far as to create and even arm Arafat's Authority. Now, though, the Palestinian war of national suicide has removed our guilt and squeamishness.

For Israelis, there is something surreal in the world's preoccupation with political solutions to the Middle East crisis. Mitchell-Tenet, the Zinni mission, the Saudi plan — all assume a conflict amenable to rational solutions, a Palestinian leadership ready to accept the legitimacy of a Jewish state. But Arafat in his besieged office proclaiming his desire to die like the Seder suicide bomber — "Oh God, give me martyrdom like this," he told al-Jazeera on March 29 — should have put to rest the fantasies. Does anyone imagine that the Israeli public — even those of us who in principle are ready for almost any concession in exchange for real peace — will accept a plan that involves "sharing" Jerusalem with Arafat?

The world asks anxiously: What will be the consequences of Israel's invasion? For Israelis, that isn't even a question. For us, the only question that matters, at least for now, is whether the fragile collective identity of "Israeli" — stretched thin over a bewildering ethnic and ideological cacophony — will continue to exist. That question will be answered not by the results of the battle, but simply by our willingness to fight it.

Rabbi Berel Wein

Israel's Strength

One of the favorite statements that is bandied about in today's confused political and diplomatic atmosphere is that "since we are so strong, we can afford to be generous in making peace with our neighbors." Without dwelling on whether or not such a statement, even if it were true, makes any real sense or is just the usual pap fed to the public, I am searching for the source of our belief that we are strong.

For strength is not only a measure of military might, of divisions and battalions and missiles and planes, but more importantly, of inner confidence and purpose. And I feel that in that strength we can still use a lot of help.

Stalin once mocked the Pope by asking: "How many divisions does he have?" And yet the truth be said, it was the current Pope who bested Communism in Eastern Europe in our time. He stared down the evil empire with a sense of moral courage and vision that all the divisions of the Soviet army could not match. So in the long run of events, the Pope was stronger than the Soviet system and its despots. For strength is not only a measure of physical prowess. It is surely a trait of purposeful behavior and inner serenity.

RABBI BEREL WEIN is a distinguished Torah scholar and author of a popular series of books and 600 audiotapes on Jewish history. He is the founder of a yeshiva and synagogue in Suffern, New York, and now resides in Jerusalem.

The Sages of the Talmud said that Israel is the strongest and boldest of all nations. This was meant both as criticism of Jewish brashness and aggressiveness, and a compliment to the tenacity and singleness of purpose of the Jewish people. Only a very strong people could have withstood and survived the events of the centuries of the Jewish story.

The strength of Israel was built upon an inner sense of self-worth, of being chosen and unique. It encompassed an iron determination to build and create and prosper and survive, no matter what the odds or the opposition. Our strength was built upon a vision of a better world and a holy future. It provided strength when we were obviously physically weak and persecuted.

I was struck by the fact that at Israel's recent Holocaust Day commemorations, almost all of the official speakers made reference to the fact that Israel is strong and, therefore, is the guarantor that the horrors perpetrated on the Jewish people in the past century will never be repeated. But that can only be true if there is real evidence that somehow we really do care about other Jews and are willing to do something about it.

We must also realize that even if we wish to do something about the persecution of Jews, we are limited no matter how strong we think we are. The case of the 13 Jews imprisoned for espionage in Iran is only one example of the impotence of the strong in difficult situations. The IDF is stronger than the Hizbullah, but our northern border is far from serene.

America was infinitely stronger than the Vietcong, but was nevertheless defeated.

King Solomon had it right when he said, "Victory in war is not necessarily to the mighty."

The source of meaningful strength lies in a shared vision of a society. It lies in a commonly held value system. It lies in a society that is unified in its understanding of itself in spite of all political, social, and religious differences. There was an old Yiddish song that summed up the feelings of Jews in such a society. Its refrain was: "Whatever we are as individuals, we are, but we are all Jews."

Somehow, that attitude of strength and unity has been lost in our current world. Today's refrain sounds like: "Whatever we are as individuals, we are, and those who are not like me are wrong." There is no national consensus any longer as to goals and vision.

Selfishness has consumed us, and the sense of sacrifice and idealistic morale that was a Jewish hallmark throughout the ages has been submerged in narrow parochial interests.

We are in a very difficult time and a very tight situation. It will require enormous strength to be able to extricate ourselves safely and securely from our present entanglements. That strength is not purely dependent upon our national will and courage.

While the expenditures on developing armed might are justified and essential for our survival, an equal expenditure of effort and wealth is necessary to build a national vision of hope and determination. To build that consensus requires honesty of expression and development of moral and spiritual resources.

We should stop boasting hollowly about how strong we are, and instead truly dedicate ourselves to attaining that inner strength which alone will guarantee serenity and peace.

Sara Yoheved Rigler

The True Face of Israeli Youth

The Western media relishes depictions of young Israeli soldiers as callous, mean, and macho. A new study of Israeli 11th and 12th graders — those who are about to become the next batch of soldiers — reveals a very different profile.

A poll conducted in April 2002 by Dr. Mina Tzemach, Israel's preeminent pollster, was published in the Hebrew weekly *Jerusalem*. It paints a portrait of teenagers whose primary value is family, who are afraid to venture out of their houses to have a good time, who are pessimistic that terror attacks will not soon end, or that the State of Israel will still exist by the time they reach middle age — yet who overwhelmingly want to remain in Israel.

Here is a sampling of the results:

What is the most important thing for you to do in life?

To raise a family	33 percent
To find love	24 percent
To help others	21 percent
To serve the country	16 percent
To make money	5 percent

Given the security situation, have you changed or not changed your recreational habits recently?

For biography of SARA YOHEVED RIGLER, see p. 28.

Yes, I go out of the house less   66 percent
Yes, I go out of the house more   1 percent
No, I haven't changed   33 percent

In your opinion, will the terror attacks in Israel continue for weeks, months, or years?

Several weeks   10 percent
Several months to one year   41 percent
At least two years   24 percent
At least ten years   18 percent
Undecided   7 percent

Ultimately, do you believe that there will be peace with the Palestinians?

Never   50 percent
Yes, but it will take many years   45 percent
Yes, soon   4 percent
Undecided   1 percent

In your opinion, will the State of Israel exist in another 50 years?

Definitely yes   54 percent
I think so   32 percent
I think not   6 percent
Definitely not   2 percent
Undecided   6 percent

In return for real peace with the Palestinians, do you support or oppose the division of Jerusalem?

Support   21 percent
Oppose   77 percent
Undecided   2 percent

As a result of the security situation, have you changed your political stand?

No, I haven't changed   58 percent
Yes, I've moved to the right 31 percent
Yes, I've moved to the left   9 percent
Undecided   2 percent

If you had the choice, would you prefer to continue to live in Israel, or would you prefer to move to a different country?

Continue to live in Israel	84 percent
Move to a different country	16 percent

In the framework of military service, which kind of unit would you like to serve in?

Combat unit	55 percent
Administrative unit	15 percent
Professional unit	29 percent
Undecided	1 percent

In the framework of military service, do you prefer to serve in a unit close to home or far from home?

Close to home	72 percent
Far from home	21 percent
Doesn't matter	6 percent
Undecided	1 percent

The pollsters' comment in comparing the last two results above was: "Even though most Israeli high school students are prepared to serve in a combat unit, even so they don't want to be far from their mothers."

Reading this poll, I was struck by the contrast with my own youth in suburban New Jersey. As high school students, our biggest worry was getting admitted to a top college. These Israeli teenagers worry that if they go out for a pizza, they could lose their hands — or their lives.

During my youth in America, gun control was a burning issue. Pro-gun control activists argued that the more guns are readily available, the more violent crimes are committed. In Israel, some two-thirds of the 18- to 21-year-olds walk around armed with an automatic rifle. (Army regulations require soldiers to carry their weapons at all times, including when they are off duty and when they go to sleep.) Yet the number of armed robberies and other crimes committed with these guns is minuscule. According to police spokesperson Susie Ben Baruch, last year there were only two

cases of armed robbery using army-issued guns (which were bran-
dished to scare but not actually fired), and no cases of off-duty soldiers using their guns against another person (domestic quarrels,
personal fights, etc.).

While my generation — the Sixties generation — was known
for its nonmaterialism, times have changed. The present mall generation sprouts more business majors than social workers. Yet only
5 percent of Israeli kids consider making money a life priority. Even
the 12 percent who aspire to become doctors must be seen in context; the standard joke in Israel is that plumbers earn more than
doctors.

As for mortality, my friends and I never gave it a thought.
Death pertained to my parents' generation, as irrelevant to us as
gray hair and paying taxes. As a teenager, I did not know a single
young person who died of any cause. Here in Israel, however, the
specter of mortality confronts every 18-year-old. Rare is the teenager who has not lost a friend, neighbor, or relative while serving
in the army. In a military helicopter collision a few years ago,
which killed 73 soldiers, five of the victims came from a single high
school. Television footage of seniors in that high school a few days
later showed young visages looking directly into the face of death.

The America of my youth was wracked by periodic race riots,
the seismic rumblings of the Civil Rights Movement, and, later, the
upheavals of the war in Vietnam. But these societal convulsions affected me only as much as I allowed. I attended demonstrations on
weekends (except, of course, during exam periods). The great tragedies of my college years — the assassinations of Robert Kennedy
and Martin Luther King, Jr. — drove me and my friends to spend
long, somber hours discussing world issues over espresso at the
Brandeis coffee house.

While I spent my youth in a land prone to occasional societal
earthquakes, young Israelis perceive themselves as building their
lives on quicksand. They are embarking on a future which, simply
put, may not be there when they arrive. Forty-six percent are not
sure their country will even exist 50 years down the road. And 95
percent expect to remain in a state of war with the Arabs for most
of their adult lives. Over 40 percent expect the terror attacks —

which make every outing to a movie or mall into a foray with fate — to last for years. These days, many Israeli 19-year-olds attend more funerals than parties.

Facing this grim scenario, one might expect most young Israelis to opt out, to want to seek a safer, more "normal" life in Los Angeles or Houston. Yet 84 percent of those polled choose to stay in Israel — at whatever cost. Why?

Although the poll included no religious nor philosophical queries, perhaps the answer lies in a result which reveals more unanimity than any of the political questions: 77 percent of Israeli teens oppose the division of Jerusalem — even for "true peace" with the Arabs.

Jerusalem, Zion, the resting place of the Divine presence, has for 3,000 years represented the core of Jewish identity, the place in this physical world which transcends the physical world, the site of our national rendezvous with God. Abdicating Jerusalem, especially the Temple Mount, means abdicating the essence of what it means to be a Jew. On some gut level, Israel's predominantly secular teenagers are not willing to sacrifice their identity as Jews, even for the sake of security, peace, and life itself.

Rabbi Nachum Braverman
and Rabbi Shraga Simmons

Why Jerusalem Matters

It is a city of little strategic value. It has no natural resources — no oil, no diamonds, not even a river or lake. It is not a center of culture, nor industry, nor trade.

And yet, Jerusalem is the heart of our world.

Throughout the millennia, Jews from far reaches of the globe have turned in prayer toward Jerusalem. At each Jewish wedding, the groom breaks a glass to commemorate the destruction of the Holy Temple. And we close each Passover Seder with the resonating words — "Next year in Jerusalem."

As voiced by the great Rabbi Judah HaLevy: "I am in the west... but my heart is in the east..." — in Jerusalem.

Jewish tradition teaches that all of creation began in Jerusalem. The epicenter is Mount Moriah, known by mystics as "the watering stone." The world flows into this spot, and from here all life force radiates outward.

Jerusalem is a preeminent theme of the Bible, mentioned 400

RABBI NACHUM BRAVERMAN studied philosophy at Yale University. He is the author of *The Bible for the Clueless but Curious* and coauthor of *The Death of Cupid*. He lives in Los Angeles with his wife and family, where he is West Coast Director for the Jerusalem Fund of Aish HaTorah.
For biography of RABBI SHRAGA SIMMONS, see p. 121.

times. It is here, on Mount Moriah, that the patriarch Isaac was bound for sacrifice. And it is here that his son Jacob dreamed of the ladder ascending to Heaven.

Three thousand years ago, King David purchased the summit of Mount Moriah and made Jerusalem his capital. It was here that his son Solomon built the Holy Temple. And it was here — three times a year on the pilgrimage festivals — that the entire Jewish nation gathered as one.

Jerusalem became the focus of the non-Jewish world as well. Ancient maps show Jerusalem at the epicenter of Asia, Europe, and Africa. Non-Jews, drawn by a magnetic spiritual power, brought offerings to the Temple. In the words of the prophet Isaiah, this was truly "a house of prayer for all nations."

Then, with the Roman conquest in the year 70, the Second Temple was destroyed and the Jewish nation sent into exile. The Romans carted off the Temple treasures and gave Jerusalem a new Latin name. Jewish life, the Romans proclaimed, had now ended.

But the Jewish connection to Jerusalem proved stronger than the will of the Roman empire.

Despite impossible conditions, Jews stubbornly refused to abandon Jerusalem. In the face of disease, lack of water, and marauding bandits, the Jewish presence remained. Barred by law from living here, Jews returned. Wiped out by Crusaders, Jews returned.

All told, Jerusalem was destroyed and rebuilt nine times. And through all this, one symbol remained intact: the Western Wall.

It became known as the "Wailing Wall" because of the centuries of endless tears, shed by Jews yearning to rebuild Jerusalem.

The Wall became the symbol of both our devastation and our hope. Just as the Wall persists in the face of countless efforts to destroy it, so too the Jewish people remain eternal.

In 1948, as Israel fought its War of Independence, Arab armies destroyed 58 synagogues in the Old City of Jerusalem and used Jewish gravestones from the nearby Mount of Olives to pave roads and build latrines.

When the cease-fire lines were drawn, Jerusalem was divided and Jews were once again banished from the Western Wall, permitted only to gaze across the barbed wire... across the endless expanse of time.

Nineteen years later in the Six Day War, Israeli paratroopers mounted an offensive against Jordanian forces in Jerusalem. Despite heavy casualties, the Israeli troops pushed on and entered the Old City through the Lion's Gate.

"Har HaBayit b'yadeinu!" came the triumphant cry — "The Temple Mount is in our hands!" Amidst shofar blasts, grown men wept and danced at the Western Wall. After 2,000 years, Jerusalem was finally liberated and united, under Jewish control, with free access for all.

Jerusalem, however, was not the only thing liberated during the Six Day War. With Jerusalem — the Jewish heart — now healthy and strong, vitality was pumped to the most distant extremities, renewing the spirit of Jews worldwide.

Millions of Jews who had been distanced from our land and our legacy felt a fresh surge of identity. Like a sleeping giant awakening from slumber, we felt Jewish oneness, we felt Jewish pride.

This pride ignited a Jewish renaissance. Millions of Jews caught behind the Iron Wall of the Soviet Union were suddenly infused with a yearning to go home. Arrested by the KGB and faced with the harshest of punishments, Natan Sharansky defiantly declared: "Next year in Jerusalem!"

In America, a grassroots movement blossomed, reconnecting thousands of Jews to their heritage.

This renaissance was possible because throughout Jewish history, our vision of Jerusalem remained unchanged.

In 1905, when Britain's Lord Balfour offered Kenya to the Jews, Chaim Weizman would accept nothing but the Holy Land. At that moment, Balfour later said, he knew that a people so determined and true to its principles would eventually triumph.

Jerusalem is no mere historical asset. It is our roots — the deepest roots that any people has. Elsewhere, we grope for insight. In Jerusalem, we achieve clarity and define who we are.

We are a nation of priests and prophets, a light unto humanity. We taught the world to dream of the day when "nation shall not lift up sword against nation, nor shall man learn war anymore...."

When Aldous Huxley said, "We have each of us our Jerusalem," he meant more than a temporal city of alleyways and olive groves, of hi-tech and taxi cabs. He meant a metaphor for the perfected world — a world in which love and justice, not power and self-interest, is the currency by which men live.

Jerusalem gives us strength to achieve that vision, to unite our people, and to sanctify the world. In Jerusalem, the Jewish heart — and soul — is restored. And that is why Jerusalem matters.

ISRAEL
DIARIES

Dvora Levin

Virtual Tourism in Israel

October 2002

Sitting with a friend in a once-popular restaurant in Ein Kerem, a neighborhood in Jerusalem, I was startled to see how empty it was. A young guard sat at the front gate. Next to him, a note was posted stating that all customers were to pay an extra two shekels to help cover his cost.

After getting the bill, I asked to speak to the manager. I told him, while the waiter hovered in the background worried about a complaint, that I would be paying three times the amount of the bill. I explained that as a visitor coming to visit family and friends during these terrible times, I had brought "virtual tourists" with me.

Most of the members of my small Jewish community in Victoria, on the far west coast of Canada, were heartfelt in their support of Israelis. However, the realities of their lives prevented them from coming personally. So they had sent me with money ($1,700) to spend on virtual drinks, meals, services, and gifts. They particularly asked me to support small businesses suffering from serious economic losses due to direct and threatened terrorist attacks and lack of tourism.

The manager and now-smiling waiter were clearly surprised

DVORA LEVIN, originally from Canada, lived in Jerusalem for 13 years. She is now a consultant in Victoria, British Columbia.

and very moved. "We in Israel feel that we are all alone in the world," he said. "It is amazing that there are others so far away who actually care about us here."

I laughed and said, "Actually they are virtually here, having virtual meals. But their money is real."

Over the next few minutes, another waiter and two waitresses came to the table to thank me and to hear the story of "virtual tourists" for themselves. The manager asked for my name and presented me a Hebrew book on the history of Ein Kerem, inscribed by the staff with a warm note of appreciation for bringing a smile to their day.

This idea of "virtual tourism" had been picked up by our rabbi, Harry Bremmer, and passed along in our synagogue and by e-mail a few days before I was to leave for Israel. During final preparations for my trip, I was constantly interrupted by calls and visitors, dropping off checks and cash. Needing to get some sleep before my departure, I finally had to ask the late callers to pass along their donations to the next community members to go.

Throughout my two-week stay in Israel, I repeated my "virtual tourist" explanation, often twice to the same stunned owner or manager of small businesses, cafés, restaurants, hairdressers, flower stores, and gift shops.

One small gift shop on Yoel Solomon Street, at the bottom of the Ben Yehudah Mall, remarked on the sweetness of this idea. She went on to tell me of one shop owner down the street who had a funeral for his closing business. He dressed in black and invited his friends and the press for a funeral — an amazing display of humor and sadness.

Half of the 500 tourist shops in Jerusalem have shut down since the increase in violence; 75 percent of hotel beds are empty. In the central area of the city, 40 restaurants have closed.

I found my own voice breaking with feeling as I repeated the story over again. One small pizza place on Emek Refa'im had just reopened that morning after a dreadful bombing of a café just up the street. After explaining "virtual tourism" to him and giving him 100 shekels (four times the bill of 25 shekels), he suggested that 50 shekels would be enough. I insisted, and he then tried to negotiate a compromise of 75 shekels. I insisted that I was obliged to give him the full 100 shekels for the other "virtual tourists" with me.

He said what a good luck sign it was, on this first day of reopening. We laughed together about the irony of someone negotiating to be paid less.

On the occasion of each small purchase, my friends joined in this delightful experience, which became a bond between us, the owners and my small community in Victoria, which grew less distant from us each day.

Some managers demanded I tell them what to do with the extra money, remarking they had no key on the cash register for such an item. I told them I had fulfilled my responsibility, and that this would be their big problem for the day. Many said they would share it with their staff. Some quickly said they would pass it along to someone "who really needs it."

The last of the funds was spent on 15 pitas (with the Jerusalem mixture of spicy shwarma meats) for the IDF negotiating team dealing with the standoff at the Bethlehem Church of the Nativity. One of my friends was on his way for reserve duty with this group and delivered the pitas.

❧❧❧

As this small idea moved into action, from my community, through me, to Israeli small-business people and friends, I became aware of it rippling out in circles beyond our knowing. One friend's son told of it in his citizenship class. Visiting relatives of another couple passed it by e-mail to their home community in America. No doubt, others would be passing it along over dinner and in phone conversations.

When asked why he thought this small act was met with such emotion, one Israeli said because it is so unexpected and completely unconditional, something for nothing, an expression of our being together.

Early in this process, I realized I had not only given, but was also being given a truly uplifting gift. My fervent hope is that others going to Israel will take along their own "virtual tourists," to leave their footprints on the shores of the turbulent sea of our homeland.

And just as our footprints are being washed away by the tides, more will be made, and Israelis will know that they are not alone. For we are with them.

Sarah Shapiro

Coffee with My Enemies

April 2003

W hen the three women walk in smiling, eyes straight ahead, my amazed gaze follows, intrusive and impolite. Twenty-five, almost 30 years here and I'm eternally a stubborn innocent, as yet to be desensitized to the unending bizarreness of it, day in, day out. My pleasant American childhood simply did not format me properly for the constant, complicated stream of this particular sort of data: in this instance, that people whose cultural abhorrence of Jews, and whose insecurity in our midst, are such that they can't enter a crowded Jerusalem coffee shop without armoring themselves against humiliation with an air of defiant nonchalance... that these women who wouldn't object to me and my family being murdered — at least that's what their chadors tell me — are chatting amiably and pulling out chairs a few inches away.

In line at the post office a half-hour earlier, I'd run into a friend and we'd gotten into a conversation about the American prisoners-of-war, whose capture in Iraq had been on the 7:00 news. They'd

For biography of SARAH SHAPIRO, see p. 102.

taken a wrong turn and were ambushed — shall we Israelis pride ourselves on being old hands at such wrong turns? — and the two of us were dwelling on the possibility of a Palestinian-style lynching. The radio had said one of them was a young mother.

We shuddered.

I invited her for a cappuccino. She didn't have time, she said. Today was her nephew's yahrtzeit, the anniversary of his death.

In my mind's eye I saw a burned-out bus. "Your nephew?"

"Yeah. My sister's son." Her sky-blue eyes filled instantly and she looked determinedly off to one side until the brimming stopped. Her expression declared that this happened a lot and she was sick and tired of it. "He was in the army."

I asked where and she said Jenin.

"Jenin?" Unlike most soldiers' deaths, the 14 which took place during the invasion of Jenin — Israel's response to last spring's suicide bombings — stood out vividly in my memory. Immediate cause: a booby-trapped house. Underlying cause: IDF policy whereby civilian Palestinian casualties are avoided by conducting house-to-house searches rather than aerial bombing.

She asked if I remembered how one of them had dismantled the Palestinian Authority computers, and I said of course, I'd read all about it. In the midst of battle, a 21-year-old soldier had sat down in the PA Office and methodically extracted their hard discs, thereby providing Israel with documentary evidence of Yasser Arafat's ongoing funding of suicide bombers. "No! That was your nephew? Devorah!"

She nodded.

"Gedalia, right? I remember the picture!"

She smirked. "Yeah, that picture. One woman called and said she just knew he had to be one of our relatives. He and my daughter had the same blue eyes, exactly." Devorah's eyes brimmed and she gave them two quick brushes with the back of her hand. "I better go. We're all meeting at the cemetery."

I wait for the waitress to finish clearing their table, then twist around in my chair to face them. They surely can't help noticing this, of course — we're sitting back to back — but they don't immediately let on. What's the Jewish woman up to? I wait awkwardly for a pause in their conversation, which doesn't come, and am feeling worse than foolish; I feel masochistic. My sense of myself as the unwanted other, the hated intruder, is surely at this moment not unlike theirs.

Finally, uncertainly, I say, "*Slichah*, excuse me. Would you like to... talk, maybe?"

There's some equally vague response that I don't catch. They exchange glances under lowered eyes, something's muttered in Arabic, then they sort of laugh to each other uncomfortably. Now that I'm looking right at them, I see that actually, only one of them is in a chador, and if not for her, it wouldn't occur to me that the others are not young middle-class Israeli housewives, sleek and stylish, in sweater-sets and slacks. Any sabra age five and up, in my experience, can differentiate instantaneously between Arab and Jew — when in doubt I've always been able to ask my children — but I'm not in possession of that elusive sixth sense.

The one in the corner, who's leaning back at an angle against the wall, one arm draped casually over the back of her chair, is now directly returning my gaze. Her glossy hair's done up in a jaunty black ponytail and she's sizing me up from behind a cool, guarded smile. "You want to talk?"

It's good that my friend Jodi can't see me right now.

"Yes, if you'd like to. I never get a chance to speak to Palestinian women. Because of — you know, the *matzav*." That all-encompassing word, meaning... everything. The situation. All the screaming, and the speeding ambulances. Shattered children, mourning parents, maimed and burned bodies. Griefs that will never depart.

Who knows what it means to these three.

With a hospitable little wave of the hand she gestures an invitation, flicking aside the past three years and all the centuries that came before. "*Bevakashah*," she offers. "*Lamah lo.*" Why not?

Why not, indeed.

I was telling Jodi about my conversation with a Palestinian taxi driver. It was the day after a suicide bombing.

"You asked him what he thought about it?" she demanded, incredulous. "Are you crazy?"

"Jodi, he said that *pigu'im* [terrorist attacks] are against the Koran. He said he wants to live in peace with Jews, that there's room enough for everyone in this beautiful country, but that he can't say so. If he were to go to Ramallah and tell Arafat he's against *pigu'im*, he said they'd go like this." I pointed a forefinger to my forehead, then drew my finger across my lips, as he had. "He said he has to remain quiet or die."

"So what?" she snapped. "You think that means something? You think he's going to tell his Jewish fare what he really thinks? I don't get it. I don't get you. What possible difference does it make what some Arab taxi driver says? I'd rather not hear it! Showing sympathy to him like that is a betrayal. If it were your brother who'd been killed, then would you be conducting these little surveys of yours?"

I slip my purse strap over one shoulder and pick up my half-drunk cappuccino for the move, one table over, into Palestinian territory, feeling obscurely embarrassed before my own self. Here we have fresh evidence, as if any were needed, of the indomitable Jewish optimism which throughout our millennia in the Diaspora has served as a crucial factor in our survival, and which in the Middle East, during the Oslo peace process, led us perilously close to self-destruction. Hope does indeed spring eternal in the human breast, especially the Jewish breast, as does my enduring, perhaps inborn belief, after all these bloody years, that when two reasonably sane individuals face each other, a potential for mutual understanding is always present; that here in this divided land, there are reachable human beings on the other side. Words from the heart speak to the heart. As I take the empty seat at their table, the unoccupied seat, that line's running through the back of my mind.

But running along, too, through the back of my mind is the other voice, caustic with disgust. *I don't get it... your little surveys....*

"So what would you like to speak about?" It's the one in the corner.

If it were your brother.... "Well..." I mutter. "What do you think about what's going on?" She's staring at me. Her eye shadow's lavender, her lipstick dark maroon. "I'd like to hear about your experience."

What kind of reply can one expect to such an idiotically broad line of inquiry? But she responds gamely with a pert nod of agreement. "That's true. We don't know what you on the other side are thinking. It would be good to know."

She introduces herself. Her name is Hulda. That is Rila, or Rala, and this — did she say Ismat? — is in the chador, seated to my right. "My name is Sarah," I tell them, expecting recognition of that standard from the Bible, but they ask me to repeat myself, as unfamiliar with my name as I am with theirs. Addressing myself to that maroon smile and instinctively avoiding the other two, I press on with more stupid questions, to which she's replying in general, cordial terms. Mutual understanding here we come! The three of them take their lunch break here often, usually around this time. Strange we've never before crossed paths. They work as secretaries. Where do they live? Ramallah. Oh! Whaddya know! Rala, sitting opposite me — demure in a smooth pageboy, her shining dark eyes positively frightened, a strand of gold at the neck, another at the wrist — can understand a little Hebrew but can't speak it, and doesn't know English. She, Hulda, speaking in Hebrew, also doesn't know English. Ismat knows both. They've got to be getting back to work soon, and Rala has to be home by 1:30 for her daughter. We navigate a back-and-forth for about five more minutes, refraining expertly from shedding any light whatsoever on the subject I said I wanted to discuss.

And now, since no summit meeting worth its salt should conclude without one of my little surveys, Hulda listens to a question and says no, of course she does not approve of the killing of innocent people.

Rala nods.

Okay, ladies! Over and out! I push my coffee cup toward the center of the table and give a little sigh, signaling that this failed experiment in Utopianism has come to an end.

"You are frightened of us?"

This from the woman on my right. I turn, seeing the face in the chador for the first time. Brown eyes. Rather prominent nose. No makeup. Hair, neck, most of the forehead concealed beneath the hood.

"You mean the three of you?" I ask.

"Yes. You are scared of us?" She's speaking in English.

"No." I tell myself to say the truth. "But I'm scared of Palestinian men."

"Why? You think we are aggressive?"

I assume she must be kidding; the set of her mouth tells me she certainly is not. I say I'm scared because of suicide bombers.

"We are not an aggressive people." Her voice is decisive but quiet. "The Palestinians are a very kind people. A very hospitable people. Go to their homes, they treat their guests like kings. Palestinians fight against Israelis because of what the Israelis do to them. Do you know what happened in Jenin?"

I'm about to say that if she's referring to the famous massacre that wasn't, the Palestinian accusations were investigated by the United Nations — not known for its support of the Jewish State — and found to be without foundation. But the futility of such a debate deflates me before I start.

"The Israelis knocked down houses with people inside them," Ismat is saying. "They buried people alive."

I ask how she knows this.

"It was on television. What would you do if your people were being attacked? If your homes were being destroyed, if your children were being shot. The Israelis make our lives very hard. You know how long it took us to get to work today through the Israeli checkpoints?"

"All of that is only because of terrorism. If the terrorism would stop, Israelis would build a normal life together with you. It's part of the Jewish character to want to make peace. We accept your presence here, and if you would accept ours" — here I take a cue from the taxi driver — "there'd be room enough for everyone in this beautiful little country. Look, you know very well what can happen if a Jew goes to one of your neighborhoods." She peers at me with an expression I can't quite identify — a mix of amused interest and reluctant agreement. "But you come here for lunch and know that nobody's going to hurt you. Right?"

A little smile's playing on her lips. "Yes. This is true."

I shift gears and ask if she likes Saddam Hussein.

"No, I don't like him, but he is strong. With the Iraqi people he has to be strong. Saddam is not bothering anyone outside his country. The Americans are there only because of oil."

I say no, they are there because of his support for terrorism, and because of what he does to his own people, and could do in the future to others.

"Saddam does not support terrorism."

"He sends support for suicide bombers here, doesn't he?"

She pauses, then says, "If you ask me what you asked them," — she points with her chin across the table, where Hulda and Rala have been conversing in undertones — "Do I approve of suicide bombings, my answer is yes, I do."

Have I misunderstood? I ask her to repeat herself, which she does, whereupon I signal to the waitress to bring my bill. As I count out change for a tip and gather up my stuff, something within me, old and familiar, has already fallen in mutely upon itself. Nothing serious, though. It will spring back up soon enough. I push back my chair and start to rise. "If you approve of suicide bombings, then I can't talk to you."

They scrutinize me with bemused expressions. And then, with what appears to be sincere curiosity, Ismat asks, "Why not?"

Alan Leventen

Fighting for Israel

July 2002

Although I'm a busy executive on Wall Street, I took time off in July 2002 to fly to Israel and serve as a volunteer with the border police. For 12 days, myself and 11 other volunteers were posted overlooking the West Bank town of Jenin, the spot where, in the last year and a half, at least 24 suicide bombers have crossed into Israel.

All day long, I wore army-issue fatigues, a flak vest, carried a full pack and an M-16 assault rifle, and patrolled cotton fields on the lookout for Palestinians crossing into Israel illegally.

They put me on the front line because I'm pushy, and I had army experience. I had served as a paratrooper in the Israeli Army 30 years earlier. In fact, when I finished high school, I didn't go to graduation exercises. I went straight to Israel to serve in the army. How did that all come about?

I was a hyperactive child who attended the Detroit public schools. In the '50s and early '60s most educational systems did not know how to deal with attention deficit, hyperactive, or dyslexic children. In my case, I was known as being smart and athletic.

ALAN LEVENTEN is first vice president with a major Wall Street financial firm. He is a former professor at Columbia University, and served as a paratrooper with the Israel Defense Forces from 1970 to 1973.

But the stigma associated with the hyperactivity had consequences. I got shifted around — to a private school, and then to a military school in Indiana.

My parents didn't know it, but this was a parochial military school, which meant that they marched us in ranks to church every day — an hour before lunch and two hours on Sunday. After a few months of this, I began speaking out in class and asking the priest some uncomfortable questions. This caused a negative reaction, even from the friends I managed to have because I was a good athlete. They'd gather around my room and call me dirty Jew, Christ killer, and similar names.

To make a long story short, I was sent back to the Detroit public schools. I spent my free time studying Jewish history. I would read almost any book I could get my hands on and I would ask my father a lot of questions. During the Six Day War, all of us became very concerned about whether or not Israel was going to survive. With the stunning victory, my Jewish pride came out and the pace of my interest picked up even more. I made a decision, at the age of 14, that after high school I was going to Israel to serve in the IDF.

My mother said, "Over my dead body." And my father thought he was going to lose a son. But no one was going to stop me.

It turned out to be a great experience. I served for three years and have never regretted it.

My "military career" lay dormant for 30 years, and then on September 11, I heard the first plane slam into the World Trade Center from my office on the 40th floor of a nearby building.

After hustling my wife, who works with me, and several colleagues out of the building, I headed toward the Twin Towers, thinking I might be able to use my medic training from the Israeli paratroopers.

I didn't know it at the time, but one of my closest friends and colleagues was having breakfast in Windows on the World, on top of the north tower, and died when it collapsed.

I decided that I wouldn't attend any more funerals without being able to say that I did everything I can to stop this from ever happening again.

You can go along in life feeling like a victim, or you can take active steps to reverse the evil.

September 11 brought home the issue that this is a global war on terror. It's not just Israel's war; it's a war between two civilizations, two cultures, two different belief systems. When I came this summer to fight for Israel, I was also fighting for my wife, colleagues, and fellow citizens in New York. Whether you fight them in Afghanistan or in Jenin, it doesn't matter. The difference is that as a Jew it's much more poignant for me to fight the terror in Israel.

I feel I'm making a contribution, not out of hatred or vengeance, but out of love.

❧

In July 2002, I showed up for my 12-day stint.

Initially the Israelis were skeptical about having an American executive in their unit. But eventually they saw I was a very good soldier. I may not be able to run as fast or as far as I once did, but my shooting is outstanding (thanks to military school) and I also have "predator's eyesight" — I can see movement at a distance. It's crucial to be constantly alert in this type of environment. We're dealing with human beings, yet at the same time, someone could blow himself up in your face.

I went on an operation in Jenin to snatch a terrorist. The guy we were after was a paymaster with a briefcase full of pay slips for the families of suicide bombers. It was a very professional operation and it was very exciting. At the time, the 28-year-old assistant commanding officer of our unit didn't know anything about me other than the fact I was a volunteer.

After the operation, an article was published about me in the *New York Daily News*. A few days later the officer said, "Aren't you the guy who was in my operation? I read about you. I was very touched when you talked about 9/11. You said that you go around with a constant sensation of having been kicked in the stomach. Let me share something with you. Do you remember in early June the bus bombing at Meggido Junction? At the back of the bus were a number of people who didn't die from the bomb, but the fuel tanks caught on fire and they burned to death. There was one young couple who, in the process of being immolated, died embracing one another. I witnessed the whole thing before my very eyes and we couldn't do anything for these people. When you described the sensation of constantly being kicked in the stomach, that's exactly how I feel."

Here was the commanding officer, and me — his rifleman. He's almost half my age. But at that moment we were more than just comrades. We connected on a level that transcended time and space. We were committed to fighting this battle together.

To me, success doesn't mean having a lot of money or fancy titles. In terms of financial resources, I do okay and live reasonably well. But I'm much more concerned about who I am as a person and whether I'm doing everything I can to improve on that.

I start with the assumption that I am deeply flawed. If you accept that premise, and you care about your life and want to bring value to yourself, then you do everything you can to improve. That means responding to the world and its challenges in a way that you can be proud of, even though it may be difficult.

If you've ever had the experience of looking in the face of someone who is hard-core Islamic Jihad or Hamas, you know they are not of this world. And once you've seen that, you realize that you can't negotiate with evil. There's only one thing you can do. You have to cut it out just like you'd cut out a cancerous mass from a human body — or the whole body dies.

This is a heavy time in the world. People have to make a choice which passport to travel on — are you traveling as a child of light, or as a child of darkness?

The Jewish people represent something very deep and important to the world, which is why the world cares so much about what we do. The Jewish people can make a huge difference in this world if we carry out our mission. God will not allow us to rest and become like every other nation. Israel will only be allowed to rest when it accomplishes its vision of being a light unto the nations.

I believe that success ultimately comes from one's sense of self-esteem, and that comes from strength of moral character. How many people do you know who are truly willing to stand up, and not just give lip service, to principles they believe in? I try to ask myself: Do I help my fellowman when he needs me? Am I courageous or am I a coward? And if I'm a coward, do I recognize it and try to overcome it?

I'm trying to balance my personal and business life. I admit that patrolling the Israeli border is an extremely odd way of doing it. It's hot, hard work. But I do it because it's bigger than the welfare of my family or myself. It gives my life added value.

And I plan to come back at least twice a year for the next few years — as long as my knees hold out.

Ester (Ellen) Katz Silvers

Tears at Rachel's Tomb

As an 18-year-old college student, I had only begun to wade in the waters of Jewish observance when I made my first visit to Israel in 1972. Coming with my Bnai Brith Youth background, I was ready to see a living Israel and did not give much thought to the Torah side of the country. Still, once I had visited the Western Wall and did all the hikes and museums that were part of my summer tour, I felt drawn to Rachel's Tomb.

Why Rachel's burial spot and not Leah's, I really couldn't say. Perhaps it was the lithograph of Rachel's Tomb hanging on my grandmother's wall that I had grown up with. Maybe it was the Sunday School notion of poor Rachel, Jacob's beloved, who had her happiness sacrificed by the wicked Lavan. Whatever the reason, I wanted to see her tomb, so one day a friend and I took the bus to Bethlehem.

I don't know what I expected from the visit, but it certainly wasn't what I found. Yes, my grandmother's picture had prepared me for the small, domed building surrounded by trees where Rachel's grave stood. And I expected the tall, stone tomb covered with a velvet tapestry inside the building. What I did not expect, though, was all the elderly women gathered around the tomb.

ESTER KATZ SILVERS is an aspiring novelist who was born and raised in Wichita, Kansas. Her favorite place to write about is Israel, where she lives with her husband and seven children.

Looking back, I wonder how old they really were — 40, 50, 60? From my youthful viewpoint they seemed ancient, and all of them seemed to have come to Rachel full of heartache. Why else did each and every one of them pour out their hearts, voices full of sobs, faces full of tears, hands clutching handkerchiefs and prayer books?

My friend and I entered the room gingerly, tiptoeing and quiet, not sure what to do with ourselves. What did one do at the burial spot of a holy person? Reciting Psalms was certainly not for us. We looked at the women as if for guidance, and finding none, we looked at each other. Suddenly, without warning, we both simultaneously burst into giggles. Both of us tried to swallow them, and if we had been alone, we probably could have succeeded. But every time we looked at each other, the laughter bubbled to the surface and escaped out of our mouths as if it controlled us.

Now it is hard to understand just exactly what struck us as funny. Growing up with a sentimental mother and a European father, tears were not uncommon in my house. We cried, believe me, we cried. We always took handkerchiefs to bar mitzvahs and weddings, to going-away parties and graduations, to tear-jerking movies and the like. Our tears, for the most part, were quiet, well-mannered tears. Sobs of prayer or despair were reserved for the privacy of our own home. I never heard anyone cry out loud while praying in a synagogue.

Here at Rachel's Tomb, these women seemed totally devoid of inhibition. They were acting at her graveside the way I would behave only in my own room, on my bed, all alone.

These women had an entirely different culture, and I guess it was the contrast that did us in. We did have enough manners to feel embarrassed and, finally, we managed to pull each other aside. Collapsing on the stone bench, we gave way to hysterics, and although we received sympathetic glances from a busload of tourists, the guard looked at us as if he was scandalized. Not wanting to offend anyone, we dragged each other out of the enclosure and to the bus stop across the road. So ended my first visit to Rachel's Tomb.

I returned not long afterward to America, dove deeper into the waters of Judaism, and married. Fourteen years later, with five children, I made aliyah and settled in Shilo, where the biblical Tabernacle had once stood. For various reasons, I never managed to return to Rachel's Tomb until Passover 1992.

It had not been an easy winter. Like every year, we had our hands full with normal family crises. What had made that year so hard was the intensification of Mideast violence. Rocks and firebombs had become passe, and our Arab neighbors had begun using firearms against us. Five months earlier, a bus full of neighbors was attacked, and my dear friend Raquela Druke was murdered. Not only did I mourn her, but I also became terrorized.

I struggled with my faith every time I or a loved one had to travel. No longer could I casually load up my family and food into our van and enjoy a day's outing. Still, it was the middle of the Passover week and hope of springtime was in the air. All of us deserved a good time and I was determined that we would have one. Swallowing my fears, we made our way south to picnic, sightsee, and to visit the burial sites of our biblical ancestors. Rachel's Tomb was our first stop and I was eager to step inside. In spite of everything that had happened, I had much to be thankful for.

We emptied out of the car, groggy from the long, hot drive. My husband took the boys to the men's side of the tomb, and I took the two girls. I entered Rachel's Tomb, my girls' hands in mine, and suddenly the tears started.

Just like the laughter 20 years earlier, I could not stop the tears. It was as if they controlled me.

"Why are you crying, Mommy?"

I could only shake my head at my three-year-old's question. Had I tried to speak, the silent tears would have turned into heartrending sobs. Besides, what could I have answered? Was I crying for our biblical mother Rachel who had died in childbirth so many years ago? Were my tears for my neighbor, Raquela, who had left behind her seven children and, in my eyes, was a symbol of all Jewish women today? Or were my tears for myself as part of the Jewish people who were still waiting, after such a long time, for "the children to return to their borders"?

Unable to talk, I squeezed my daughters' hands tighter. My

tears continued to flow unchecked, and in my imagination I envisioned two college coeds, dressed in clothing of the '70s, staring at me and trying to control their laughter. Was I now so comfortable in a synagogue or holy site that I could let my private feelings show? How had the "me" I had been 20 years earlier changed so much?

Thankful for the metamorphosis I had undergone, I suddenly felt a sense of hope and healing that I had not felt in all the time since Raquela's murder. Surely if God had changed me from the giggling teenager I had been into the weeping mother I am, He could change the violent world that we live in to one of peace and redemption.

Yaffa Ganz

A Place to Sigh

I once went to a funeral — a spring funeral — at the Mount Herzl military cemetery in Jerusalem. An Israeli soldier had been killed. Another name was added to a list, a long list of Jews who have given their lives in the past 50-plus years so that the Jewish State of Israel might live.

I didn't know this particular soldier, but it didn't matter. He was one of ours — our children, our soldiers, our sons, our people. His name was Yehoshua Yehudah Friedberg, but he was more commonly known by his English name, Jason. He had come to Israel alone, from Montreal, and had joined the IDF. Now his parents, stunned, bewildered, jet-lagged, disoriented, had hurriedly come to join him one last time — for his funeral.

The mother who brought forth a child from her womb would now return him to the womb of the earth. The father who dreamed of escorting his son to the marriage canopy now followed him to the grave.

YAFFA GANZ is the award-winning author of more than 40 books for Jewish children, two books of essays for adults, and many articles of Jewish interest in publications worldwide. Her newest books are *The Travels and Tales of Dr. Emanuel J. Mitzvah, Doctor of Mostly Everything*; *Savta Simcha and the Roundabout Journey to Jerusalem*; and *The Adventures of Jeremy and Heddy Levi*. The Ganzes live in Jerusalem and are the happy grandparents of a growing clan.

He was so young, their son. Old enough to be a soldier; old enough to have made aliyah; but barely finished with the business of being a boy. He thought he was returning to his ancient homeland to begin a new life. How could he know that he was coming home to end his short sojourn in this world?

The funeral should have taken place a week earlier, but it took four or five days to find his body. You see, Jason had been kidnapped and then brutally slaughtered by terrorists. Then a huge snowstorm in Canada grounded all planes. No one knew if his parents would arrive on time.

So thousands of strangers came in their place. They did not know Jason personally, but they claimed him as their own, perhaps because he had come to them alone. Like our father Abraham, Jason had left the safe and familiar to follow his God and to join his people in the Promised Land.

He wore their khaki uniform and stood side by side with his brothers and sisters, willing to endanger his life and, if need be, make the ultimate sacrifice for their welfare. In ancient Egypt, Pharaoh had buried Jewish infants in the walls and monuments memorializing Egypt's dead. Now, Jewish soldiers stood shoulder to shoulder, forming a living wall to protect Jewish children and keep them alive. Jason stood with them.

He was kidnapped, tortured, and killed because of a khaki uniform, a blue and white flag, a Star of David. Because "in every generation, they rise up against us to destroy us." Because he was a glowing, living stone in our protective wall. Because he was a son of Abraham, a son of the covenant, a Jew in a Jewish land.

His parents spent 20 years or so raising him — through fevers and vaccinations and summer vacations and birthday parties and worries and hopes — many, many hopes. They were all laid to rest on that gray, spring afternoon in the Holy City of Jerusalem.

I was swept along in the sea of silent marchers. They edged silently forward, crunching the gravel of well-tended paths beneath their feet. The air was heavy with their silence and their sighs. All along the paths they sighed. Old people and young. Thousands and thousands of them, parents carrying babies, students holding books, soldiers toting guns.

They stopped before the freshly dug gravesite and the sweeping, communal sigh was heard again. They huddled together, each one alone, before that awful gap in the ground. The earth lay open and exposed, its surface turned back like flaps of skin on a human chest, ready for surgery. Was the gaping hole a wound in the heart of the land? Or had the land opened its heart to embrace yet another son, and gather in his war-torn body as his soul journeyed onward?

No one spoke. There were no words. Only heavy, heart-weary sighs.

The almond trees were in bloom. Frothy white blossoms covered the mountaintop like spring brides hovering over still, sleeping grooms. Life and death mingled like old friends at a party. For some, life in all its turbulence would, meanwhile, go on. For others, time was forever stilled. The exact date was etched on stone.

Even the birds were still that day. Hundreds of trees grace Mount Herzl and thousands of birds fill the mountainside with their music. But that day all were strangely mute. Suddenly, one lonely songbird pierced the wall of silence with a stunning serenade.

"Do not despair! This is not the end! A soul has returned to his Maker, but there is still work waiting to be done, worlds to be built, songs to be sung. The world is alive with the promise of spring. God wills that life go on!"

Jason was no more, but *Am Yisrael Chai* — his people are alive.

The crowd listened to the Kaddish prayer and in a hushed, muted voice, answered Amen. And they sighed.

It is not easy to carry the burden of the Land of Israel. It is no simple matter to be deserving of this ancient, holy, demanding homeland. For the Wandering Jew, even a small plot of land, just big enough to hold a military coffin, comes with a steep price. Even when the land is ours.

The cemetery is peaceful, quiet, very beautiful. The mountain is terraced with waves of neatly tended, low, square stones, each one lovingly landscaped and decorated, bordered with bright flowers and green plants. Each stone is carefully lettered with a name, parents' names, date of birth, place of birth, date of death. The letters are silent, but the stones cry — for those who died so that after 2,000 years, the Jewish people might finally live — in peace — in their own Promised Land.

Those who lie here have a right to this lovely hill, this exclusive piece of land overlooking the Holy City of Jerusalem. They have paid for it with precious life's blood.

And we have a right to our Promised Land. But there is a price, even for a promise. When, I wonder, will the price be paid in full? My eyes wander across the seemingly endless rows of stones. They fill with tears.

It begins to rain. Even in Heaven, the tears will flow.

Esther Wachsman

His Name Was
Nachshon Wachsman

I was born in a DP camp in Germany in 1947 to parents who had survived the ovens of Nazi Germany, in which their entire families had perished. We — my parents, my sister (who had been hidden by a Catholic family during the war) and I — sailed to America in 1950. I grew up as a child of survivors, and became a true JAP — Jewish American Princess. But the cloud of depression, of a deep sadness and melancholy, hung over our home.

As is typical of the "Second Generation Syndrome," I was my parents' sole reason for existence. Their hope, their future, all their expectations were wrapped up in me. I knew without their ever having said anything that I had to be the smartest, the prettiest, the most popular, the most obedient and best of all children.

That was a tough burden for a little girl, a young lady, and later a wife and mother, to carry. I, too, demanded excellence and perfection of myself — and later of my children.

In 1969 I immigrated to Israel and came to Jerusalem, where I attended Hebrew University, going for my master's degree in history, specializing in the Holocaust. My parents were Zionists, and their sole remaining relatives lived in Israel. I came to study with

ESTHER WACHSMAN lives in Jerusalem.

their blessing, though when I met my future husband and knew that only here in Jerusalem did I wish to raise my family, I'm not sure they were too thrilled.

I had caught the bug. I was going to be part of the history of our old-new homeland, and I would raise proud, independent, believing Jewish children in their homeland after 2,000 years of exile. I could no longer simply pray for the "Return to Zion" and the "Building of Jerusalem" when I knew I was a plane ticket away from fulfilling those prayers.

And so I was married to Yehudah in 1970, and we had seven sons between 1971 and 1986. Our sons were raised on a threefold love — of their people, their land, and their heritage, the Torah. Our lives were complete, my dreams fulfilled, and I felt privileged to be able to live my life and raise my children in this, our sacred city, in this, our God-given land.

I taught English at the Hebrew University High School for 28 years. My children grew up, attended yeshivot, and in time served their country, proudly wearing the uniform of the Jewish army. How proud I was — the Jewish immigrant from Brooklyn, mother of soldiers of Israel!

My two oldest sons — named after ancestors, grandparents who had perished in the Holocaust — served in the Golani Brigade. When the time came for my third son, Nachshon, to be drafted, he wanted to outdo his two older brothers and volunteered for an elite commando unit of Golani. His brothers mocked him, for he was shorter and slighter than the big staffing soldiers in that unit, but he persevered and became a soldier in the Orev Golani. He was the pride of his brothers, of his entire family.

Nachshon was not named after any ancestors. We chose his name because he was born on the last day of Passover, just after we'd read the Torah portion about the Jews crossing the Red Sea. Nachshon, the son of Aminadav, the head of the tribe of Yehudah, was the first to jump into the water, thereby expressing complete belief in God's promise that the water would turn into dry land, and all of the Children of Israel followed him. It was also at this time of the year, in Passover of 1948, that Operation Nachshon took place — the maneuver that opened the road to Jerusalem. So

we felt that the name *Nachshon* incorporated all of our ideals —
faith and belief in God and love of our people and our land.

Nachshon did us proud, as did all our sons and, thank God,
lived up to his name.

After serving in the army for a little over a year, with two stints
in Lebanon, Nachshon came home for a week's leave on Friday, October 7, 1994, just before the Sabbath. On Saturday night, he got a
call from the army informing him that the following day, Sunday,
he was to report up north, where he and another soldier would
learn to operate a special military vehicle, and in a one-day course
receive a license.

Nachshon found this offer very prestigious, and got a ride with
a friend to take the course up north. He left us late Saturday night
and told us he would be back home the following night.

Nachshon did not come home on Sunday night. Perhaps because of my background with overprotective parents, I always
want to know where my children are and when to expect them
home. They always notify me of any delay or change of plans.

When by midnight Nachshon did not call or arrive home, I
feared the worst. We notified the military authorities, we traced his
movements, we spoke to his army friends. We discovered from one
of them that he had been dropped off after completing the course
at the Bnai Atarot junction — one of the most populated areas in
the center of Israel — where he could either catch a bus or hitch-
hike (as all soldiers do) to Jerusalem. This friend was the last one to
have seen him.

On Monday we sent search parties to the area where he had
last been seen. At this point the army was still unconcerned, and
was more or less making inquiries at resorts in Eilat to see if he had
just taken off. The fact that I told them such a thing was simply out
of the question in my family just seemed to amuse them as the attitude of a typical Jewish mother. To me, on Monday, my child was
dead.

On Tuesday, we were contacted by Israeli Television, who told
us that they had received a videotape from a Reuters photographer
showing my son being held hostage by Hamas terrorists. They said
they were coming directly to our home to show us the video before

broadcasting it to the entire nation, and the world.

On that videotape, Nachshon was seen, bound hand and foot, with a terrorist whose face was covered with a keffiyeh, holding up Nachshon's identity card. The terrorist recited his home address and identity number, and then Nachshon spoke at gunpoint. He said that he had been kidnapped by Hamas, who were demanding the release of their spiritual leader, Achmed Yassin, from an Israeli prison, as well as the release of 200 other imprisoned Hamas terrorists. If these demands were not met, he would be executed on Friday at 8 p.m.

At that point I did not have the "luxury" of breaking down. We were all mobilized for the next four days, 24 hours a day, to do everything in our power to save our son's life. We spoke to Prime Minister Rabin, who informed us that he would not negotiate with terrorists, nor would he yield to blackmail. We announced Nachshon's American citizenship, and President Clinton intervened. Both Secretary of State Warren Christopher, who was in the area, and the United States consul in Jerusalem, Ed Abbington, went to Gaza — where it was believed Nachshon was being held — and brought us messages from Yasser Arafat.

Arafat called our home and told us that he would leave no stone unturned to locate our son and return him to us safe and sound.

We appealed to world leaders everywhere and to Muslim religious leaders, all of whom stated unequivocally on the media that they must not harm our son.

We appealed to our brethren — to Jews throughout the world — and asked them to pray for our son. The Chief Rabbi of Israel designated three chapters of Psalms to be said every day, and people everywhere, including schoolchildren who had never prayed before, did so for the sake of one precious Jewish soul.

I asked women throughout the world to light an extra Shabbat candle for my son. From about 30,000 letters that poured into our home, I learned of thousands of women who had never before lit Shabbat candles, but who did so for the sake of our son — who had become a symbol of everyone's son, brother, friend.

On Thursday night, 24 hours before the ultimatum, a prayer

vigil was held at the Western Wall and, at the same hour, prayer vigils were held throughout the world in synagogues, schools, community centers, street squares... and, yes, churches too. People of good faith everywhere hoped and pleaded and prayed for Nachshon.

At the Western Wall, 100,000 people arrived with almost no notice. Chassidim in black frock coats and long side curls swayed and prayed and cried, side by side with young boys in torn jeans, ponytails and earrings. There was total unity and solidarity of purpose among us — religious and secular, left wing and right wing, Sephardi and Ashkenazi, old and young, rich and poor — an occurrence unprecedented in our sadly fragmented society.

On Friday night before we ushered in Shabbat, I spoke to my son on the media and begged him to be strong, for all our people were with him. We sat rooted to our Shabbat table; my eyes were glued to the door, somehow expecting Nachshon to walk in at any moment.

We were not aware of the fact that Israeli Intelligence had captured the driver of the car that picked Nachshon up, who told our intelligence that the terrorists had all worn *kippot*, there were a Bible and siddur on the dashboard, and chassidic music was playing on the tape deck. An unsuspecting soldier got into the car.

We were not aware that Israeli intelligence had discovered from their informant that Nachshon was being held in a village called Bir Nabbalah, under Israeli rule, located about 10 minutes from our home in Ramot. We were not aware that Prime Minister Rabin had made a decision to launch a military action to attempt to rescue our son.

At the hour of the ultimatum, 8 p.m. Friday, General Yoram Yair, not Nachshon, walked through our door and brought us the terrible news. The military rescue attempt had failed — Nachshon had been killed and so had the commander of the rescue team, Captain Nir Poraz.

At the same hour, people had returned to synagogue, after their Shabbat meal, to recite Psalms for Nachshon's rescue. We called our sons home from the synagogue and together we all sat frozen, unbelieving, shocked, and devastated for the rest of Shabbat.

On Saturday night at midnight we buried our son.

That same microcosm of our people who had come to pray for Nachshon's rescue at the Western Wall came to Mount Herzl at midnight to attend Nachshon's funeral. Many had never before set foot a military cemetery.

My husband's greatest concern when burying his son was that there would be a crisis in faith. My husband asked Nachshon's *rosh yeshiva*, Rabbi Mordechai Elon, who gave the eulogy, to please tell all our people that God did listen to our prayers and that He collected all our tears. He asked Rabbi Elon to tell everyone that just as a father would always like to say "yes" to all his children's requests, yet sometimes has to say "no," though the child may not understand why, so too our Father in Heaven heard our prayers. And though we don't understand why, His answer was "no."

The entire nation mourned with us. Thousands came to comfort us, though no one can comfort a bereaved parent. Israeli radio began each morning's broadcast with the words, "Good morning Israel, we are all with the Wachsman family." Food and drink were delivered nonstop to our home. Bus drivers and taxi drivers who brought people from all over the country to express their condolences left their vehicles and joined their passengers in our home. That unity, solidarity, caring, compassion, and love which was showered upon us gave us strength and filled our hearts with love for our people.

After the shiva mourning period, we all returned to our routines. Our son who had just gotten out of the army attended Hebrew University, another went back to the army, two others returned to yeshiva. The two youngest, twins who turned eight on the day of the funeral, went back to school.

For that is what the Jewish people have always done. We rebuild after destruction and begin new lives from the ashes and blood of the old.

Through all this, I gained a new respect for my parents, who had lost everyone and relocated to a strange land, a foreign tongue, and built a new family, a new life. I was in my own country, my own homeland. My son died wearing his country's uniform, and, God willing, my other sons will serve their country proudly as well.

Among my people I dwell, and that for me is a privilege and a blessing. My threefold love of my people, my land, and my Torah has never wavered.

Sarah Shapiro

Preserve the Vessel

Hatred is like acid; it destroys the vessel that contains it.

(Anonymous)

Blessed are You... our God... Who recalls the kindnesses of our forefathers.... I will always recall the deeds that were done.... A snake [Haman] descended from serpents [Amalek]. When his vileness is recalled, may his memory decay for angering God. That thorny enemy blossomed from the nation that was a constant threat to Israel... generation after generation....

(Yotzer prayer for Parshat Zachor)

Dear Sarah,

I hope that you and yours are well and healthy after the terrible bombing so near your home.

On a magnificent morning in spring, I've just finished lodging my whole litany of complaints, pleas, thanks, worries, fears, and regrets at the Kotel. Walking backwards a few steps, as is the custom, so as not to immediately turn my back to the Wall, I'm thinking of an e-mail I got last night.

For biography of SARAH SHAPIRO, see p. 102.

I spent the day in one of the semi-intensive care rooms at Hadassah, rushing through my routine activities and waiting for the imminent arrival of one of the wounded, a seven-year-old boy with burns over 70 percent of his body.

It was from my friend Chana Siegel, a nurse at Hadassah, and the e-mail happened to arrive the same day we'd had a rug put in one of the bedrooms. On the phone with the store, I'd said something I can't recall having ever said so flatly before, in all these years: "I don't want Arab workers." That shift can probably be attributed to the bombing the night before, which, as Chana said, took place close to our home. Our 15-year-old daughter later realized that it had probably been the suicide bomber whom she and her friends, sitting on a bench outside, late Shabbos afternoon, had seen about a half-hour before the explosion. He'd been wandering around, probably hoping to come across a crowd — which soon he did. One of those who died was a little girl in a carriage. When the child went up in flames, her mother reached madly to pull her out, but couldn't, because her own hand had been blown off.

You clear out a space in the room, which means picking which patient is most suitable to move to a lower level of observation, you move the bed and the dresser out, get the cleaning people to mop up and you try to snag an electric eye IV pump that is not in use. You fill up the nebulizer unit with distilled water, and you make sure you have both an oxygen mask and an oxygen hose, because the patient will almost certainly need supplementary oxygen.

"No, no, *geveret*, don't worry," the man at the carpet store assured me. "Only Jewish workers."

But when I opened the door — who knows how these things happen — it was two young Palestinian men who stood there facing me. One was in his 20s, one a teenager. I showed them in — their eyes averted, as were mine — with all their tools, and buckets, and the roll of carpet.

They worked all day, steadily, with a break for lunch out on the porch. Eyes averted, I had served them Turkish coffee. Every once in a while, tense, I'd looked in on them as the work progressed.

They were doing a good job.

At six o'clock the older one told me they were done. I was out
of checks, so I paid in cash. "Can you give me a receipt?" I asked.

He shook his head, no.

"But —" I didn't know what to make of this. "I'll need a receipt."

"No." He shrugged slightly. "I can't."

"You don't have any from the store?"

He shook his head.

"You can just write it on a piece of paper, then. I'll give you paper."

"No, no." He seemed to be reddening. His eyes, brown,
glanced into mine. "I — can't write." He was ashamed.

"Oh!" He was a very slender, olive-skinned young man. "That's
all right." He looked like one of my cousins, Michael, at that age.
"So I'll write it and you can sign it."

He shook his head. "I can't write Hebrew."

"Oh!" I exclaimed, still trying to get this straight. "So you
mean you can't write in Hebrew. What about Arabic?"

*You rush through the burn treatments of the two burn pa-
tients you already have in the room, and you try to rush the doctors of the various staffs who are planning to release patients today into finishing their release letters so you can hurry up and
check the patient out on the computer, and then explain the release letter to the patient's family. You do whatever you can to
thin out or finish the workload so that you'll be free to deal with
the transfer of what will be a difficult, physically, and emotionally demanding patient, and a family that is bound to be an ex-
hausted emotional wreck.*

Shrugging maybe, he shook his head, no.

"Really, Arabic would be fine. It would be interesting for me!"

I went to get some paper and a pen and pulled out a chair for
him at the dining room table, then watched, over his shoulder,
how the Arabic writing appeared, as if of its own volition, and then
the numbers. He signed it, rose, and handed me the note. I looked
at his signature.

"May I ask what your name is?"

He told me the name (which I've forgotten). Something occurred to me, to ask him. "What do you think of what's happening?"

*And then the boy burned in the suicide bombing does not
come. Because he is not doing so well, after all, and because in
spite of two terrorist attacks (you heard the helicopters coming in
with the wounded from Ofra), he still cannot be released from the
Pediatric Intensive Care Unit. Who were we kidding, anyway?
Seventy percent second and third degree burns is a big deal, a
disaster to the body's ecological system. Thank God they could still
keep him in PICU.*

*Heaven knows, you will get to know him well enough in the
weeks and weeks and weeks he will be with you all in semi-intensive
care, assuming, God willing, he makes it that far. You know, within
certain parameters, what will be, and it will not be pretty.*

Pain flitted over his face. He shook his head, lifting both
hands, palms up. "I don't know," he said, pressing one hand lightly
to his heart. "I am just a small person."

*It will involve oceans and oceans of pain, for the child, for his
family, and, to a more limited extent, for you.*

"Does it hurt you at all, what's happening?" My mind veered
crazily into the thought of the woman reaching for her little girl
and ricocheted crazily away. "When your people do things, when
they hurt children?"

You wish you could just be doing appendectomies and hernias.

"Yes," he said, as I wondered if he meant it. "I don't want to
die. I don't want to send my children to die."

The self-preservation instinct? Could one safely assume, then,
that this was not a likely candidate for martyrdom?

"Oh," I said, "so you have children?"

"Would you like to see?"

*You try to prepare a face for Arab faces you will also meet at the
hospital.*

He took out his wallet. First, a girl, two years old, but it was the
little boy, aged seven, that got me. A sweet face. Disturbingly sweet.

Faces of children you will care for, about whom you will also bring yourself to care.

Once again, "I don't want my children to die."

The Western Wall Plaza stretches out before me. As I head toward the long flight of stairs that I'll be climbing to the Jewish Quarter of the Old City, I notice two Arab women on their way down, arm in arm, one leaning on the other for support.

It's a slow, laborious descent. I slow down as I approach, watching.

You remind yourself that you do this for you, not necessarily for them, because this is part of what it means to be rachmanim b'nei rachmanim — *merciful ones, the children of merciful ones. Because at the end of the day, this is what makes you different from them.*

I see them better now. The difficulty of the older one's walking, and the younger one's difficulty, supporting the weight. A scarf's wrapped around the younger one's head and tied under the chin, as is the custom, but the other one's dressed in secular fashion.

You put your anger in a box and nail the top on tight, because this is not the place, this is not the forum to let it out.

Amazing how hard a mundane thing like going downstairs can be when you're in pain. At the foot of the stairs is a wheelchair, waiting. The younger one must have brought it down and gotten it set up there beforehand.

And you know that tomorrow will be another day in the ward, that no matter how tempting it may be to fall apart, you will continue to function, just as you did today, because tomorrow that little boy, or another one, will be there, and will need you, and a lot of other people who can keep the lid on the box and just get on with it.

They get to the bottom. The older one's not so old, after all — maybe in her mid-50s.

You will try to stop dramatizing yourself by doing things like writing in the second person.

Grimacing, she grips the armrests as the other woman lowers her down. For all I know, the one in the chair, in pain, has dedicated her motherhood to raising suicide bombers. The younger one could very well view it as her sacred duty to hate — or who knows, kill — this Jewish infidel coming their way, who for some unknown reason seems to be looking in their direction.

Even to be civil to these people might be a betrayal of myself, of my people's blood, but if the two of them are blossoms of Amalek, here and now there's no way for me to know. All I can do is to practice self-preservation — Jewish self-preservation — and perpetuate our survival as *rachmanim b'nei rachmanim*.

I nod politely towards the wheelchair. A shadow of the bombing looms up, blocking the sun. "Shalom, *geveret*. Good morning."

The younger one's face is a hard steely surface; her lowered gaze darts instantly away. But the other woman's bleakly stricken countenance tips up towards me from under her body's pain and the deadweight hatred of 3,000 years.

Suspicion flickers under her skin.

Stay well.

But for a fraction of a moment,

Stay healthy.

an uncertain moment

We are all in God's hands.

her face dawns tentatively in grateful surprise.

Love,

Chana

Liba Pearson

Mother Brigade

June 2001

My mother stands all of five-foot-two, but sometimes she seems like a giant.
     The same week that the largest movement in American Judaism cancelled its summer youth trips to Israel, my mom showed up at Ben Gurion Airport ready to make up the difference.

My mother is a cute little woman who, at age 56, has retained something of the air of a wide-eyed cheerleader, and when she gets hold of an idea, she just won't let go. Although it happened to coincide with the painful canceling announcement, her trip was hastily planned a few weeks ago, squeezed in between major projects at work. Sure, she wanted to check up on her only daughter. But she really wanted to do whatever she could to stand in solidarity with the people of Israel.

At first, I found this quite funny.

As the e-mails flew back and forth hatching the details of her trip, I'd snort to friends about my mom's mission: She wants to spend as much money here as possible. Understand, much as I might wish otherwise, my mom is no Michael Steinhardt. She's a generous woman, but the thought of her disposable income mak-

For biography of LIBA PEARSON, see p. 51.

ing any serious dent in the shortfall left by the tourism drought seemed laughable.

Yet when I chuckled affectionately about this one-woman-solidarity-mission, I was met not with grins, but with pauses, long moments in which indecipherable emotions crossed my Israeli friends' faces.

"Wow," they'd say after the pause. "That's great."

The emotion behind the pause, I came to realize, was gratitude.

In normal years, Jerusalem overflows with tourists — mostly Jewish tourists — during the summer months. There are entire swaths of downtown I customarily avoid, lest I be crushed by hordes of baseball-cap wearing kids from NFTY teen tours. At the Western Wall, synagogue after synagogue trips pose for group pictures. Tour buses clog the already-crowded streets and we American *olim* (immigrants) cringe listening to our visiting countrymen trying to bargain down shopkeepers' set prices.

Not so this year. We practically had Ben Yehudah, the pedestrian mall in the center of Jerusalem, to ourselves. The square in the middle of the Jewish Quarter of the Old City, ringed by stores, stood empty.

The economic effects are devastating. Tourism is down by 46 percent, and the Ministry of Tourism estimates the loss for the last quarter of 2000 alone at $1 billion. Hotels and restaurants have laid off staff, closed wings or branches, or even shut down altogether. Tour operators and tour guides are almost completely without work. In the hotel industry alone, at least 20,000 jobs have already been eliminated or furloughed.

Even if the situation improved dramatically tomorrow, it would take 12 to 18 months for the tourist trade to begin to recover. Groups book that far in advance, so filling up the hotels and empty tour guide schedules won't happen overnight.

The absence of tourists hits deeper than mere economics. Israelis feel abandoned.

We are going about our daily lives, expectantly listening to the news every hour, hoping and praying that the latest cease-fire violation won't take anyone's life along with it. We're losing sleep when our husbands, sons, friends, and brothers are called for reserve duty in greater frequency. We grimace at the sensation that, no matter what we do, the whole world is going to condemn us.

And then comes the news that our American brothers and sisters are staying home.

During her visit, my mother mortified me time and again as she whipped out her camera to take pictures of the lines of people at the newly opened Ikea in Netanya. Yes, there's a crisis going on here, but that doesn't stop the entire country from massing on a reasonably-priced Scandinavian furniture store.

Nor did it stop people from filling Jerusalem's shopping mall in Malcha. There, my mother snapped shots of two cherubic-looking soldiers, telling them sternly to "Be safe!" as she walked away.

"I want people to know that life is going on here, that life is normal," she would explain to shopkeepers and passersby as she documented their comings and goings, while I stood, face burning, in the corner.

"I want people to know that it's safe here!" she would declare, insisting that she feels less safe on the streets of Phoenix than she does on the streets of Jerusalem. She would explain to them how I walk my dog around my neighborhood in the middle of the night without a second thought.

"You'd need an armed guard for that in the States!" she'd exclaim.

She told everyone who would listen that she is angry with other American Jews for staying home, for leaving hotels empty, beaches abandoned, tourist sites barren, and an economy devastated. She is angry at them for staying home at the very time Israelis need to feel that someone in the world stands with them.

And, like every good daughter, I rolled my eyes when she said all this. And then I realized something: While I imagined that her cheerleading sounded silly and overdramatic and maybe even condescending to the tough Israelis, the Israelis themselves didn't see it that way.

Hearing her homily, a cab driver tried to refuse her money for a ride. He was overwhelmed and she had to force him to accept payment. Storekeepers, instead of taking advantage of a willing customer, gave her incredibly fair prices. The $15 or $150 she spent in each store isn't going to make up the huge losses businesses have been suffering. But her attitude — I saw slowly on the faces of storekeepers — made a huge impact.

The Torah portion that we read the Shabbat she was here told of the spies who scoped out the Land of Israel and came back bearing tales of a foreboding and dangerous land. The Jews cried and lost faith in the land that God had promised them. For this sin, they were forced to wander in the desert.

It dawned on me: My spunky little mother was enacting a modern-day *tikkun*, repair, of what the spies did. They came to Israel and scared people off, as some do today, whether it's talking about terrorism or inflation. But my mother came here to document the vitality and beauty and energy that is Israel. She came to scope out the land and go back to tell her fellow Jews how wonderful a land it is that God gave us, and how excited we should be at the opportunity to enter it.

At every store we passed, she marched in and bought some sort of trinket, big or small. "I am here to show solidarity with the Israelis!" she'd chirp.

She'd proudly explain to the storekeeper how she came here to make a difference.

And amazingly, she did.

Sue Tedmon

Insidious
Palestinian Television

Tis week I went to my friend Fatima's house to visit her and see her new baby. It was the first time in three weeks, and the second time in two months, that I'd been there. Before the violence started, I was popping in about once a week or so, and Fatima would stop at my house for coffee and a chat.

Since the violence, Fatima hasn't been coming to visit. She stopped working because of the pregnancy, but still might have come to visit if it hadn't been for the big boulders set in the road to block the way from her village to our town. A few times she called, or I called her, and we'd arrange a time to meet by the boulders — she in her car, me in mine. We'd park on our respective sides, then she would clamber over the rocks to sit in my car, or I'd clamber over and sit in hers, and we'd talk.

I wasn't comfortable going into the village, so I put off her invitations, made excuses about the kids, my husband, the army. One day she asked me to come, and so, impetuously, I just went. I drove around the roadblock, following her in her little car. I had

SUE TEDMON, originally from upstate New York, now lives in Efrat where she teaches English and has been an active participant in Muslim-Jewish dialogues.

my baby with me but wasn't worried about our safety. Once I got into the village, I could see that everything was normal and friendly, just as it had always been.

But everything wasn't the same. Talking with Fatima and her family, I learned that her oldest daughter, in her last year of high school, has had trouble getting to school, and switched to a different school that was easier to get to. She still ends up missing a lot of days because every time there's a Palestinian "martyr's" funeral, the PA cancels school so everyone can go to the funeral and riot afterwards. Fatima doesn't allow her children to participate in such things, so they spend a lot of time at home.

That's where I saw things were different. Fatima's kids have always watched what seems to me to be a lot of television — several hours a day. Her husband, who doesn't work, watches pretty much all day. Usually when my kids and I visited, there'd be some silly soap opera on, all the kids glued to the screen. But for the past few months, it was all "news." I put it in quotation marks because it's not really news. It's propaganda. To my college-educated, Western eyes, it's the most blatant, offensive, obvious kind of junk — bad actors and bad commentators reading from gory scripts of the most inflammatory kind, plainly seeking to inflame the senses of anyone watching.

At first I thought, "No one pays attention to it, it doesn't mean anything" — even though I was bothered by the one-sided, negativity, and falsehood of it all. But what I've seen is that it does have an effect on those who watch it. I can't even blame the viewers: They were seeing it for so many hours, and with no alternative point of view, how could they know enough to question it, let alone criticize or recognize it for what it was?

Fatima called me in a panic one night, saying they had just heard that Jewish residents of our neighborhood near Jerusalem were marching on their villages and shooting everyone. I looked out the window, saw nothing, then sent my husband up the street to check things out. It was perfectly quiet and peaceful, not a soul in sight, not a sound to be heard. I told her then that she should not believe everything on Palestinian TV and radio, that they lied in order to get people upset and angry.

Even as I told her, I could sense her skepticism: "Oh, sure, Sue. You don't know anything more than I do, and of course you don't want to believe that your neighbors would shoot us!"

It was when I spoke with her daughter that same night that I realized the extent of the damage those lies on television had caused. I have known Shiruk for years, ever since she was 11. She is now nearly 18. We have hiked together, cooked, danced, and sang together. She taught my daughter Arabic every week for a couple of months. She is a beautiful, bright, talented girl who hopes to go to college. To put that ambition in perspective, Fatima can barely read Arabic, and in her village few girls finish high school.

Whenever the subject of politics came up, which it inevitably did over the years, Shiruk would wave a hand dismissively at all politicians, Arabs and Israelis alike. They were all the same, she'd say, interested only in putting money in their own pockets instead of serving the people. It wasn't a subject we pursued for very long. We would voice our opinion on areas we could agree on, and let the rest drop.

But the night that Fatima called, I could hear Shiruk shouting in the background. Fatima kept telling her what I was saying, then Shiruk would argue with her mother, saying, "But they're showing it on TV right now! They're cutting off his head!" Finally, Fatima put Shiruk on the phone. I told her, "Listen to me. It is not true. I am here in our town and there is nothing like that going on. Turn off the TV and stop watching that!"

She replied, "But I want to watch and be with my people."

Never before, in the years I had known her, had I heard Shiruk identify with "her people." Her people had always meant her family, her relatives, her village — in that order, with loyalties sharply dropping for each category. Now she wants to be with "her people," the ones who are making Molotov cocktails, the ones who teach small children to throw rocks and fire guns.

If anyone could be immune to political propaganda, I would have thought it was Shiruk. She has spent a lot of time with Jews. After all, she has eaten in our home, been to our parties and synagogue, held our babies. She has a good head on her shoulders, knows English, reads books. But it seems that even the brightest mind is susceptible to hate-mongering, given enough exposure to it.

Kept out of school, Shiruk spends many, many hours watching television. She has seen dramatized, studio-fabricated decapitations, gang rapes, and children being maimed and murdered — all at the hands of "Israeli soldiers." Her younger siblings watch, too, and I imagine that this is the norm in most homes in hundreds of villages throughout the West Bank.

What will the future bring?

Mara (Frei) Goldblatt

A Different Kind of
Independence

What is independence? My dictionary gives me the words liberty, freedom, and self-rule. Which only conjures up more questions: Independent of what? Liberated from whom? And who is the self that is ruling us anyway?

Perhaps by understanding better what freedom is, both at the national and the personal level, we can appreciate the day more deeply.

Life has given me a deep understanding of what it is to be enslaved. On the night of September 5, 1995, an Arab terrorist broke into our home in Ma'aleh Michmas, north of Jerusalem. My husband, Danny Frei, while saving my life and that of our baby daughter, was killed along with our unborn child.

In the blink of an eye, literally, I went from being a happy wife and mother of a little family, to a maimed widow with an orphaned daughter. I was enslaved to the pain, and imprisoned by my new position in life, restrained at various levels physically and emotionally.

With the help of God and of family and friends, I am managing to rise above the deep river that constantly threatens to pull me

MARA (FREI) GOLDBLATT holds a master's degree from Hebrew University in Environmental Chemistry. She presently lives in Chicago with her husband and three children.

under. Almost five years later I am remarried to a kind, gentle soul; my daughter Rachel is now six years old, and I also have twin babies and a beautiful *bayit ne'eman b'Yisrael*, a "faithful house in Israel," in another Jewish town.

I've worked hard at finding my smile, and with it, freedom from my wounds.

Today, I took our kids to an indoor playground in Jerusalem. Rachel was at a friend's house and I was helping my toddlers play in the large box of colorful balls. There was a six-year-old boy who insisted on playing there, too, and playing hard. Cute as he was, I was there to protect my children. An elderly Israeli gentleman who was looking after the boy tried to coax him into the other areas designated for bigger kids, or to at least be careful of those around him. But a little while later, the boy managed to jump on my kids quicker then I could stop him, and both of my toddlers started crying at once. Like any mother bear protecting her children, I acted fast. I couldn't remove both of them from the danger at the same time, so instead I acted to remove the danger.

I wasn't gentle, and the grandfather didn't hesitate to tell me so.

Words ensued and the tough-looking Israeli had a stunned look on his face. I believe he was shocked that a woman with such an American accent could think to answer back a man of his stature — and in Hebrew, no less.

For the first time, I was seeing up close the Israeli attitude of: "I drained the swamps. Give me respect."

And in one sense it's a legitimate attitude. How many veteran Israelis have lost dear ones or have been physically maimed in war? And what have we Anglo-Saxons really gone through, anyway?

Yet if only he could see my scars, I thought to myself. If only we had the ability to see into others' backgrounds, and thus be able to better appreciate their position. That's what I really wanted to say to this man and to all the onlookers. How long does it take to say, "I've made it"? Ten, 20, or 30 years? Must I lose a husband through a terror attack? Or a child in war? Only then do I have the right to demand respect?

That is what part of me felt like saying. But I held back. Because I have been working on freeing myself of that bondage. If what I have to say is important and has meaning, then it doesn't matter who I am. I want it to stand on its own. If I had said today that I, too, am a veteran — with all its ramifications — they would have looked at me differently, and I would have gained respect. But how flimsy such respect would have been.

We all stayed a while longer at the indoor playground. I approached the gentleman and apologized for being rough with his grandchild, saying that I have little doubt that my baby, too, will one day have to learn the meaning of "gentle," just as his grandson did. He accepted the apology and walked away.

A group that supports victims of Arab terror has approached me on numerous occasions to inquire about my state and ask if I need help in any way. It is a fantastic group. But I never became active or used their services, and it's only recently that I realized why.

My approach is different. I am not a victim of Arab terror, but rather a survivor. My first husband, Danny, of blessed memory, is a victim. I am growing independent of the enslavement of terror. I try to liberate myself from using my background to further my needs.

I am ruling myself with God as my Master. No one person or country rules over my destiny. When we celebrate our freedom from slavery on Passover, the physical part is the fluff. Our spiritual freedom of thought and choice are the key points. When the State of Israel celebrates Independence Day, we need to realize what the "rule of self" is and, in turn, Who it is that is sovereign over us.

I was only able to learn this lesson because I am here in a Jewish state. I recognize my good fortune in learning this lesson and growing from it.

King David writes in Psalms:

> Out of my distress I called out to God. God answered me with liberation.... O give thanks to God for He is good. His unwavering love endures forever.

This is what I would really have liked to say to that grandfather at the playground.

Sarah Shapiro

The Flowers

A s my mother was dying far away in America, growing weaker
month by month, the flowers on our porch were dying, too.
It couldn't be helped. It was Israel's sabbatical year; by
Jewish law, the earth lay fallow. I couldn't weed them, couldn't
drown them with fertilizer to make up for my frequent absences.
No one else in the family loved them as much as I; and while my
mother was dying, they kept slipping my mind. I didn't love them
myself.

They weren't getting fed at their appointed times: the tiny
white blossoms with orange at the center were supposed to be watered every morning, before the day got hot; the pink geraniums,
twice a week; the purple nasturtiums, every other day. The leaves
turned yellow, then brown. I didn't care. I'd return from a trip to
Los Angeles (where I'd run up my mother's long distance bill:
"Don't any of you dare take buses! Don't go anywhere!"), and after
a few days would notice that the plants were starving. Who cared?
The intifada was in full swing. Mothers were being shot as they
drove to work, men had been lynched; father after father after father, gone; children were being torn out by their roots. I was losing
Mommy. The land was filling with orphans. They were crying everywhere. Hands and legs were blown off. Our souls turned dry to

For biography of SARAH SHAPIRO, see p. 102.

the touch. Mothers were screaming. Blood soaked the soil.

The flowers withered, and shriveled. They said goodbye.

When the ambulances were shrieking crazily and my electrified heart jumped out of its socket whenever the children left for school; when it would have been an act of heroism or insanity to go downtown for a cappuccino and I didn't want anyone out of my sight, wanted everybody to just stay home for crying out loud; when there was nowhere to go but out on the porch and nowhere to turn but into our own hearts, I remembered the flowers.

My mother had died. It was *erev Pesach*, the day before Passover. We were turning to stone. From the porch we heard the explosions. Sometimes we saw plumes of smoke. The kitchen cabinets had turned white with bleach and our hands were turning red. I stole out of the house. I wanted to forget. I wanted the flower boxes to overflow.

The Russian woman behind the counter dispensed instructions: these, she said, you have to water only when the soil gets dry to the touch, and these, every day; these can get direct sunlight, but these just light, no sun. As she rang up 12 plants and a big bag of moist black dirt, the infants stood in their innocence before me, their tightly shut blossoms all in a row, their glossy, small leaves like green hearts, and my heart sprouted hope. "What do you think of all this?" I asked her, gesturing out the store window to Jerusalem, and the sky. She shrugged. "The world likes us more now, don't you think," I said, "now that we're being killed?" She smiled.

Back home, it took all morning to complete the transplanting. It was hot out there on the porch. Inside, everyone else in the family was scrubbing away. When I finished, I sneaked off to take a nap... a deep, deep sleep. I wanted to dream about my mother but she didn't show. When I woke, I went out to check if any of them had blossomed.

Not yet.

The sky was so intensely gentle, and the evening breeze like a mother's caress.

Just as we sat down for the Seder, the world echoed with thunder as if we were being bombed. Lightning flashed and crashed around us. How strange, in this season. Hail shot down like bullets.

We read: These are the Ten Plagues which the Holy One, Blessed is He, brought upon the Egyptians: blood, frogs, vermin, wild beasts, pestilence, boils, hail.... In every generation, it is each person's duty to regard himself as though he personally had gone out of Egypt. How would they fare out there in the punishing downpour, my little blossoms, out in the cold? At dawn I paid them a visit. They were wilting, but hadn't been destroyed. "They're so fragile," I said. "I wonder why they don't die."

"Because they don't fight against the rain," said my husband.

When the holiday departed, we turned on the radio and heard about the suicide bombing in Netanya.

My flowers blossomed and bloomed and multiplied and died and budded, the endless unfolding of sheer, unnecessary beauty a synonym for God's extravagant kindness. The IDF entered Ramallah and the suicide bombings stopped. What joy! Just to be alive! Back in the store, I got more dirt, more plants. I told the Russian woman that I wanted tiny white blossoms, the kind that spread. She nodded. I was probably one of her best customers. I said, "I get so mad reading the paper, what the world is saying about us. Thank God for the flowers. They're cheaper than a therapist."

"Yes, I know. My son, too. He's 31. He was in Jenin last week. A reservist. He sees CNN, he reads the paper. He gets so furious at what they say, he is furious at their ludicrous stories. He doesn't know what to do with himself. He's jumping out of his skin. I tell him, this is the power of a lie. Why watch it? This one looks not so good," she said, pointing to a wilting white pansy. "You can have it for free. My son and I, ever since we got here 11 years ago, always, this terrorism. If not for that, we would live with them. Why not? Have a state next door, who cares?"

The tiniest flowers opened their secret faces, petal by petal, and greeted me. The black loss of my mother kept blossoming over and over again, new buds born amidst long-buried memories. Spring doesn't die. Once, as I was watering the weak one, the pansy, the runt of the litter, I remembered something in the paper, that in one of the bombings, a few blocks from our apartment, a father found his son on the street and kneeled over him crying, "Don't die! Daddy loves you! Don't die!" But he died. Lo and behold, the pansy bloomed.

What magnificent mornings! We've set up the porch table, put up the umbrella. I make myself cappuccino, or something like it, and drift through all the bad news in the morning paper. The sunshine dapples the trees, the flowers are smiling, and after all, isn't it written in Psalms... Truth will come out of the ground.

Rabbi Shraga Simmons

Missing in Action

The Talmud says that after one year, a person is consoled over the death of a loved one. But the biblical Jacob mourned unendingly for 22 long years following the disappearance of his son Joseph — given the uncertain evidence whether Joseph was dead or alive.

A similar ordeal confronts those Israeli families whose loved ones have been captured by Arab militias and their fates remain unknown.

Since Israeli independence in 1948, 420 Israeli soldiers have been declared "Missing in Action" (MIA). Every year, a state ceremony is held at Mount Herzl, Israel's military cemetery in Jerusalem. The ceremony is on Adar 7, the Hebrew anniversary of the death of Moses, whose final resting place is also not known.

Currently, six of the MIAs are listed as "missing but presumed alive." The IDF follows Jewish law that without concrete evidence of a person's death, he is presumed to be alive.

Over the years, a steady flow of information supports the presumption that some of these MIAs may be alive and held under Syrian and Iranian control. Yet despite the diplomatic and military efforts of over seven successive Israeli governments, almost no progress has been made in determining the fate of the missing men.

For biography of RABBI SHRAGA SIMMONS, see p. 121.

There is no way of knowing their situation — who exactly is holding them, where, and under what conditions. Representatives of international relief organizations have not been allowed to visit them, nor do captors allow the delivery of even a brief note from the MIAs to their families (or from family members to them).

All the while, the families suffer with nagging questions: Was their loved one wounded? Have they received proper medical treatment? What conditions are they being kept in? Are they under interrogation and torture?

Penina Feldman, the mother of one of the MIAs, says: "I cried on Yom HaZikaron (Israeli Memorial Day). I don't even belong to this day. I have nothing. I sit and cry. I don't even have a grave. I want the Jewish people not to forget these boys. Lately, many mothers are mourning their children. For us, to remain not knowing is the worst thing that can be."

The ransoming of captives is closely connected to the commandment of saving a life and occupies a place of supreme importance in Jewish law. Even if there is only a remote chance of finding the person, Jewish law obligates us to search relentlessly until we find him, dead or alive. "Never leave a soldier behind" is the policy of the Israeli army.

Even if there is for certain no chance for survival, Jewish law obligates us to persevere, to try and retrieve the body for burial and identification purposes.

Indeed, the search never stops. In 2001, after an amateur diver found the remnants of an IDF plane that crashed at sea in 1953, the IDF recovered the bodies of the plane's two pilots. After 48 years, the pilots were accorded proper burial.

❦

For the families of MIAs, the pain of being plunged into deep unknown darkness is unspeakable. As long as the bodies of missing soldiers are not brought home, the families know no comfort, have no closure. Jewish law maintains that we are not allowed to say Kaddish or mourn for anyone who is missing.

Yosef Fink and Rahamim Alsheikh were kidnapped by

Hizbullah in 1986 while serving in Lebanon. For five years, the families believed they were alive, until the IDF told them in 1991 that new intelligence indicated the two soldiers were actually dead. Only five years later, after agony for the families and toil for the defense establishment, were their bodies returned in a deal involving the release of Hizbullah prisoners.

"When we were told the boys were dead, we had mixed feelings," Yosef's mother Hadassah Fink told Israeli newspaper *Ha'aretz*. "On the one hand, we were relieved because there was an end to the mystery that had been plaguing us, and we knew that at least the boys weren't suffering anymore — all the while we believed and hoped they were alive, we worried about the conditions of their captivity. On the other hand, it was difficult to accept a final conclusion that ended all our hopes.

"My husband and I had different reactions to the announcement. He immediately accepted it and began mourning the boy. I refused to accept what they said without proof. I wanted them to give me at least something so I could believe it was final.... I allowed myself five more years of illusion that maybe he was alive, that he would suddenly show up. I only began to mourn in 1996, when the bodies were returned."

Hadassah Fink has experienced the anguish before. Her father disappeared toward the end of World War Two, and his body was never recovered, Yair Sheleg of *Ha'aretz* writes. "The uncertainty is maddening," Mrs. Fink says. "The most difficult thing when there's no grave is that everything is up in the air. As much as you know there's no chance he's alive, the fact there's no sign, and no body, makes it difficult to accept he's gone."

"Measuring success is very difficult," says Brigitte Silverberg, who is active on behalf of the MIAs. After the bodies of two MIAs were returned to Israel for burial, someone wished her, "*Mazel tov* (congratulations)."

Silverberg said, "*Mazel tov*?! I'm going to a funeral! On the other hand, the enormous significance of bringing back a missing soldier, even in the most tragic of circumstances, cannot be overstated."

❧❧

Here are the stories of the six Israeli soldiers currently listed as "missing but presumed alive":

Zachary Baumel, Tzvi Feldman, and Yehudah Katz

On June 11, 1982, Israeli soldiers were under heavy fire in a battle near the Lebanese village of Sultan Yaqub. As religious soldiers fighting for their lives, they ran from rock to rock reciting Psalms. Their positions were coordinated over the radio using Hebrew numerology (*gematria*) as a code.

At least five Israeli soldiers were captured, and several hours later, journalists from *Time* magazine, Associated Press, and others reported that Israeli soldiers and tanks were being publicly paraded through the streets of Damascus.

Several years later, two of the captured soldiers were returned to Israel in prisoner exchanges, but three soldiers — Zachary Baumel, Yehudah Katz, and Tzvi Feldman — are still missing. Baumel is an American citizen; Katz and Feldman are the children of Holocaust survivors.

Indications over the years show the men are being held under Syrian control and may still be alive. Riffat Assad, uncle of Syrian President Bashar Assad, and Syrian Defense Minister Mustafa Tlass both stated that Syria is holding Israeli prisoners. As late as 2000, Ibrahim Suliman, a Syrian-American and close friend of (now-deceased) Syrian President Hafez Assad, stated that Zachary Baumel is alive.

Baumel's parents, Yona and Miriam Baumel, are an elderly American couple who made aliyah in 1970 when Zachary was nine. In 1994, they held a hunger strike outside the Prime Minister's office in Jerusalem — insisting that the answer to their son's fate lie in the hands of Yasser Arafat, who in 1993 handed over a broken piece of Baumel's IDF dog tag to an Israeli envoy in Tunisia. Where did Arafat get the dog tag from? Why did he deny he had it for so many years? What else does he know about the MIAs?

Sarah Katz, the mother of Yehudah Katz, says: "I have not given up regarding my son and I am hopeful for good developments. Although so many years have gone by, we believe that our son is hidden in some place, even though he can't let us know. I feel him every day and I don't forget him — and that's the best sign that he's alive."

Ron Arad

On October 16, 1986, Israeli Air Force navigator Ron Arad and a pilot parachuted to the ground when their F-4 Phantom warplane went down over Syrian-controlled Lebanon. The pilot was flown to safety under fire, holding onto the bottom of an Israeli helicopter in a spectacular rescue operation. Arad was taken captive by Amal, a Shi'ite militia group led by Nabih Berri, who later served as speaker of the Lebanese Parliament.

One year after the capture, two photos and three letters — in Arad's handwriting — arrived. "Try to do whatever you can for me," he wrote to his family. "I don't know how, but please say something to our leaders, to the government, to anyone who could do something to get me out of here...."

Arad had been held with Syrian knowledge and approval, and negotiations for his release ended after Arad was "sold" to Iranian-backed forces in Lebanon. The 1949 Geneva Convention (Section 2, Articles 11 & 12) holds Syria responsible for his fate.

Arad's daughter Yuval, an infant at the time of his capture, is now 17 years old.

Guy Hever

On August 17, 1997, IDF soldier Guy Hever was last seen at his army base in the southern Golan Heights. The area was searched thoroughly but no trace of him was found. Today, six years later, there is still no clue what happened.

His mother, Rina Hever, cannot rest until the matter is solved. She told *Ha'aretz*: "As a mother, I still dream and hope that Guy would suddenly open the door and come home. My gut feelings are that he might be held somewhere by some hostile element, waiting for us to come to his rescue."

Elchanan Tannenbaum

On October 15, 2000, Hizbullah announced that an Israeli reserve officer, 54-year-old Elchanan Tannenbaum, had been taken captive while on a business trip to Belgium. Tannenbaum is chronically ill and on medication, but Hizbullah has refused to let anyone see him.

In September 2003, Hizbullah agreed in principle to release Tannenbaum, in exchange for Israel's release of Palestinian and Lebanese prisoners.

Tannenbaum's daughter, Keren Tannenbaum, noted the many years that have passed since the disappearance of Israeli airman Ron Arad, saying, "We don't want to have to wait that long."

The MIA issue has the broadest consensus in Israeli society, where almost every household has a loved one serving in the armed forces. A 1999 Gallup poll showed that the overwhelming majority of Israelis (75.2%) demand that Syria must provide all information about the MIAs before any peace treaty can be signed. The MIA issue continues to make headlines, and Israeli schoolchildren know the names and personal histories of the missing men.

Yet some had a growing sense that not enough was being done. So in 1994, Danny Eisen, an American who made aliyah, founded the International Coalition for Missing Israeli Soldiers (ICMIS), an organization that works tirelessly on behalf of MIAs and their families (www.mia.org.il).

"When the Oslo negotiators first met in 1993, a cornerstone of Palestinian demands was the release of thousands of Palestinians being held in Israeli prisons," says Eisen. "What we got in return was half of Baumel's dog tag. It was obvious that much more needed to be done from our side."

Many people ask: Is it reasonable to believe that after so many years, the MIAs are still alive? If they are alive, why haven't the Arabs used the MIAs as negotiating leverage?

Eisen explains that thugs and dictators are driven by the need to control; by murdering or releasing a prisoner they lose control.

Deceased Syrian President Hafez Assad was once quoted as saying that he "likes the idea of getting up in the morning having something that the Israelis want." It is not unusual to hold prisoners for decades; last year, North Korea released some prisoners it had been holding for 40 years (and others still remain).

"Humans are better-equipped to deal with death than with the unknown," says Eisen. "Our enemies know that and have exploited it."

ICMIS has taken the cause globally, and in 1999 United States President Clinton signed into law House of Representatives Bill #1175, calling for the release of Zachary Baumel and other Israeli MIAs.

Yet what is needed is more than politicians issuing statements, or international bodies volunteering to mediate. Every caring individual must speak out and demand that the terrorists (and the governments that support them) make information on the captives open and available.

To this end, ICMIS has an on-line petition to gather one million signatures in support of Israel's missing soldiers, and another petition of doctors demanding medical care for Elchanan Tannenbaum.

Until the issue is resolved, the agony will endure. "We can't forget," says Penina Feldman, Tzvi's mother. "I once had a dream about the matriarch Rachel. I told her: 'My destiny is your destiny.' [Rachel's son Joseph remained missing for 22 years.] When I woke up, I saw it was the day of Rachel's *yahrtzeit*. We went to her grave and lit a candle."

Prayers for the MIAs can be said:

- Yekutiel Yehudah Nachman ben Sarah (Katz)
- Zecharia Shlomo ben Miriam (Baumel)
- Tzvi ben Penina (Feldman)
- Ron ben Batya (Arad)
- Guy ben Rina (Hever)
- Elchanan ben Rivka (Tannenbaum)

The author thanks Rosally Saltsman for key source material.

Professor Laurie Zoloth

Dear Jewish Studies Faculty at San Francisco State

On campus, incitement against Israel reached a fever pitch in the first few months of 2002, with over 50 documented cases of anti-Semitic acts in and around the Bay Area, including an attempted arson at a synagogue in Berkeley and the firebombing of a San Francisco synagogue. At UC Berkeley, a brick was thrown through the Hillel windows, Hillel property spray-painted with "Hate Jews," and a rabbi's son was beaten up, requiring stitches to his head. Meanwhile, at Concordia University in Montreal, a lecture by Benjamin Netanyahu had to be cancelled when pro-Palestinian groups vandalized a public building and threatened violence against the 650 attendees — forcing police to use pepper spray and tear gas.

The following is a private letter that became public, regarding events at San Francisco State. The accuracy of this letter is supported by police videotapes.

PROFESSOR LAURIE ZOLOTH is former director of the Jewish Studies Program at San Francisco State University. She is now at Northwestern University, as Professor of Medical Humanities and Bioethics and of Religion, and Director of Bioethics, Center for Genetic Medicine.

May 9, 2002

Today, all day, I have been listening to the reactions of students, parents, and community members who were on campus yesterday. I have received e-mail from around the country, and phone calls, worried for both my personal safety on the campus, and for the entire intellectual project of having a Jewish Studies program, and recruiting students to a campus that in the last month has become a venue for hate speech and anti-Semitism.

After nearly seven years as director of Jewish Studies, and after nearly two decades of life here as a student, faculty member, and wife of the Hillel rabbi, after years of patient work and difficult civic discourse, I am saddened to see SFSU return to its notoriety as a place that teaches anti-Semitism, hatred for America, and hatred, above all else, for the Jewish State of Israel, a state that I cherish.

I cannot fully express what it feels like to have to walk across campus daily, past maps of the Middle East that do not include Israel, past posters of cans of soup labeled "canned Palestinian children meat, slaughtered according to Jewish rites under American license," past poster after poster calling out "Zionism = Racism," and "Jews = Nazis."

This is not civic discourse, this is not free speech, and this is like the Weimar Republic with brown shirts it cannot control. This is the casual introduction of the medieval blood libel and virulent hatred smeared around our campus in a manner so ordinary that it hardly excites concern — except if you are a Jew, and you understand that hateful words have always led to hateful deeds.

Yesterday, the hatred coalesced in a hate mob. Yesterday's "Peace in the Middle East Rally" was completely organized by Hillel students, mostly 18 and 19 years old. They spoke about their lives at SFSU and of their support for Israel, and they sang of peace. They wore new Hillel T-shirts that said "peace" in English, Hebrew, and Arabic.

A Russian immigrant, in his new English, spoke of loving his new country, a haven from anti-Semitism. A sophomore spoke about being here only one year, and about the support and community she found at the Hillel House. Both spoke of how hard it was to live as a Jew on this campus, how isolating, how terrifying. A surfer guy, who was a born-again Christian student with long bleached hair, spoke of his support for Israel. And as a young freshman earnestly asked for a moment of silence, all the Jews stood still, listening as the shouted hate of the counterdemonstrators filled the air with abuse.

As soon as the community supporters left, the 50 students who remained — praying in a minyan for the traditional afternoon prayers, or chatting, or cleaning up after the rally — were surrounded by a large, angry crowd of Palestinians and their supporters. But they were not calling for peace. They screamed at us to "go back to Russia" and they screamed that they would kill us all, and other terrible things. They surrounded the praying students, and the elderly women who are our elder college participants, who survived the Holocaust, who helped shape the Bay Area peace movement, only to watch as a threatening crowd shoved the Hillel students against the wall of the plaza.

I had invited members of my Orthodox community to join us, members of my Board of Visitors, and we stood there in despair. Let me remind you that in building the SFSU Jewish Studies program, we asked the same people for their support and that our Jewish community, who pay for the program once as taxpayers and again as Jews, generously supports our program. Let me remind you that ours is arguably one of the Jewish Studies programs in the country most devoted to peace, justice, and diversity since our inception.

As the counterdemonstrators poured into the plaza, screaming at the Jews to "Get out or we will kill you" and "Hitler did not finish the job," I turned to the police and to every administrator I could find and asked them to remove the counterdemonstrators from the plaza, to maintain the separation of 100 feet that we had been promised.

The police told me that they had been told not to arrest anyone, and that if they did, "It would start a riot."

I told them that it already was a riot.

Finally, Fred Astren, the Northern California Hillel Director, and I went up directly to speak with Dean Saffold, who was watching from her post a flight above us. She told us she would call in the

SF police. But the police could do nothing more than surround the Jewish students and community members who were now trapped in a corner of the plaza, grouped under the flags of Israel, while an angry, out-of-control mob, literally chanting for our deaths, surrounded us. Dr. Astren and I went to stand with our students.

This was neither free speech nor discourse, but raw, physical assault.

Was I afraid? No, really more sad that I could not protect my students. Not one administrator came to stand with us. I knew that if a crowd of Palestinian or black students had been there, surrounded by a crowd of white racists screaming racist threats, shielded by police, the faculty and staff would have no trouble deciding which side to stand on.

In fact, the scene recalled for me many moments in the Civil Rights movement, or the United Farm Workers movement, when, as a student, I stood with black and Latino colleagues, surrounded by hateful mobs. Then, as now, I sang peace songs, and then, as now, the hateful crowd screamed at me, "Go back to Russia, Jew." How ironic that today's event all took place under the picture of Cesar Chavez, who led the very demonstrations that I took part in as a student.

There was no safe way out of the plaza. We had to be marched back to the Hillel House under armed SF police guard, and we had to have a police guard remain outside Hillel. I was very proud of the students, who did not flinch and who did not, even one time, resort to violence or anger in retaliation. Several community members who were swept up in the situation simply could not believe what they saw.

One young student told me, "I have read about anti-Semitism in books, but this is the first time I have seen real anti-Semites, people who just hate me without knowing me, just because I am a Jew." She lives in the dorms. Her mother calls and urges her to transfer to a safer campus.

Today is advising day. For me, the question is an open one: what do I advise the Jewish students to do?

David Arenson

Hidden Hero

K oby Azoulay wears a brave face when the subject of autumn vacation arises. He doesn't spend his vacation time
the way many Israelis do, relaxing with his family. Azoulay
spends it putting his life on the line, serving in a combat unit of the
IDF. Every year he leaves his wife, two daughters, and business to
defend his country by doing *milium* — army reserve service. With
the constant terror threat, the need for ex-servicemen to do reserve
duty is paramount.

Azoulay operates a dry-cleaning service in Jerusalem. Behind
this innocuous facade is a humble man of few words. He gets paid
to return clothes to their original condition — to preserve things.
No one notices him as long as he does his job. But should he fail to
remove a stain, he is noticed.

So too with his job as a reservist. He puts his life on the line,
and yet the only time he is noticed is if something goes wrong.

Azoulay has been barely noticed lately, because he was instrumental in preventing three separate terror attacks.

On the night of November 16, 2002, Koby and his fellow reservists were stationed at the Tapuach junction. "We stopped a sus-
picious-looking taxi with an Israeli Arab driver and five other Arabs

DAVID ARENSON, a native of South Africa, has worked as a web designer,
writer, and Israel activist. His travels led him to Jerusalem, where he now
studies at Aish HaTorah.

inside. One of my colleagues noticed that a passenger was agitated," he explains.

The reservists instructed all the passengers to get out of the taxi, and they began checking papers. Upon discovering that one of the Arabs was on the list supplied to them by the Shabak, the Israel secret police, their search intensified. Their alertness uncovered a large quantity of explosives hidden inside two computers in the car.

Sappers destroyed the bomb-laced computers in a controlled explosion. "It was very scary," Koby recalls. "There was something like 20 kilograms of explosives. When we exploded it, everything in sight was destroyed. Imagine the damage it could have done!"

This led to the IDF's subsequent arrest of a leading Hamas figure who was responsible for planning the attempted attack.

That same month, Azoulay's unit thwarted two other attacks. The first occurred at the same Tapuach junction. "We saw a suspicious car about to pass the checkpoint, signaled the car to stop, and instructed the two passengers to get out. Again, one of them was on our list of suspects, so we knew something wasn't right. We told him to open up everything. He had boxes of clothing. The last one was so heavy that he could barely pick it up. He left it, and put his hands up."

The reservists found an explosive belt hidden among the clothes. The terrorists were on their way to perpetrate a suicide attack in Jerusalem.

The other incident occurred when soldiers from the same unit caught two Hamas terrorists driving a stolen Israeli car on the Nablus bypass road. "We found a plastic bag with M-16 and Kalashnikov rifles, bullets, and equipment inside. Thank God we were able to apprehend them in time!"

The West Bank Division Commander honored Azoulay's unit for their actions.

When speaking about his successes, Azoulay is characteristically modest. "It didn't change anything for me. We serve our country. I don't think we're heroes. We have a job to do — fighting terror."

Azoulay gives all the credit to the reservists' wives. "They are the real heroes, taking care of the children and the home while we're away."

Morale amongst soldiers is at an all-time high. In April 2002, during Operation Defensive Shield, the IDF had 110 percent turn-out for its reserve call-up. That means people reported for duty who weren't supposed to — many who were over age 54, when reserve duty no longer applies.

Azoulay sees the spiritual component as well. "When I'm on duty I see the hand of God guiding me. He is always on my mind. Every minute that we're here, we have miracles from Heaven. When you see how many terrorists in Nablus want to kill you, you know for sure that God is saving you.

"You have to be focused all the time, not afraid. We keep our eyes wide open for any potential threat. The atmosphere is tense. You know what can happen if you hesitate in a situation. The consequences of failure are too horrible to contemplate."

Azoulay hopes that Palestinians will soon understand that terrorism achieves nothing. "We want to live in peace. I can't understand how Palestinians think. Why don't they want peace, or to build something? The terrorists bring their life and our life to hell. When Palestinians understand this and start fighting terrorists, then we will have a platform to talk about peace."

Azoulay's goals are modest — to support his family, keep his dry cleaning customers coming back, and keep his country safe from terror.

As long as nobody notices him, he knows he is doing his job well.

Sherri Mandell

Birthday for the Bereaved

June 2001

Y ou may have heard of my son Koby. In May 2001, he and a
friend were brutally murdered near our home in Tekoa, Israel. He was bludgeoned to death in a cave.

He was an innocent 8th grader. He and his friend had cut
school to go hiking in the wadi, the dry riverbed. They wanted to
know the wadi like the back of their hands, his friends told us during the shiva.

June 14 would have been Koby's 14th birthday. On that day, I
was in terrible pain. How do you celebrate the birthday of your oldest child, who is no longer with you? How do you mark the day
that would have brought him closer to high school and to college,
to manhood and marriage, to children?

How do you mark the day that reminds you that your son is no
longer alive?

My kids and I did errands in Jerusalem in the morning, and
then we decided to go to Burger King to mark Koby's birthday, because one thing Koby loved about Israel was being able to eat kosher hamburgers there. My son loved to eat — especially hamburgers. He made the screensaver on our computer say, "I'm hungry,

---

For biography of SHERRI MANDELL, see p. 32.

give me something to eat now!!!" His hunger was a force to be reckoned with.

My three kids — Daniel, 12, Eliana, 10, and Gavi, 6 — and I would have had to walk about five blocks to get to Burger King. We were hungry and tired and cranky, so when we passed a vegetarian restaurant, we decided to stop there to eat. I think we were all relieved not to have to feel the sadness of eating hamburgers without Koby.

As we ate, I cried and cried. I miss him so much — the way he hugged me at night, the way he dropped his backpack on the living room floor when he walked in, even the way he kept his room a total disaster zone. I miss the way he read each article I wrote and commented on it. I miss the jokes he was sure to tell me every day. I miss him and I miss my previous life, one where pain wasn't my constant companion, one where horror wasn't the undertone of my dreams.

I closed my eyes and held a napkin against my eyes as I cried, and I thought: *How am I going to go on? How am I going to get the strength to leave this restaurant and get through the day?*

And suddenly I realized. On my birthday I like to swim a mile. What was I going to do on Koby's birthday? Swim 14 laps? We were in downtown Jerusalem; Koby would have been 14. I said to my kids, "Let's go give charity to 14 beggars in Koby's name."

At that instant, a gentleman with a clean-shaven face and puffy white hair put a card down on our table. With a glance, I knew that the card said that the man was deaf and was looking for a contribution.

In the past cards like that had annoyed me — I was trying to eat a meal in peace, and suddenly some beggar had interrupted me.

Now my kids and I were thrilled to see him. "Here," we said, "here's money." He looked at us with a grin on his face.

We got change and exited the restaurant, energized by our mission. The only problem was it was so hot and there were so few people in downtown Jerusalem because of the fear of terrorism. We saw a man giving charity to an old stooped man. The old man walked away and we ran after him to give him money. We actually went up to two people who had broken legs and were resting on a bench because we thought they were beggars. We strode purposefully up to them but didn't see a cup or change basket.

Up in Heaven, I thought, Koby was laughing at our escapades. There was nothing he loved more than irony and this was supreme irony: We needed beggars because we were desperate for someone to give to. We were begging for beggars. But just when we needed them, there weren't any.

Perhaps this was Koby's message to us, his birthday adventure. His spirit was alive and connected to us.

It was too hot to stay out much longer. We thought about visiting the Western Wall, where there is usually a good group of beggars, but it was the middle of the afternoon and it was just too hot to be out more. So we decided that next year on Koby's birthday, we would get up early, go downtown, and visit the Wall, and make sure to give away money in Koby's name.

When I later told my husband about the 14 beggars, he said, "Next year, we'll gather the beggars and take them out to a restaurant for a meal."

What do you do with tragedy and pain? Either you become bitter, hardened, and despondent, or you go forward and try to make beauty and joy in the world.

Koby would have wanted us to create joy in his name. Koby would have rejoiced to sit with the beggars at a table.

Excerpted from the author's book The Blessing of a Broken Heart *(Toby Press, 2003).*

THE
MIDDLE
EAST
CONFLICT

William J. Bennett, Jack Kemp,
and Jeane Kirkpatrick

Twenty Facts about Israel and the Middle East

Τ he world's attention has been focused on the Middle East. We are confronted daily with scenes of carnage and destruction. Can we understand such violence? Yes, but only if we come to the situation with a solid grounding in the facts of the matter — facts that too often are forgotten, if ever they were learned. Below are 20 facts that we think are useful in understanding the current situation, how we arrived here, and how we might eventually arrive at a solution.

Roots of the Conflict

1. When the United Nations proposed the establishment of two states in the region — one Jewish, one Arab — the Jews accepted the proposal and declared their independence in 1948. The Jewish state constituted only one-sixth of one percent of what was known as "the Arab world." The Arab

WILLIAM J. BENNETT is former United States Secretary of Education; JACK KEMP is former United States Secretary of Housing and Urban Development; JEANE KIRKPATRICK is former United States Representative to the United Nations. All three are codirectors of EmpowerAmerica.org.

states, however, rejected the UN plan and since then have waged war against Israel repeatedly, both all-out wars and wars of terrorism and attrition. In 1948, five Arab armies invaded Israel in an effort to eradicate it. Jamal Husseini of the Arab Higher Committee spoke for many in vowing to soak "the soil of our beloved country with the last drop of our blood."

2. The Palestine Liberation Organization (PLO) was founded in 1964 — three years before Israel controlled the West Bank and Gaza. The PLO's declared purpose was to eliminate the State of Israel by means of armed struggle. To this day, the website of Yasser Arafat's Palestinian Authority (PA) claims that the entirety of Israel is "occupied" territory. It is impossible to square this with the PLO and PA assertions to Western audiences that the root of the conflict is Israel's occupation of the West Bank and Gaza.

3. The West Bank and Gaza (controlled by Jordan and Egypt from 1948 to 1967) came under Israeli control during the Six Day War of 1967 that started when Egypt closed the Straits of Tiran and Arab armies amassed on Israel's borders to invade and liquidate the state. It is important to note that during their 19-year rule, neither Jordan nor Egypt had made any effort to establish a Palestinian state on those lands. Just before the Arab nations launched their war of aggression against the State of Israel in 1967, Syrian Defense Minister (later President) Hafez Assad stated, "Our forces are now entirely ready... to initiate the act of liberation itself, and to explode the Zionist presence in the Arab homeland.... The time has come to enter into a battle of annihilation." On the brink of the 1967 war, Egyptian President Gamal Nassar declared, "Our basic objective will be the destruction of Israel."

4. Because of their animus against Jews, many leaders of the Palestinian cause have long supported our enemies. The Grand Mufti of Jerusalem allied himself with Adolf Hitler during World War II. Yasser Arafat, chairman of the PLO and

chairman of the PA, has repeatedly targeted and killed Americans. In 1973, Arafat ordered the execution of Cleo Noel, the American ambassador to the Sudan. Arafat was very closely aligned with the Soviet Union and other enemies of the United States throughout the Cold War. In 1991, during the Gulf War, Arafat aligned himself with Saddam Hussein, whom he praised as "the defender of the Arab nation, of Muslims, and of free men everywhere."

5. Israel has, in fact, returned most of the land that it captured during the 1967 war, and right after that war offered to return all of it in exchange for peace and normal relations; the offer was rejected. As a result of the 1978 Camp David accords — in which Egypt recognized the right of Israel to exist and normal relations were established between the two countries — Israel returned the Sinai desert, a territory three times the size of Israel and 91 percent of the territory Israel took control of in the 1967 war.

6. In 2000, as part of negotiations for a comprehensive and durable peace, Israel offered to turn over all but the smallest portion of the remaining territories to Yasser Arafat. But Israel was rebuffed when Arafat walked out of Camp David and launched the current intifada.

7. Yasser Arafat has never been less than clear about his goals — at least not in Arabic. On the very day that he signed the Oslo accords in 1993, in which he promised to renounce terrorism and recognize Israel, he addressed the Palestinian people on Jordanian television and declared that he had taken the first step "in the 1974 plan." This was a thinly veiled reference to the "phased plan," according to which any territorial gain was acceptable as a means toward the ultimate goal of Israel's destruction.

8. The recently deceased Faisal al-Husseini, a leading Palestinian spokesman, made the same point in 2001 when he declared that the West Bank and Gaza represented only "22 percent of Palestine" and that the Oslo process was a "Trojan

horse." He explained, "When we are asking all the Palestinian forces and factions to look at the Oslo Agreement and at other agreements as 'temporary' procedures, or phased goals, this means that we are ambushing the Israelis and cheating them." The goal, he continued, was "the liberation of Palestine from the river to the sea," i.e., the Jordan River to the Mediterranean Sea — all of Israel.

9. To this day, the Fatah wing of the PLO (the "moderate" wing that was founded and is controlled by Arafat himself) has as its official emblem the entire state of Israel covered by two rifles and a hand grenade — another fact that belies the claim that Arafat desires nothing more than the West Bank and Gaza.

10. While criticism of Israel is not necessarily the same as "anti-Semitism," it must be remembered that the Middle East press is, in fact, rife with anti-Semitism. More than 15 years ago the eminent scholar Bernard Lewis could point out that "The demonization of Jews [in Arabic literature] goes further than it had ever done in Western literature, with the exception of Germany during the period of Nazi rule." Since then, and through all the years of the "peace process," things have become much worse. Depictions of Jews in Arab and Muslim media are akin to those of Nazi Germany, and medieval blood libels — including claims that Jews use Christian and Muslim blood in preparing their holiday foods — have become prominent and routine. One example is a sermon broadcast on PA television where Sheik Ahmad Halabaya stated, "They [the Jews] must be butchered and killed, as Allah the Almighty said: 'Fight them: Allah will torture them at your hands.' Have no mercy on the Jews, no matter where they are, in any country. Fight them, wherever you are. Wherever you meet them, kill them."

11. Over three-quarters of Palestinians approve of suicide bombings — an appalling statistic but, in light of the above facts, an unsurprising one.

The State of Israel

12. There are 21 Arab countries in the Middle East and only one Jewish state: Israel, which is also the only democracy in the region.

13. Israel is the only country in the region that permits citizens of all faiths to worship freely and openly. Twenty percent of Israeli citizens are not Jewish.

14. While Jews are not permitted to live in many Arab countries, Arabs are granted full citizenship and have the right to vote in Israel. Arabs are also free to become members of the Israeli parliament (the Knesset). In fact, several Arabs have been democratically elected to the Knesset and have been serving there for years. Arabs living in Israel have more rights and are freer than most Arabs living in Arab countries.

15. Israel is smaller than the state of New Hampshire and is surrounded by nations hostile to her existence. Some peace proposals — including the recent Saudi proposal — demand withdrawal from the entire West Bank, which would leave Israel nine miles wide at its most vulnerable point.

16. The oft-cited UN Resolution 242 (passed in the wake of the 1967 war) does not, in fact, require a complete withdrawal from the West Bank. As legal scholar Eugene Rostow put it, "Resolution 242, which as undersecretary of state for political affairs between 1966 and 1969 I helped produce, calls on the parties to make peace and allows Israel to administer the territories it occupied in 1967 until 'a just and lasting peace in the Middle East' is achieved. When such a peace is made, Israel is required to withdraw its armed forces 'from territories' it occupied during the Six Day War — not from 'the' territories nor from 'all' the territories, but from some of the territories."

17. Israel has, of course, conceded that the Palestinians have legitimate claims to the disputed territories and is willing to engage in negotiations on the matter. As noted above, Israeli Prime Minister Ehud Barak offered almost all of the territories to Arafat at Camp David in 2000.

18. Despite claims that the Israeli settlements in the West Bank are the obstacle to peace, Jews lived there for centuries before being massacred or driven out by invading Arab armies in 1948–49. And contrary to common misperceptions, Israeli settlements — which constitute less than 2 percent of the territories — almost never displace Palestinians.

19. The area of the West Bank includes some of the most important sites in Jewish history, among them Hebron, Bethlehem, and Jericho. East Jerusalem, often cited as an "Arab city" or "occupied territory," is the site of Judaism's holiest monument. While under Arab rule (1948–67), this area was entirely closed to Jews. Since Israel took control, it has been open to people of all faiths.

20. Finally, let us consider the demand that certain territories in the Muslim world must be off-limits to Jews. This demand is of a piece with Hitler's proclamation that German land had to be *"Judenrein"* (empty of Jews). Arabs can live freely throughout Israel, and as full citizens. Why should Jews be forbidden to live or to own land in an area like the West Bank simply because the majority of people is Arab?

In sum, a fair and balanced portrayal of the Middle East will reveal that one nation stands far above the others in its commitment to human rights and democracy, as well as in its commitment to peace and mutual security. That nation is Israel.

Benjamin Netanyahu

The Root Cause of Terrorism

D o not be fooled by the apologists of terror.
These apologists tell us that the root cause of terrorism is the deprivation of national and civic rights, and that the way to stop terror is to redress the supposed grievances that arise from this deprivation.

But the root cause of terrorism, the deliberate targeting of civilians, is not the deprivation of rights. If it were, then in the thousands of conflicts and struggles for national and civil rights in modern times we would see countless instances of terrorism. But we do not.

Mahatma Gandhi fought for the independence of India without resorting to terrorism. So too did the peoples of Eastern Europe in their struggle to bring down the Berlin Wall. And Martin Luther King Junior's campaign for equal rights for all Americans eschewed all violence, much less terrorism.

If the deprivation of rights is indeed the root cause of terrorism, why did all these people pursue their cause without resorting to terror? Put simply, because they were democrats, not terrorists. They believed in the sanctity of each human life, were committed to the ideals of liberty, and championed the values of democracy.

BENJAMIN NETANYAHU, former prime minister of Israel and ambassador to the United Nations, now serves as the Israeli finance minister.

But those who practice terrorism do not believe in these things. In fact, they believe in the very opposite. For them, the cause they espouse is so all-encompassing, so total, that it justifies anything. It allows them to break any law, discard any moral code, and trample all human rights in the dust. In their eyes, it permits them to indiscriminately murder and maim innocent men and women, and lets them blow up a bus full of children.

There is a name for the doctrine that produces this evil. It is called totalitarianism.

Indeed, the root cause of terrorism is totalitarianism. Only a totalitarian regime, by systemically brainwashing its subjects, can indoctrinate hordes of killers to suspend all moral constraints for the sake of a twisted cause.

That is why from its inception totalitarianism has always been wedded to terrorism — from Lenin to Stalin to Hitler to the ayatollahs to Saddam Hussein, right down to Osama bin Laden and Yasser Arafat.

It is not merely that the goals of terrorists do not justify the means they choose, it is that the means they choose tell us what their true goals are. Osama bin Laden is not seeking to defend the rights of Muslims, but to murder as many Americans as possible, and ultimately to destroy America. Saddam Hussein is not seeking to defend his people, but to subjugate his neighbors. Arafat is not seeking to build a state but to destroy a state; the many massacres of Jews he sponsors tells us what he would do to all the Jews of Israel if he had enough power.

Those who fight as terrorists rule as terrorists. People who deliberately target the innocent never become leaders who protect freedom and human rights. When terrorists seize power, they invariably set up the darkest of dictatorships — whether in Iraq, Iran, Afghanistan, or Arafatistan.

In short, the reason why some resort to terror and others do not is not any absence of rights, but the presence of a tyrannical mindset. The totalitarian mind knows no limits. The democratic mind sets them everywhere.

The essential steps to defeat international terrorism are being courageously undertaken by President Bush. By declaring that terrorism is never justified, and by deterring or destroying those regimes that support terror, President Bush has bravely charted a course that will lead the free world to victory.

But to assure that this evil does not reemerge a decade or two from now, we must not merely uproot terror but also plant the seeds of freedom. Only under tyranny can a terrorist mind-set be widely cultivated. It cannot breed in a climate of democracy and freedom.

The open debate of ideas and the respect for human life that are the foundation of all free societies are a permanent antidote to the poison that the terrorists seek to inject into the minds of their recruits.

That is why it is imperative that once the terrorist regimes in the Middle East are swept away, the free world, led by America, must begin to build the institutions of pluralism and democracy in their place. This will not happen overnight, and it is not likely to result in liberal, Western-style democracies. But given an option between Turkish-style freedom and Iranian-style tyranny, the choice is clear.

We simply can no longer allow parts of the world to remain cloistered by fanatic militancies. Such militancies, if armed with nuclear weapons, could destroy our civilization. We must begin immediately to encourage the peoples of the Arab and Islamic world to embrace the idea of pluralism and the ideals of freedom — for their sake, as well as ours.

Rabbi Ken Spiro

Jerusalem:
Jewish and Muslim Claims

The Jews of Israel are currently locked into a conflict with their Palestinian Arab neighbors. While the media bombards us with constant reports of violence in the West Bank and Gaza, there is no doubt that the epicenter of the conflict lies in Jerusalem, and more specifically, on the Temple Mount in the Old City.

Palestinians constantly repeat that there can be no peace without Jerusalem as the capital of Palestine, and without total Muslim sovereignty over the Temple Mount. Indeed, the last Camp David Summit floundered over Arafat's uncompromising position on the issue of controlling the site.

Israeli leaders, on the other hand, say that Jerusalem will remain under Israeli sovereignty, even as Ehud Barak offered significant autonomy over the Temple Mount, as well as Palestinian Authority control over Arab sections of Jerusalem.

What historical or religious claim do both sides make? Is either

RABBI KEN SPIRO has a master's degree in history and did graduate studies at the Pushkin Institute in Moscow. He lives outside of Jerusalem where he is a licensed tour guide, and a senior lecturer and researcher for Aish HaTorah outreach programs.

party's claim for Jerusalem stronger, or is it merely a case of "might makes right"?

The purpose of this article is not to prove or disprove anyone's claim to Jerusalem, but rather to clear up some of the fog surrounding this controversy, and to enable us to better understand both the Jewish and Muslim connection to this holy site.

∝

To understand the Jewish connection to Jerusalem we must begin with the Jewish Bible. From the Jewish perspective, the area of special holiness is Mount Moriah, today known as the Temple Mount. This area is located beneath the platform on which the Muslim Shrine, the Dome of the Rock, now stands.

In the Jewish Bible, Jerusalem has many names: Salem (Shalem), Moriah, Jebuse (Yevuse), Jerusalem (Yerushalayim), and Zion (Tziyon). The most common term for the city, Yerushalayim, is mentioned 349 times in the Jewish Bible, while Tziyon is mentioned an additional 108 times.

The earliest mention of the site is Genesis 4:18, when Abraham interacts with Malchi-tzedek, King of Shalem. According to Jewish tradition, the story of the Binding of Isaac (Genesis 22:1–19) also took place in the "land of Moriah" on the site of the present-day Temple Mount. Abraham chose the site specifically because he sensed that God's presence is strongly connected to this site.

In Kabbalah, the Jewish metaphysical tradition, the rock of Mount Moriah is known as the Evven Shetiyah, the Drinking Stone. This is the spiritual center of the universe, the place from where the world is spiritually "watered."

Later patriarchal stories in Genesis are also connected with the site:

- When Isaac goes out into the fields to pray, prior to meeting Rebecca for the first time, he is standing on Mount Moriah (Genesis 24:63–67).

- Jacob's dream of the ladder to Heaven, on which angels are ascending and descending, takes place on this site (Genesis 27:10–22).

We see from this that for thousands of years, the Jewish people have always identified Mount Moriah as the place where God's presence can be felt more intensely than any other place on Earth. That is why, for the Jewish people, the Temple Mount is the single holiest place.

This connection is still very much alive and well in contemporary Jewish practice:

- When religious Jews pray three times a day, they always turn toward Jerusalem. (Someone praying in Jerusalem faces the direction of the Temple Mount.)

- Jerusalem is mentioned numerous times in Jewish daily prayers and in the "Grace After Meals."

- Jews close the Passover Seder with the words "Next year in Jerusalem." These same words are invoked to conclude the holiest day of the Jewish year, Yom Kippur.

- The Jewish national day of mourning, Tisha B'Av, commemorates the destruction of the First and Second Temples.

- During a Jewish wedding ceremony, the groom breaks a glass as a sign of mourning to commemorate the destruction of the Holy Temples which stood on Mount Moriah. The breaking of the glass is accompanied by the recitation of part of Psalm 137: "If I forget thee, O Jerusalem, let my right hand forget its cunning. If I do not remember thee, let my tongue cleave to the roof of my mouth, if I do not set Jerusalem above my highest joy."

- Many Jews keep a small section of one wall in their house unplastered and unpainted, as a sign of mourning for the destruction of the Temple.

The early history of Jerusalem is also rooted in the Bible. In addition to the events already mentioned, the Book of Joshua (ch. 10) describes how Adoni-Tzedek, the Canaanite king of Jerusalem, waged war against the Jews.

During the approximately 400-year period from the entrance

of the Jewish people into the land, and throughout the period of the Judges, Jerusalem remained a non-Jewish city. It was not until the reign of King David (ca. 1,000 BCE) that Jerusalem was captured from the Canaanites (2 Samuel ch. 5) and converted into the political-spiritual capital of the Jewish people. (Archaeologists agree that the original Canaanite city and the City of David was located in what is now the Arab village of Silwan, a few meters south of the "modern" walls of the Old City.)

David purchased the peak of Mount Moriah (2 Samuel 24:18–25) as the site for the future Temple and gathered the necessary building supplies. The first Book of Kings (ch. 6–8) describes in great detail how David's son, King Solomon, built and dedicated the Temple: "And it came to pass after the 408th year after the Children of Israel left Egypt, in the fourth year of Solomon's reign over Israel... that he began to build the house of God" (1 Kings 6:1).

Solomon's Temple is also known as the Beit HaMikdash (First Holy Temple). While all archaeologists agree that it stood on Mount Moriah, probably on the site of the present Gold Dome of the Rock, its exact location is unknown.

Four hundred and ten years after its completion, the Temple was utterly destroyed by the Babylonians when they besieged Jerusalem, and no trace of it remains.

After the Babylonian destruction, most of the Jewish population of Israel was forcibly exiled from the land. This forced exile on the road to Babylon is mentioned in the famous verse from Psalm 137: "By the rivers of Babylon, there we sat down and wept when we remembered Zion."

Fifty years later, after Babylon was captured by Persia, the Jews were allowed to return to Jerusalem. Under the leadership of Zerubavel and Nechemiah, the Jews rebuilt both the Temple and the walls around the city (Nechemiah ch. 4–6).

This rebuilt temple is known as the Second Temple (*Bayit Sheni*). It stood for 420 years on the same site as the First Temple, on Mount Moriah. The Second Temple was remodeled several times, but reached its most magnificent form during the reign of King Herod the Great (37–4 BCE). The great Jewish historian, Josephus, who lived during the end of the Second Temple period, gives detailed descriptions of both Herod's construction and the layout of the Temple compound (see Antiquities ch. 15 and Jewish Wars ch. 5).

During both the First and Second Temple periods, the Temple was the central focus of the Jewish world, both in Israel and the Diaspora. Its upkeep was paid for by all Jews worldwide. The *kohanim* (priests) and Levites served in the Temple, and three times a year — during the holidays of Passover, Shavuot, and Sukkot — all Jews were commanded to come to Jerusalem and visit the Temple.

The Second Temple period ended with the Roman destruction of Jerusalem in 70 CE. It is possible that the Jews tried to rebuild the Temple at later periods, but they were never successful, and for over 600 years the site of the Temple Mount lay in ruins. The only remains are the massive retaining walls that encompass Mount Moriah, built by Herod to support the platform on which the Temple stood.

Although the Temple hasn't stood for almost 2,000 years, Jerusalem continues to be the focus of the Jewish world. The Temple may not be there, but Jews believe that the intrinsic holiness of the site always remains. Jewish tradition also maintains that in the End of Days, during the Messianic Era, a third and final Temple will be built on Mount Moriah.

It is often stated that the holiest site in the world to Jews is the Western Wall. This is incorrect. The holiest spot for Jews is Mount Moriah itself, behind the Wall. The Western Wall is merely a small section of Herod's massive retaining wall and has significance only as it relates to the Temple Mount itself.

So why do Jews pray at the Wall? Since the destruction of the Temple, the Sages decreed that due to the sanctity of the site, Jews (and non-Jews) should not go up on the actual Temple Mount. Therefore, the Western Wall became the site of prayer for Jews wishing to get as close as possible to their holiest site, the Temple Mount. It earned the moniker "Wailing Wall" because Jews coming to this site would shed tears over the loss of the Holy Temple.

The Islamic connection to Jerusalem began much later in history, during the 7th century CE. The central personality of Islam, Mohammed, was born and raised in the area of present-day Saudi Arabia and founded Islam in the early 7th century. (The first year of the Muslim calendar, or the *Hajira*, corresponds to the year 622 CE of the Christian calendar.)

Scholars agree that Mohammed was influenced by Judaism (and Christianity). This influence was significant enough that Mohammed's original plan for the direction of prayer (*Qibla*) was also Jerusalem. Mohammed later changed the direction of prayer to Mecca in Saudi Arabia — a place that was converted from a pagan pilgrimage site to the "eternal city," and the center of the Muslim religion. (Muslims also identified Mecca as the spot where Abraham nearly sacrificed Isaac's brother Ishmael.)

After founding Islam and leading his Islamic armies to victory over pagan rivals, Mohammed died. Although Mohammed never made it to Jerusalem with his conquering armies, his successor, the Caliph Omar, captured Jerusalem from the Byzantines in 638. When Omar first visited the ruined Temple mount, he deliberately prayed south of the ruins of the Temple, toward Mecca, so that no one should think he was praying in the same direction as the Jews.

The holiest book of Islam is the Koran, which according to Muslim tradition contains the teachings of Mohammed. Unlike the Jewish Bible, which contains hundreds of references to Jerusalem, the word *Jerusalem* appears nowhere in the Koran. So what is the Islamic spiritual connection to the site? To answer that question we must understand more of early Islamic history.

By the time the Omar arrived in Jerusalem in 638, the Islamic direction of prayer was toward Mecca, and the two holiest sites, Mecca and Medina, were already well established. Islam, like Christianity, has many of its spiritual roots in Judaism, and it recognizes the Jewish connection to the Temple Mount. One early Islamic name for the Temple Mount was *Bayt al-Maqewdis* — literally "Holy Temple." The name used today, *al-Quds*, is based on the Hebrew word for "holy." Muslims have also used the term *Sahyun* or *Sihyun*, the Arabic form of "Zion."

Historians suggest several reasons for the construction of Muslim holy sites on the Temple Mount. The establishment of the Umayyid Islamic Dynasty in 658 corresponds to a period of instability in the Islamic world, characterized by power struggles and assassinations. One of the Five Pillars (commandments) of Islam is *Hajj* — pilgrimage to the holiest Islamic city, Mecca. In the late 7th century, the Damascus-based Umayyid Caliphate lost control of Mecca. This need to diminish the importance of Mecca and create an alternative Muslim holy site closer to Damascus may well have pushed the Umayyid Caliph Abd al-Malik, in 688, to begin construction of the Dome of the Rock on the former site of the Jewish Temple.

Another reason suggested by historians for a Muslim presence in Jerusalem is that the Caliph wished to compete with the impressive Church of the Holy Sepulcher, the traditional burial place of Jesus in Jerusalem. It is interesting to note that the present dimensions of the Dome of Rock are identical to those of the rotunda of the Holy Sepulcher.

Yet given that Jerusalem isn't mentioned in the Koran, what is the uniquely Islamic connection to the site? The answer is found in the Sura (chapter) 17 of the Koran. This chapter recounts the story of a dream Mohammed has where he takes a midnight ride (*al-Isra*) on his flying horse (*al-Buraq*, which had the face of a woman, the body of a horse, and the tail of a peacock). The narrative of the Koran in Sura 17 describes it as follows:

> Glory be to Him, who carried His servant by night from the Holy Mosque (in Mecca) to the further mosque (*al-masjid al-Aqsa*), the precincts of which we have blessed.

The actual location of al-Aqsa (the "further mosque") in Mohammed's dream ride is never mentioned. Some early Muslims understood al-Aqsa metaphorically, or as a place in Heaven.

In the late 7th century, the Umayyids claimed that the actual site of al-Aqsa was in fact the Temple Mount. Later, the site of al-Aqsa was restricted to the mosque area at the southern end of the Temple Mount (the site of the current al-Aqsa Mosque). The original mosque, probably located on the site where Omar first prayed when he arrived in Jerusalem in 638, was built by the Umayyid Caliph al-Walid in the early 8th century. It was destroyed by earthquakes several times and later rebuilt.

The narrative of the Koran then describes how Mohammed, having arrived at al-Aqsa, ascended to heaven (*al-Mi'raj* — "the ascension") accompanied by the angel Gibril (Gabriel), where he then traveled around the heavens and spoke with Allah and other prophets. The Umayyids in Jerusalem claimed that the actual site of Mohammed's ascension to heaven was the exposed piece of bedrock at the top of Mount Moriah. Thus Caliph Abd-al-Malik's beautiful Dome of the Rock was built to commemorate the location of this important event.

From 638 CE until 1917 (with the exception of the Crusader occupation from 1099–1187), Jerusalem was controlled by various Islamic dynasties based in Syria, Egypt, and Turkey. While Jerusalem remained a city of pilgrimage, none of these Islamic dynasties made Jerusalem their capital. Besides the Jews, the only other people in the last 3,000 years to have Jerusalem as a capital were the Crusaders, who founded the Latin Kingdom of Jerusalem from 1099 to 1187.

For most of this 1,300-year period, despite its status as the third holiest Islamic city, Jerusalem remained a backwater, a run-down town under Islamic control. Exceptions to this were the Umayyid period (seventh to mid-eighth century) and the Mamluk period (mid-13th to early-16th century), during which major Islamic building projects were carried out in the city.

From 1918 through 1948, the Land of Israel was under the control of the British, who conquered it from the Ottoman Turks in World War I. The State of Israel was established in 1948, when half of Jerusalem — including the entire Old City and Temple Mount — was under the control of the Kingdom of Jordan.

During the Six Day War in 1967, Israel captured the Old City. For the first time in nearly 2,000 years, the Temple Mount was back under Jewish control.

It is worth noting that the inaugural PLO Covenant of 1964 does not mention Jerusalem. Only after the city reverted to Jewish control did the updated PLO Covenant of 1968 mentioned Jerusalem by name.

One might have expected that the Israelis would immediately expel the Muslims and reestablish control of the single holiest Jewish site. But in an act of what can only be described as unprecedented tolerance, Israel handed over control of the site to the Wakf, the Muslim Religious Trust.

Today, although Israel technically claims sovereignty over the site, the de facto reality since 1967 has been that the Muslims control the site, to the point where Jews are forbidden to pray on the Temple Mount (and permitted to visit based on the political climate).

Within the Hebrew word *Jerusalem* is the word for peace — *shalom*. It is ironic that Jerusalem, often referred to as the City of Peace, sits at the heart of the Arab-Israeli conflict.

There are no simple solutions to complex problems, especially when religious beliefs and national identities are at stake. But only through an objective understanding of the intricacies that surround the history of Jerusalem can we hope to arrive at a just and lasting solution.

Sources and Suggested Reading

Bahat, Dan. *The Illustrated Atlas of Jerusalem.* New York: Simon & Shuster, 1990.

Ben-Dov, Meir. *In the Shadow of the Temple Mount: The Discovery of Ancient Jerusalem.* New York: Harper and Rowe, 1982.

Gil, Moshe. *A History of Palestine, 634–1099.* Cambridge: Cambridge University Press, 1992.

Mazar, Benjamin. *The Mountain of the Lord: Excavating in Jerusalem.* Garden City, New York: Doubleday and Co., 1975.

Murphy-O'Connor, Jerome. *The Holy Land: An Oxford Archaeological Guide from Earliest Times to 1700.* Oxford: Oxford University Press, 1998.

Prawer, J. and Ben-Shammai, H. *The History of Jerusalem: The Early Muslim Period 638–1099*. New York: New York University Press, 1996.

Shanks, Hershel. Jerusalem: *An Archaeological Biography*. New York: Random House, 1995.

Efraim Karsh

History of the Territories

July 2002

N o term has dominated the discourse of the Palestinian-Israeli conflict more than "occupation." For decades now, hardly a day has passed without some mention in the international media of Israel's supposedly illegitimate presence on Palestinian lands. This presence is invoked to explain the origins and persistence of the conflict between the parties, to show Israel's allegedly brutal and repressive nature, and to justify the worst anti-Israel terrorist atrocities. The occupation, in short, has become a catchphrase, and like many catchphrases it means different things to different people.

For most Western observers, the term "occupation" describes Israel's control of the Gaza Strip and the West Bank, areas that it conquered during the Six Day War of June 1967. But for many Palestinians and Arabs, the Israeli presence in these territories represents only the latest chapter in an uninterrupted story of "occupations" dating back to the very creation of Israel on "stolen" land. If you go looking for a book about Israel in the foremost Arab bookstore on London's Charing Cross Road, you will find it in the section labeled "Occupied Palestine." That this is the prevailing view

EFRAIM KARSH is head of Mediterranean studies at Kings College, University of London.

not only among Arab residents of the West Bank and Gaza but among Palestinians living within Israel itself as well as elsewhere around the world is shown by the routine insistence on a Palestinian "right of return" that is meant to reverse the effects of the "1948 occupation" — i.e. the establishment of the State of Israel itself.

Palestinian intellectuals routinely blur any distinction between Israel's actions before and after 1967. Writing recently in the Israeli daily *Ha'aretz*, the prominent Palestinian cultural figure Jacques Persiqian told his Jewish readers that today's terrorist attacks were "what you have brought upon yourselves after 54 years of systematic oppression of another people" — a historical accounting that, going back to 1948, calls into question not Israel's presence in the West Bank and Gaza but its very legitimacy as a state.

Hanan Ashrawi, the most articulate exponent of the Palestinian cause, has been even more forthright in erasing the line between post-1967 and pre-1967 "occupations." "I come to you today with a heavy heart," she told the now-infamous World Conference Against Racism in Durban in 2001, "leaving behind a nation in captivity held hostage to an ongoing *naqba* [catastrophe].

"In 1948, we became subject to a grave historical injustice manifested in a dual victimization: on the one hand, the injustice of dispossession, dispersion, and exile forcibly enacted on the population... On the other hand, those who remained were subjected to the systematic oppression and brutality of an inhuman occupation that robbed them of all their rights and liberties."

This original "occupation" — that is, again, the creation and existence of the State of Israel — was later extended, in Ashrawi's narrative, as a result of the Six Day War:

"Those of us who came under Israeli occupation in 1967 have languished in the West Bank, Jerusalem, and the Gaza Strip under a unique combination of military occupation, settler colonization, and systematic oppression. Rarely has the human mind devised such varied, diverse, and comprehensive means of wholesale brutalization and persecution."

Taken together, the charges against Israel's various "occupations" represent — and are plainly intended to be — a damning indictment of the entire Zionist enterprise. In almost every particular, they are also grossly false.

In 1948, no Palestinian state was invaded or destroyed to make way for the establishment of Israel. From biblical times, when this territory was the state of the Jews, to its occupation by the British army at the end of World War I, Palestine had never existed as a distinct political entity but was rather part of one empire after another, from the Romans, to the Arabs, to the Ottomans. When the British arrived in 1917, the immediate loyalties of the area's inhabitants were parochial — to clan, tribe, village, town, or religious sect — and coexisted with their fealty to the Ottoman sultan-caliph as the religious and temporal head of the world Muslim community.

Under a League of Nations mandate explicitly meant to pave the way for the creation of a Jewish national home, the British established the notion of an independent Palestine for the first time and delineated its boundaries. In 1947, confronted with a determined Jewish struggle for independence, Britain returned the mandate to the League's successor, the United Nations, which in turn decided on November 29, 1947, to partition mandatory Palestine into two states: one Jewish, the other Arab.

The State of Israel was thus created by an internationally recognized act of national self-determination — an act, moreover, undertaken by an ancient people in its own homeland. In accordance with common democratic practice, the Arab population in the new state's midst was immediately recognized as a legitimate ethnic and religious minority. As for the prospective Arab state, its designated territory was slated to include, among other areas, the two regions under contest today — namely, Gaza and the West Bank (with the exception of Jerusalem, which was to be placed under international control).

As is well known, the implementation of the UN's partition plan was aborted by the effort of the Palestinians and of the surrounding Arab states to destroy the Jewish state at birth. What is less well known is that even if the Jews had lost the war, their territory would not have been handed over to the Palestinians. Rather, it would have been divided among the invading Arab forces, for the simple reason that none of the region's Arab regimes viewed the Palestinians as a distinct nation. As the eminent Arab-American historian Philip Hitti described the common Arab view to an Anglo-American commission of inquiry in 1946, "There is no such thing as Palestine in history, absolutely not."

This fact was keenly recognized by the British authorities on the eve of their departure. As one official observed in mid-December 1947, "It does not appear that Arab Palestine will be an entity, but rather that the Arab countries will each claim a portion in return for their assistance [in the war against Israel], unless [Transjordan's] King Abdallah takes rapid and firm action as soon as the British withdrawal is completed." A couple of months later, the British high commissioner for Palestine, General Sir Alan Cunningham, informed the colonial secretary, Arthur Creech Jones, that "the most likely arrangement seems to be Eastern Galilee to Syria, Samaria and Hebron to Abdallah, and the south to Egypt."

The British proved to be prescient. Neither Egypt nor Jordan ever allowed Palestinian self-determination in Gaza and the West Bank — which were, respectively, the parts of Palestine conquered by them during the 1948–49 war. Indeed, even UN Security Council Resolution 242, which after the Six Day War of 1967 established the principle of "land for peace" as the cornerstone of future Arab-Israeli peace negotiations, did not envisage the creation of a Palestinian state. To the contrary: since the Palestinians were still not viewed as a distinct nation, it was assumed that any territories evacuated by Israel would be returned to their pre-1967 Arab occupiers — Gaza to Egypt, and the West Bank to Jordan. The resolution did not even mention the Palestinians by name, affirming instead the necessity "for achieving a just settlement of the refugee problem" — a clause that applied not just to the Palestinians but to the hundreds of thousands of Jews expelled from the Arab states following the 1948 war.

At this time — we are speaking of the late 1960s — Palestinian nationhood was rejected by the entire international community, including the Western democracies, the Soviet Union (the foremost supporter of radical Arabism), and the Arab world itself.

"Moderate" Arab rulers like the Hashemites in Jordan viewed an independent Palestinian state as a mortal threat to their own kingdom, while the Saudis saw it as a potential source of extremism and instability. Pan-Arab nationalists were no less adamantly opposed, having their own purposes in mind for the region. As late as 1974, Syrian President Hafez al Assad openly referred to Palestine as "not only a part of the Arab homeland but a basic part of southern Syria"; there is no reason to think he had changed his mind by the time of his death in 2000.

Nor, for that matter, did the populace of the West Bank and Gaza regard itself as a distinct nation. The collapse and dispersion of Palestinian society following the 1948 defeat had shattered an always fragile communal fabric, and the subsequent physical separation of the various parts of the Palestinian diaspora prevented the crystallization of a national identity. Host Arab regimes actively colluded in discouraging any such sense from arising. Upon occupying the West Bank during the 1948 war, King Abdallah had moved quickly to erase all traces of corporate Palestinian identity. On April 4, 1950, the territory was formally annexed to Jordan, its residents became Jordanian citizens, and they were increasingly integrated into the kingdom's economic, political, and social structures.

For its part, the Egyptian government showed no desire to annex the Gaza Strip but had instead ruled the newly acquired area as an occupied military zone. This did not imply support of Palestinian nationalism, however, or of any sort of collective political awareness among the Palestinians. The local population was kept under tight control, was denied Egyptian citizenship, and was subjected to severe restrictions on travel.

What, then, of the period after 1967, when these territories passed into the hands of Israel? Is it the case that Palestinians in the West Bank and Gaza have been the victims of the most "varied, diverse, and comprehensive means of wholesale brutalization and persecution" ever devised by the human mind?

At the very least, such a characterization would require a rather drastic downgrading of certain other well-documented 20th-century phenomena, from the slaughter of Armenians during World War I and onward, through a grisly chronicle of tens upon tens of millions murdered, driven out, crushed under the heels of despots. By stark contrast, during the three decades of Israel's control, far fewer Palestinians were killed at Jewish hands than by King Hussein of Jordan in the single month of September 1970 when, fighting off an attempt by Yasser Arafat's PLO to destroy his monarchy, he dispatched (according to the Palestinian scholar Yezid Sayigh) between 3,000 and 5,000 Palestinians, among them anywhere from 1,500 to 3,500 civilians. Similarly, the number of innocent Palestinians killed by their Kuwaiti hosts in the winter of 1991, in revenge for the PLO's support for Saddam Hussein's brutal occupation of Kuwait, far exceeds the number of Palestinian rioters and terrorists who lost their lives in the first intifada against Israel during the late 1980s.

Such crude comparisons aside, to present the Israeli occupation of the West Bank and Gaza as "systematic oppression" is itself the inverse of the truth. It should be recalled, first of all, that this occupation did not come about as a consequence of some grand expansionist design, but rather was incidental to Israel's success against a pan-Arab attempt to destroy it. Upon the outbreak of Israeli-Egyptian hostilities on June 5, 1967, the Israeli government secretly pleaded with King Hussein of Jordan, the de-facto ruler of the West Bank, to forgo any military action; the plea was rebuffed by the Jordanian monarch, who was loathe to lose the anticipated spoils of what was to be the Arabs' "final round" with Israel.

Thus it happened that, at the end of the conflict, Israel unexpectedly found itself in control of some one million Palestinians, with no definite idea about their future status and lacking any concrete policy for their administration. In the wake of the war, the only objective adopted by then-Minister of Defense Moshe Dayan was to preserve normalcy in the territories through a mixture of economic inducements and a minimum of Israeli intervention. The idea was that the local populace would be given the freedom to administer itself as it wished, and would be able to maintain regular contact with the Arab world via the Jordan River bridges. In sharp contrast with, for example, the United States occupation of postwar Japan, which saw a general censorship of all Japanese media and a comprehensive revision of school curricula, Israel made no attempt to reshape Palestinian culture. It limited its oversight of the Arabic press in the territories to military and security matters, and allowed the continued use in local schools of Jordanian textbooks filled with vile anti-Semitic and anti-Israel propoganda.

Israel's restraint in this sphere is only part of the story. The larger part, still untold in all its detail, is of the astounding social and economic progress made by the Palestinian Arabs under Israeli "oppression." At the inception of the occupation, conditions in the territories were quite dire. Life expectancy was low; malnutrition, infectious diseases, and child mortality were rife; and the level of education was very poor. Prior to the 1967 war, fewer than 60 percent of all male adults had been employed, with unemployment among refugees running as high as 83 percent. Within a brief period after the war, Israeli occupation had led to dramatic improvements in general well-being, placing the population of the territories ahead of most of its Arab neighbors.

In the economic sphere, most of this progress was the result of access to the far larger and more advanced Israeli economy: the number of Palestinians working in Israel rose from zero in 1967 to 66,000 in 1975 and 109,000 by 1986, accounting for 35 percent of the employed population of the West Bank and 45 percent in Gaza. Close to 2,000 industrial plants, employing almost half of the work force, were established in the territories under Israeli rule.

During the 1970s, the West Bank and Gaza constituted the fourth fastest-growing economy in the world — ahead of such "wonders" as Singapore, Hong Kong, and Korea, and substantially ahead of Israel itself. Although GNP per capita grew somewhat more slowly, the rate was still high by international standards, with per-capita GNP expanding tenfold between 1968 and 1991, from $165 to $1,715 (compared with Jordan's $1,050, Egypt's $600, Turkey's $1,630, and Tunisia's $1,440). By 1999, Palestinian per-capita income was nearly double Syria's, more than four times Yemen's, and 10 percent higher than Jordan's (one of the better off

Arab states). Only the oil-rich Gulf states and Lebanon were more affluent.

Under Israeli rule, the Palestinians also made vast progress in social welfare. Perhaps most significantly, mortality rates in the West Bank and Gaza fell by more than two-thirds between 1970 and 1990, while life expectancy rose from 48 years in 1967 to 72 in 2000 (compared with an average of 68 years for all the countries of the Middle East and North Africa). Israeli medical programs reduced the infant-mortality rate of 60 per 1,000 live births in 1968, to 15 per 1,000 in 2000 (in Iraq the rate is 64, in Egypt 40, in Jordan 23, in Syria 22). And under a systematic program of inoculation, childhood diseases like polio, whooping cough, tetanus, and measles were eradicated.

No less remarkable were advances in the Palestinians' standard of living. By 1986, 92.8 percent of the population in the West Bank and Gaza had electricity around the clock, as compared to 20.5 percent in 1967; 85 percent had running water in dwellings, as compared to 16 percent in 1967; 83.5 percent had electric or gas ranges for cooking, as compared to 4 percent in 1967; and so on for refrigerators, televisions, and cars.

Finally, and perhaps most strikingly, during the two decades preceding the intifada of the late 1980s, the number of schoolchildren in the territories grew by 102 percent, and the number of classes by 99 percent, though the population itself had grown by only 28 percent. Even more dramatic was the progress in higher education. In 1967, not a single university existed in these territories. By the early 1990s, there were seven such institutions, boasting some 16,500 students. Illiteracy rates dropped to 14 percent of adults over age 15, compared with 69 percent in Morocco, 61 percent in Egypt, 45 percent in Tunisia, and 44 percent in Syria.

All this, as I have noted, took place against the backdrop of Israel's hands-off policy in the political and administrative spheres. Indeed, even as the PLO (until 1982 headquartered in Lebanon and thereafter in Tunisia) proclaimed its ongoing commitment to the destruction of the Jewish state, the Israelis did surprisingly little to limit its political influence in the territories. The publication of pro-PLO editorials was permitted in the local press, and anti-Israel activities by PLO supporters were tolerated so long as they did not involve overt incitements to violence. Israel also allowed the free flow of PLO-controlled funds, a policy justified by Minister of Defense Ezer Weizmann in 1978 in these (deluded) words: "It does not matter that they get money from the PLO, as long as they don't build arms factories with it." Nor, with very few exceptions, did Israel encourage the formation of Palestinian political institutions that might serve as a counterweight to the PLO. As a result, the PLO gradually established itself as the predominant force in the territories, relegating the pragmatic traditional leadership to the fringes of the political system.

Given the extreme and even self-destructive leniency of Israel's administrative policies, what seems remarkable is that it took as long as it did for the PLO to entice the residents of the West Bank and Gaza into a popular struggle against the Jewish state. Here Israel's counterinsurgency measures must be given their due, as well as the low level of national consciousness among the Palestinians and the sheer rapidity and scope of the improvements in their standard of living. The fact remains, however, that during the two-and-a-half decades from the occupation of the territories to the onset of the Oslo peace process in 1993, there was very little "armed resistance," and most terrorist attacks emanated from outside — from Jordan in the late 1960s, then from Lebanon.

In an effort to cover up this embarrassing circumstance, Fatah, the PLO's largest constituent organization, adopted the slogan that "there is no difference between inside and outside." But there was a difference, and a rather fundamental one. By and large, the residents of the territories wished to get on with their lives and take advantage of the opportunities afforded by Israeli rule. Had the West Bank eventually been returned to Jordan, its residents, all of whom had been Jordanian citizens before 1967, might well have reverted to that status. Alternatively, had Israel prevented the spread of the PLO's influence in the territories, a local leadership, better attuned to the real interests and desires of the people and more amenable to peaceful coexistence with Israel, might have emerged.

But these things were not to be. By the mid-1970s, the PLO had made itself into the "sole representative of the Palestinian people," and in short order Jordan and Egypt washed their hands of the West Bank and Gaza. Whatever the desires of the people living in the territories, the PLO had vowed from the moment of its founding in the mid-1960s — well before the Six Day War — to pursue its "revolution until victory," that is, until the destruction of the Jewish state. Once its position was secure, it proceeded to do precisely that.

By the mid-1990s, thanks to Oslo, the PLO had achieved a firm foothold in the West Bank and Gaza. Its announced purpose was to lay the groundwork for Palestinian statehood, but its real purpose was to do what it knew best — namely, create an extensive terrorist infrastructure and use it against its Israeli "peace partner." At first it did this tacitly, giving a green light to other terrorist organizations like Hamas and Islamic Jihad; then it operated openly and directly.

But what did all this have to do with Israel's "occupation"? The declaration signed on the White House lawn in 1993 by the PLO and the Israeli government provided for Palestinian self-rule in the entire West Bank and the Gaza Strip for a transitional period not to exceed five years, during which Israel and the Palestinians would negotiate a permanent peace settlement. During this interim period the territories would be administered by a Palestinian Council, to be freely and democratically elected after the withdrawal of Israeli military forces both from the Gaza Strip and from the populated areas of the West Bank.

By May 1994, Israel had completed its withdrawal from the Gaza Strip (apart from a small stretch of territory containing Israeli settlements) and the Jericho area of the West Bank. On July 1, Yasser Arafat made his triumphant entry into Gaza. On September 28, 1995, despite Arafat's abysmal failure to clamp down on terrorist activities in the territories now under his control, the two parties signed an interim agreement, and by the end of the year Israeli forces had been withdrawn from the West Bank's populated areas with the exception of Hebron (where redeployment was completed in early 1997). On January 20, 1996, elections to the Palestinian Council were held, and shortly afterward both the Israeli civil administration and military government were dissolved.

The geographical scope of these Israeli withdrawals was relatively limited; the surrendered land amounted to some 30 percent of the West Bank's overall territory. But its impact on the Palestinian population was nothing short of revolutionary. At one fell swoop, Israel relinquished control over virtually all of the West Bank's 1.4 million residents. Since that time, nearly 60 percent of them — in the Jericho area and in the seven main cities of Jenin, Nablus, Tulkarm, Qalqilya, Ramallah, Bethlehem, and Hebron — have lived entirely under Palestinian jurisdiction. Another 40 percent live in towns, villages, refugee camps, and hamlets where the Palestinian Authority exercises civil authority, but, in line with the Oslo accords, Israel has maintained "overriding responsibility for security." Some 2 percent of the West Bank's Palestinians continue to live in areas where Israel has complete control, but even there the Palestinian Authority maintains "functional jurisdiction."

In short, since the beginning of 1996, and certainly following the completion of the redeployment from Hebron in January 1997, 99 percent of the Palestinian population of the West Bank and the Gaza Strip have not lived under Israeli occupation. By no conceivable stretching of words can the anti-Israel violence emanating from the territories during these years be made to qualify as resistance to foreign occupation. In these years there has been no such occupation.

⚙⚙

If the stubborn persistence of Palestinian terrorism is not attributable to the continuing occupation, many of the worst outrages against Israeli civilians likewise occurred — contrary to the mantra of Palestinian spokesmen and their apologists — not at moments of breakdown in the Oslo "peace process" but at its high points, when the prospect of Israeli withdrawal appeared brightest and most imminent.

Suicide bombings, for example, were introduced in the atmosphere of euphoria only a few months after the historic Rabin-Arafat handshake on the White House lawn: eight people were murdered in April 1994 while riding a bus in the town of Afula. Six months later, 21 Israelis were murdered on a bus in Tel Aviv. In the following year, five bombings took the lives of a further 38 Israelis. During the short-lived government of the dovish Shimon Peres (November 1995–May 1996), after the assassination of Yitzhak Rabin, 58 Israelis were murdered within the span of one week in three suicide bombings in Jerusalem and Tel Aviv.

Further disproving the standard view is the fact that terrorism was largely curtailed following Benjamin Netanyahu's election in May 1996 and the consequent slowdown in the Oslo process. During Netanyahu's three years in power, some 50 Israelis were murdered in terrorist attacks — a third of the casualty rate during the Rabin government and a sixth of the casualty rate during Peres's term.

There was a material side to this downturn in terrorism as well. Between 1994 and 1996, the Rabin and Peres governments had imposed repeated closures on the territories in order to stem the tidal wave of terrorism in the wake of the Oslo accords. This had led to a steep drop in the Palestinian economy. With workers unable to get into Israel, unemployment rose sharply, reaching as high as 50 percent in Gaza. The movement of goods between Israel and the territories, as well as between the West Bank and Gaza, was seriously disrupted, slowing exports and discouraging potential private investment.

The economic situation in the territories began to improve during the term of the Netanyahu government, as the steep fall in terrorist attacks led to a corresponding decrease in closures. Real GNP per capita grew by 3.5 percent in 1997, 7.7 percent in 1998, and 3.5 percent in 1999, while unemployment was more than halved. By the beginning of 1999, according to the World Bank, the West Bank and Gaza had fully recovered from the economic decline of the previous years.

Then, in still another turnabout, came Ehud Barak, who in the course of a dizzying six months in late 2000 and early 2001 offered Yasser Arafat a complete end to the Israeli presence, ceding virtually the entire West Bank and the Gaza Strip to the nascent Palestinian state together with some Israeli territory, and making breathtaking concessions over Israel's capital city of Jerusalem. To this, however, Arafat's response was war. Since its launch, the Palestinian campaign has inflicted thousands of brutal attacks on Israeli civilians — suicide bombings, drive-by shootings, stabbings, lynching, stonings — murdering more than 500 and wounding some 4,000.

In the entire two decades of Israeli occupation preceding the Oslo accords, some 400 Israelis were murdered; since the conclusion of that "peace" agreement, twice as many have lost their lives in terrorist attacks. If the occupation was the cause of terrorism, why was terrorism sparse during the years of actual occupation, why did it increase dramatically with the prospect of the end of the occupation, and why did it escalate into open war upon Israel's most far-reaching concessions ever? To the contrary, one might argue with far greater plausibility that the absence of occupation — that is, the withdrawal of close Israeli surveillance — is precisely what facilitated the launching of the terrorist war in the first place.

There are limits to Israel's ability to transform a virulent enemy into a peace partner, and those limits have long since been reached. To borrow from Baruch Spinoza, peace is not the absence of war but rather a state of mind: a disposition to benevolence, confidence, and justice. From the birth of the Zionist movement until today, that disposition has remained conspicuously absent from the mind of the Palestinian leadership.

It is not the 1967 occupation that led to the Palestinians' rejection of peaceful coexistence and their pursuit of violence. Palestinian terrorism started well before 1967, and continued — and intensified — after the occupation ended in all but name. Rather, what is at fault is the perduring Arab view that the creation of the Jewish state was itself an original act of "inhuman occupation" with which compromise of any final kind is beyond the realm of the possible. Until that disposition changes, which is to say until a different leadership arises, the idea of peace in the context of the Arab Middle East will continue to mean little more than the continuation of war by other means.

Originally published in Commentary Magazine *(July/August 2002).*

Faisal's Trojan Horse

Faisal Husseini, who died of a heart attack in May 2001, was a darling of the Western world, hailed as a "moderate voice of peace." But recent evidence suggests that Husseini — the PLO representative in Jerusalem and a PA minister — saw negotiations with Israel as just an interim strategy to liberate the entire land.

In a speech in Beirut in April 2001, Husseini said:

> There is a difference between the strategic goal of the Palestinian people, which is not willing to give up even one grain of Palestinian soil, and the political [tactical] effort that has to do with the [present] balance of power and with the nature of the present international system. The latter is a different effort than the former.

> We may lose or win [tactically] but our eyes will continue to aspire to the strategic goal, namely, to Palestine from the river to the sea. Whatever we get now cannot make us forget this supreme truth.

On his way to Kuwait, where he died of a heart attack, Husseini gave what would be his last interview to the Egyptian daily *Al-*

The Middle East Media Research Institute (MEMRI), headquartered in Washington, D.C., bridges the language gap between the West and the Middle East by providing translations of Arabic media.

Arabi. Husseini speaks metaphorically of the Trojan horse as a Palestinian tactic for the elimination of the Jewish state. Following are excerpts from the interview, published on June 24, 2001.

[The ancient] Greek Army was unable to break into Troy due to [internal] disputes and disagreements [among themselves]. The Greek forces started retreating one after the other, and the Greek king ended up facing the walls of Troy all by himself, and he too suffered from illnesses and [internal] disputes, and ended up leading a failed assault on Troy's walls.

[Following these events] the people of Troy climbed on top of the walls of their city and could not find any traces of the Greek army, except for a giant wooden horse. They cheered and celebrated thinking that the Greek troops were routed, and while retreating left a harmless wooden horse as spoils of war. So they opened the gates of the city and brought in the wooden horse. We all know what happened next.

Had the United States and Israel not realized, before Oslo, that all that was left of the Palestinian National movement and the Pan-Arab movement was a wooden horse called Arafat or the PLO, they would never have opened their fortified gates and let it inside their walls.

Despite the fact that we entered these walls in order to build, unlike the Greeks who entered them in order to destroy, I now tell you all, all these to whom I spoke in a secret meeting during the days of Oslo: "Climb into the horse and don't question what type of material the horse is made of. Climb into the horse, and we shall transform your climbing into that horse into a beginning of a building era, rather than an era of the end of hope."

And indeed, there are those who climbed onto the horse and are [now] inside [the PA territory] whether they supported the Oslo accords or not....

So come down out of the horse and start working for the goal for which you entered the horse to begin with. In my opinion, the intifada itself is the coming down out of the horse. Rather than getting into the old arguments... this effort [the intifada] could have been much better, broader, and more significant had we made it clearer to ourselves that the Oslo agreement, or any other agreement, is just a temporary procedure, or just a step towards something bigger....

When we are asking all the Palestinian forces and factions to look at the Oslo Agreement and at other agreements as "temporary" procedures, or phased goals, this means that we are ambushing the Israelis and cheating them. However, the truth is that we are doing exactly what they are doing. The proof for that is that they are aware of, and are not trying to hide, the fact that there is nothing that unites them more around the territory which extends from the Nile to the Euphrates, than their slogan, which was taken from the Torah, and reads: "These are the borders of the greater land of Israel...."

Similarly, if we agree to declare our state over what is now only 22 percent of Palestine, meaning the West Bank and Gaza — our ultimate goal is [still] the liberation of all historical Palestine from the [Jordan] River to the [Mediterranean] sea, even if this means that the conflict will last for another thousand years or for many generations.

In short, we are exactly like they are. We distinguish the strategic, long-term goals from the political phased goals, which we are compelled to temporarily accept due to international pressure. If you are asking me as a Pan-Arab nationalist what are the Palestinian borders according to the higher strategy, I will immediately reply: "From the river to the sea."

Palestine in its entirety is an Arab land, the land of the Arab nation, a land no one can sell or buy, and it is impossible to remain silent while someone is stealing it, even if this requires time and even [if it means paying] a high price.

If you are asking me, as a man who belongs to the Islamic faith, my answer is also "from the river to the sea," the entire land is an Islamic Waqf which cannot be bought or sold, and it is impossible to remain silent while someone is stealing it....

If you are asking me as an ordinary Palestinian, from the "inside" or from the Diaspora, you will get the same answer and without any hesitations. However, what I am able to achieve and live on right now, due to [constraints of] the international system, is not, of course, Palestine "from the river to the sea." In order for us to fulfill all of our dreams regarding Palestine, we must, first of all, wake up and realize where we are standing. On the other hand, if we will continue to behave as if we are still dreaming, we will not find a place to put our feet on....

As I once said in the past: our eyes must continue to focus on the higher goal. The real danger is that I might forget [it], and while advancing towards my short-term goal I might turn my back on my long-term goal, which is the liberation of Palestine from the river to the sea....

Dan Gillerman

The Problem, Not the Solution

September 15, 2003 — As the Israeli cabinet decides to remove Yasser Arafat, the UN Security Council drafts a resolution to protect him.

On September 13 we commemorated the 10th anniversary of the signing of the Declaration of Principles on the White House lawn. That was a time of hope for the people of the region and of the world, that the leadership on both sides was committed to a peaceful and negotiated resolution of the Israeli-Palestinian conflict. At that time, and despite well-founded reservations, Israel was willing to believe that Yasser Arafat had abandoned the path of terrorism and embarked on the road to true reconciliation and mutual recognition....

Unfortunately, as we have all known for some time, Mr. Arafat lied. Israel, like other members of the international community, has come to this conclusion reluctantly and painfully. More than any other state, we invested a great deal in Mr. Arafat's word, and were willing, against our better judgment, to heed calls from other states to forgo or forgive Mr. Arafat's failures even at the earliest stages of the peace process.

As much as we all hoped for the opposite result, it is abun-

AMBASSADOR DAN GILLERMAN is the permanent representative of Israel to the United Nations.

dantly clear that the person with the standing to deliver a fair and genuine peace on the Palestinian side has done the most to bury its chances. We cannot ignore the facts. His continuing rejection of Israel's right to exist, his denial of the ancient ties of the Jewish people to its homeland, and his support of terrorists and their tactics has brought untold suffering to the region and denied the promise of peace and prosperity for Israelis and Palestinians alike... Among the litany of deliberately missed opportunities, the Palestinian leadership, under Mr. Arafat's control, rejected at Camp David the opportunity for the establishment of a Palestinian state side-by-side with Israel, in favor of the path of terrorism that he, as one of its masterminds, has never really abandoned....

There is hardly a single Israeli citizen today who has not been affected, directly or indirectly, by Palestinian terrorism. The equivalent number of casualties in a country with a population of that of the United Kingdom would be 84,609 citizens. This figure may give us all some pause in comprehending the devastating impact that the Palestinian leadership's refusal to confront the terrorists in its midst has had on the people of the region....

The brazen refusal of the Palestinian leadership to fulfill its obligations to dismantle terrorist organizations, and join the global campaign against terrorism has exacted a heavy toll on Palestinian society. By allowing terrorists to set up shop in the heart of Palestinian civilian areas, in grave violation of international humanitarian law, Mr. Arafat has seriously endangered the lives of innocent Palestinian civilians. By stifling dissent, preventing the emergence of democratic institutions, and violating the human rights of Palestinians, including the Palestinian Christian community, he has set back the development of a vibrant and responsible Palestinian society. By allowing only one voice, while nurturing a myriad of competing security and terrorist organizations, he has succeeded in perpetuating his own corrupt rule at the expense of the welfare of Palestinian civilians....

He is amongst a select group of terrorist entrepreneurs who have brought airplane hijackings, massacres of Olympic athletes, the killing of children sleeping in the shelter of their own beds, and suicide terrorism, to a region that yearns for peace and stability.

And he is at the helm of those who have been supporting mega-terror attacks, in the style of the bombing of the Twin Towers, to bring the region to the brink of catastrophe. Today such immoral tactics, stamped with Mr. Arafat's label of origin, are callously and indiscriminately exported beyond our region.

Knowing all this, for how long will there be states among us who are willing to continue the charade of touting Mr. Arafat as a legitimate leader committed to the welfare of his people and peaceful relations with his neighbors?...

Since efforts have been underway to restart the peace process through the road map, Mr. Arafat has played a wholly destructive role at every step of the way. He has actively sought to prevent the Palestinian Prime Minister from fulfilling the Palestinian obligations under the road map. He has sabotaged attempts to establish new and different leadership in the Palestinian Authority, which stood at the basis of President Bush's vision.

He has refused to allow the consolidation of security forces under the control of an empowered minister for internal security, so that finally, responsible Palestinians can act to completely dismantle the terrorist infrastructure, as they are morally and legally obligated to do. After voicing his active objection to the appointment of Mr. Mahmoud Abbas, Mr. Arafat pressured members of the Palestinian legislative council to narrow Mr. Abbas's control. He has acted to undermine Mr. Abbas from the beginning of his tenure to the very end, until Mr. Abbas was compelled to resign and admit publicly that Mr. Arafat had not given him the authority to fulfill the obligations that the Palestinians had taken upon themselves.

He has continued to encourage acts of terrorism and violence and kept renegade terrorist groups like the Tanzim under his direct control so that at any given moment he could scuttle efforts to renew dialogue by directing the murder of innocent civilians. And he has worked to prevent efforts made to introduce transparency and accountability in Palestinian Authority finances, so that money can continue to be funneled into his private accounts. He has signed peace agreements with one hand and signed checks to terrorists and suicide bombers with the other....

In other instances, members of the international community

have recognized that certain leaders are so destructive to the rights of their own people and to the security and stability of their region, that their legitimacy must be questioned. Mr. Arafat is no exception.

How many more children have to die? How many more concerted peace efforts need to be scuttled before the world is willing to denounce Mr. Arafat's role in a clear voice?

And yet, when is the UN Security Council galvanized into action? Was it galvanized to act after the horrific suicide bombings which killed 22 and injured 135 on a crowded bus in downtown Jerusalem filled with families and children returning from prayers at the Western Wall? Was it galvanized to act when two suicide bombings, at a café in Jerusalem and a bus stop in central Israel, killed a total of 15 and injured more than 70 Israelis, just hours apart?

The Council may have already heard that these latest attacks were perpetrated by terrorists recently released by Israel as part of a goodwill gesture toward the Palestinian leadership. They are further evidence that every gesture made by Israel, and every risk taken for the sake of peace has been answered with criminal action and inaction on the part of the Palestinian leadership, under Mr. Arafat's control....

It would be a grave error if the Council were to come to the aid not of the victims of terrorism, but of their sponsor and perpetrator....

In perpetuating this game of legitimizing Mr. Arafat, we fundamentally undermine our efforts to allow an empowered Palestinian Prime Minister to work to implement the road map and reach a peaceful solution. Such a policy serves the interests of no one other than the terrorists that Mr. Arafat continues to support. It is time we expressly admitted that he is part of the problem and not part of the solution.

Israel holds out hope that a new and different Palestinian leadership that categorically abandons the ways of Mr. Arafat, will be ready to fully and responsibly implement its obligations to fight terrorism and incitement. If it does so, it will find in Israel a willing partner ready to make painful compromises, as it has proven before, to realize President Bush's vision....

In the two years following September 11, Mr. Arafat has continued to demonstrate that he is on the wrong side of history and that he refuses to learn any lessons about the effects of terrorism for both Israelis and Palestinians. Rather than taking responsibility to build a genuine, democratic Palestinian society that can live in peace with its neighbors, he has turned Palestinian victim-hood into a professional enterprise and Palestinian suffering into a source of power and personal prosperity. We will bring no benefit today to the cause of peace, if we come to the defense of someone who has brought only suffering and the promise of further bloodshed.

David Arenson and Simon Grynberg

Anti-Globalization and Anti-Semitism

February 2003

W hat do international banks, sweatshops, soft drink makers, and Israel all have in common?
The attention of the anti-globalization movement.
The phenomenon of anti-globalization first appeared in Seattle in 1999 at the World Trade Organization meeting and gained steam at demonstrations during meetings of the World Bank, the G7, and the UN. The pattern of disrupting international conferences and trade summits is now firmly entrenched.

While globalization — the internationalization of market capitalism — is seen by many as a ray of hope for solving the world's economic problems, it is also blamed for problems plaguing nations and individuals. A new umbrella movement has emerged to oppose "capitalist globalization." It is a broad-based, motley gathering of groups who aim to reduce corporate power and global inequity, and bring about social justice. It is decentralized, multinational, opposed to hierarchy, and by nature chaotic. Among the

SIMON GRYNBERG lives in Toronto and holds a degree in Global Political Studies.
For biography of DAVID ARENSON, see p. 258.

very few goals shared universally among its members is the need for radical reform of the World Trade Organization and International Monetary Fund.

Israel has recently been added to that list, becoming the global "whipping boy" of the movement. This serves to unify the anti-globalization movement despite its obvious complexities and contradictions.

The roots of the shift toward Israel were amplified at the Durban Conference on Racism, which ended only three days before the September 11 attacks. This controversial conference, ostensibly to combat racism and xenophobia, quickly dissolved into a forum to prove that Israel is an apartheid state engaged in oppression of Palestinians. At Durban, terms like "genocide," "fascism," "apartheid," and "holocaust" were bandied about at every opportunity to describe Israeli actions; the infamous forgery *Protocols of the Elders of Zion* was included in the discourse; and Nazi symbols were freely juxtaposed with the Star of David.

The avalanche of anti-Israel sentiment was made particularly credible by the legitimacy of the United Nations. Most NGO's (nongovernmental organizations) look toward the UN for moral guidance, leadership, and responsible governance. The UN is supposed to represent the common goal of truth and justice brought forth by all nations.

However, Arab states have a disproportionate voice in setting the agenda at the UN General Assembly and have made it a bastion for anti-Israel resolutions. For 53 years, Israel was the only member state at the UN denied a seat on the Security Council and the only state not included in any UN regional group. Of the 690 General Assembly resolutions voted on before 1990, 429 were directed against Israel. Of the 175 Security Council resolutions passed during that time, 97 were directed against Israel. The UN Commission on Human Rights has issued fully a quarter of its official condemnations against (democratic) Israel.

The second largest employer after the PA in the West Bank and Gaza is UNRWA, a UN flagship organization which administers Palestinian camps that fester as centers of terror activity — most notably in Jenin, the "suicide bombers' capital." And following the nonmassacre in Jenin, UNRWA commissioner general Peter Hansen spoke of "wholesale obliteration," "a human catastrophe that has few parallels in recent history," "helicopters... strafing civilian residential areas," and "bodies... piling up" in "mass graves."

The UN's stance against despotic Arab regimes is particularly troubling. Syria now sits on the UN Security Council. The head of the UN Human Rights Commission is from Libya. And in May 2003, Iraq is to assume the rotating chairmanship of the UN Conference on Disarmament, established in 1979 as "the single multilateral disarmament negotiating forum of the international community."

Durban was the catalyst that legitimized anti-Israel rhetoric on a grand scale. The ideas disseminated placed Israel as the sole antagonist in the conflict, raising anti-Israel emotion across the globe.

And the anti-globalization movement took on Israel-bashing as its cause and mantra. A large anti-globalization demonstration in Washington in April 2002 was supposed to be a protest against the G8. Instead it turned predominantly into a show of solidarity for the Palestinian cause and a mobilization against Israel. Movements aligned to the anti-globalization movement called for a "global intifada" to protest against "Israeli aggression."

The anti-globalization movement blames Israel for creating desperate conditions that lead to violent resistance. Yet Palestinian violence in 2000 increased while economic conditions were improving, and a recent study from the independent National Bureau of Economic Research in Cambridge, Massachusetts concludes: "Any connection between poverty, education, and terrorism is indirect and probably quite weak."

Anti-globalization activists claim that Zionism is a form of apartheid and a racist ideology forced on the Palestinian people. The claim that anti-Zionism is not anti-Semitism, but a legitimate criticism of Israel's policies, is difficult to understand in the context of the anti-globalization movement making no pronunciations about any other country in the world. Why is Jewish nationalism exclusively described as racism — do Jews not deserve a national homeland? The only satisfactory answer is that anti-Zionism is really anti-Semitism on a national scale. Instead of targeting the Jew as individual, now his national homeland bears the brunt of hatred.

Indeed, is not Islamic fundamentalism, which promotes jihad as a legitimate religious protocol, the most serious threat to Western democratic values and the values of peace expounded by the anti-globalization movement?

Palestinian society is strangled by the dictatorial rule of Arafat, with extremist elements like Islamic Jihad and Hamas controlling the streets. Palestinians are directly responsible for a large percentage of the Palestinian death toll as "suspected collaborators" are publicly lynched. Where is the outcry over the suffering inflicted upon them by the Arafat regime?

The anti-globalization movement engages in selective amnesia when it comes to other countries, particularly Israel's neighbors who consistently ignore its citizens' human rights, democratic values and freedoms. "Justice" in Saudi Arabia involves the flogging of women, no matter what the crime. The religious intolerance of many Arab nations, or the oppression meted out by African crackpot dictatorships, fails to show up on the radar screen of this movement. How about subjugated Cypriots, Tibetans, Balkan refugees, and the litany of displaced peoples in Africa?

The hypocrisy was perhaps most evident in February 2003, when activist Michael Lerner was banned from speaking at a peace rally in San Francisco. Lerner, an outspoken critic of President Bush's planned invasion of Iraq, wrote in the *Wall Street Journal* that the war "is bound to increase the threat of terrorism to American citizens and provoke more violence. It will also fuel American fantasies of world economic and political domination."

So why was Lerner blackballed over the peace rally? Because Lerner, a Jew, was perceived as being "pro-Israel." Bottom line, the "peace" activists' hatred for Israel was higher on its agenda than the alleged "core cause" of world peace.

If the anti-globalization movement is to be taken seriously in the future, it needs to stop its implicit support of terrorists and despotic regimes. And rather than battle against Israel, it should support Israel as a staging ground for Western values and democracy in the Middle East.

Jeffrey Dunetz

Except When You're Targeting Jews

June 2003

When I was in grade school, spelling traumatized me. I couldn't get the knack — all those exceptions. "I" before "e" except after "c," except for weigh and weird. The rules have so many exceptions, that even the exceptions have exceptions. I still get heart palpations just thinking about it. That's probably why I studied international politics in college — it's so much easier than spelling.

On the world political stage, there is only one exception and it's the same for each rule. It's called, "Except when you're targeting Jews." Let me explain how it works.

Take for example targeted assassinations, like the first lightning strike in the recent war against Saddam Hussein, which was followed up with more targeted strikes against Saddam, his sons, and others such as "Chemical Ali." These hits were hailed as

JEFFREY DUNETZ is a 20-year marketing veteran and a freelance writer. He is married and the father of two kids who ask lots of questions about being Jewish that he can't answer. Jeffrey has been active in Jewish organizations since his USY days. Presently he is a member of the Board of Trustees of the Dix Hills Jewish Center.

masterstroke by the media. United States leaders said that they were instrumental in shortening the war.

On the other hand, when Israel pursues terrorist leaders with targeted strikes, they are criticized by the world community as excessive and provocative. That is because Exception #1 of world politics states: Targeted killings of terrorists are okay, except when the terrorist is killing Jews.

Civilian casualties? This week, the Associated Press reported there were over 3,200 civilian deaths in the recent Iraq war. The United States government says as much as they have tried, civilian deaths are unavoidable because the Iraqi military is breaking the rules of Geneva Convention by deploying in civilian areas.

It was just a year ago that an Israeli Air Force jet dropped a bomb on a Gaza apartment building housing Salah Shehadeh, the commander of Hamas who had ordered scores of terrorist acts. In the bombing, 15 civilians perished. Israel was severely rebuked.

Obviously the IDF never read Exception #2 of world politics: Civilian deaths are to be avoided, but cannot be criticized when the enemy is using civilians as human shields... except when you are targeting someone who is killing Jews.

There is another rule which relates to terrorism. Everyone knows that September 11 was terrorism, that the Bali nightclub was terror, that the airline shoe bomber was a terrorist. Terrorism is defined as "intentionally targeting civilians to advance a political cause." Simple, right?

But open up your local paper and see how perpetrators of the following attacks are described: bus bombing in Jerusalem, Seder massacre in Netanya, bat mitzvah shooting in Hadera, shopping mall bombing in Haifa. Instead of "terror," the media uses terms like "militant" and "activist."

Which brings us to Exception #3 of world politics: Do not hesitate to call terrorists "terrorists" — except when they're targeting Jews.

And then there's the whole issue of eliminating terror from our global landscape. After September 11, President Bush declared war on terrorists and "all who harbor them." The issue is black and white. There is no negotiating with terrorists. After the recent terror attacks in Saudi Arabia, Vice President Cheney declared, "The only way to deal with this threat ultimately is to destroy it. There's no treaty that can solve this problem. There's no peace agreement, no policy of containment or deterrence that works to deal with this threat. We have to go find the terrorists."

Throughout the 1990s, Yasser Arafat enjoyed full immunity, despite not arresting terrorists, stopping funding, or confiscating weapons. Under his watchful eye (and often with his signature), Palestinian terror groups organized, trained, armed — and killed hundreds. And now as the road map begins, Palestinian Prime Minister Abbas has declared that he will not forcibly disarm Hamas, preferring instead to work with them so that they agree to go along (temporarily) with the diplomatic route.

This week, faced with 53 separate terror alerts, Israel finally decided to take out Hamas cofounder and terror chief Abdel Aziz Rantisi. After the missile strike (which Rantisi narrowly escaped), world condemnation of the IDF was resounding; President Bush called Israel's action "troubling."

It highlighted Exception #4 of world politics: Weed out and fight terrorism wherever you may find it... except if the terrorists are targeting Jews.

Without knowing these basic exceptions to the rules of world politics, how can anyone make sense of the Mideast situation? If only spelling were so easy....

Rabbi Shraga Simmons

Seven Principles of
Media Objectivity

September 2001

Since the outbreak of violence in September 2000, it has become increasingly clear that a key factor in Israel's struggle is the media's ability to influence public opinion.

We expect journalists to maintain independence and objectivity — and certainly not pledge "cooperation" with one side of an armed struggle. But when a representative of Italian state television issued an apology in Arabic over the filming of a brutal lynching of two Israelis in Ramallah, and promised to cooperate more fully with the Palestinian Authority in the future, the trust of the consumer public was shaken.

Why is the media biased? It could be they are intimidated by Palestinian strongmen into covering only the "positive" side, while Israeli democracy permits more open coverage of the Israeli position. Or it could be that the world applies a double standard of morality to Israel. Or it could simply be that it's more exciting to root for the underdog.

Whatever the reason, it's important to become a discerning

For biography of RABBI SHRAGA SIMMONS, see p. 121.

media consumer. As Mark Twain once said, "If you don't read the newspaper, you are uninformed; if you do read the newspaper, you are misinformed."

How can readers discern the truth between the lines? Here are seven common methods employed by the media — intentionally or not — to influence public opinion. By being aware of these methods, we can avoid being unwittingly shaped by someone else's agenda.

1. Misleading Terminology

By using terminology and definitions in a way that implies accepted fact, the media injects bias under the guise of objectivity.

In March 2001, two separate acts of terrorism occurred a few days apart, providing the opportunity to compare the media's selective use of terminology. The BBC's article on an IRA car bomb in London carried the headline "BBC Bomb Prompts Terror Warning," and the word "terror" (or its derivatives) was used five other times in the article. (One man was slightly injured in the blast.)

One day later, when a Palestinian homicide bomber killed three Israeli civilians in Netanya, the BBC avoided the label "terrorist," and instead used the far milder term "militant."

In actuality, the term "terrorist" would have applied more appropriately to the Palestinian attack, which targeted innocent civilians, as opposed to the IRA attack on BBC, a quasigovernmental institution.

When questioned about this inequity, BBC responded:

> It has long been the policy of the domestic service to refer to terrorists in Northern Ireland of any religious persuasion as [terrorists], but the policy of the [BBC] World Service is not to refer to anyone in those terms.

BBC claims different rules for attacks inside the UK and outside. Yet BBC World Service freely applied the term "terrorist" to the perpetrators of the World Trade Center attacks. Why the double standards?

2. Imbalanced Reporting

Media reports frequently skew the picture by presenting only one side of the equation.

An editorial cartoon on the *Los Angeles Times* website (October 3, 2000) depicts a Jew praying at the Western Wall, with the stones of the wall forming the word "hate." The caption reads: "Worshipping Their God."

When thousands of readers complained, *LA Times* artist Michael Ramirez said the cartoon was balanced, claiming that second man in the cartoon (sprawled on the ground and much less noticeable) is supposed to be a Muslim praying (though the keffiyeh headdress which would identify him as a Muslim is practically invisible).

But why did Ramirez choose as his venue of "hate" the Western Wall, a site sacred only to Jews, which has never been a place of Muslim prayer? Claimed Ramirez: This is a generic wall, not the Western Wall — despite the unique Herodian frame depicted on the stones, and even the trademark bushes growing out of the Wall.

Following reader protest, the *Los Angeles Times* altered its cartoon, deleting the unique Herodian frame around the stones, to make it look more like a generic wall.

3. Opinions Disguised as News

Reporters often adopt a partisan position, even though opinions should only be reported when quoting a spokesperson.

On February 7, 2001, "The Early Show" cohost Bryant Gumbel interviewed former Middle East envoy Dennis Ross about the impact of Ariel Sharon's election victory. Gumbel repeatedly asked Ross leading questions, loaded with negative descriptions of Sharon. Gumbel said:

> But does [Arafat] even have a chance with — with Sharon, when many objective observers view [Sharon] as — as not only a racist, a terrorist, a murderous war criminal?

4. Lack of Context

By failing to provide proper context and full background information, journalists can dramatically distort the true picture.

In February 2001, a Palestinian killed eight Israelis by ramming his bus into a crowd. The front page of the *Los Angeles Times* carried an Associated Press photo which shows the damaged bus, and the Palestinian driver still behind the wheel, lying back with a sad face. The caption read:

> Palestinian bus driver Khalil abu Olbeh, 35, sits wounded after leading police on a 19-mile chase. Family members said he was distraught over financial problem and upset by current unrest.

The LA Times presented the Palestinian terrorist as a victim. Here he sits, looking sad and injured. His bus has been ruined. Why? The police just chased him for 19 miles! He is portrayed as a victim of Israeli aggression — "distraught over financial problems and upset by the current unrest." The caption made no mention of his killing eight innocent people.

Meanwhile, the *Guardian* (UK) defended the bus driver as "a sort of Palestinian everyman who finally snapped because of the combined pressure of the four-month uprising and Israel's economic blockade." Despite his having admitted to carefully planning the attack, the *Guardian* says the attack was "far from being the calculated aim of a dedicated terrorist," and dismissed the killer as being drowsy from medication.

5. Selective Omission

By choosing to report one detail over another, the media controls access to information and manipulates public sentiment.

On October 24, 2000, *The New York Times* referred to a case of Palestinian incitement:

> Israelis cite as one egregious example a televised sermon that defended the killing of the two [lynched] soldiers. "Whether Likud or Labor, Jews are Jews," proclaimed Sheik Ahmad Abu

Halabaya in a live broadcast from a Gaza city mosque the day after the killings.

But *The Times* failed to convey the main message of the televised sermon, the call for the eradication of the Jewish state:

> Even if an agreement for Gaza is signed, we shall not forget Haifa, and Acre, and the Galilee, and Jaffa, and the Triangle and the Negev, and the rest of our cities and villages. It is only a matter of time.... Have no mercy on the Jews, no matter where they are, in any country. Fight them, wherever you are. Wherever you meet them, kill them.

None of this was mentioned in *The Times* article. Instead, *The Times* went out of its way to choose a one-sentence quotation that is innocuous when taken out of context.

6. Using True Facts to Draw False Conclusions

Media reports frequently use true facts to draw erroneous conclusions.

In February 2001, when Ariel Sharon was elected Prime Minister, the *Christian Science Monitor* tried to delegitimize his leadership by claiming that voter turnout "was an unprecedentedly low 60 percent," and that "at least 62 percent of eligible Israeli voters did not vote for Sharon."

Taken out of context, this statement is technically accurate. But in reality, only despotic countries like North Korea or Iraq report 99 percent voter turnout. Truly free elections mean that citizens are also free not to vote. In the United States, for example, only 51 percent of eligible voters participated in the November 2000 presidential elections. This means that President George W. Bush received fewer than 25 percent of the eligible votes (he did not even win the popular vote). In years when only congressional elections are held, American voter turnout drops to 36–38 percent.

But the *Christian Science Monitor* takes the Israeli election out of context, presenting it as a fluke, without comparing it to other democratic elections.

7. Distortion of Facts

In today's competitive media world, reporters frequently do not have the time or inclination to verify information before publication.

In reporting on violence at Joseph's Tomb in October 2000, CNN writes:

> Meanwhile, at least 77 people, mostly Palestinians, have died during several fierce clashes at Joseph's Tomb during the past week. The lone Israeli soldier to die during the clashes bled to death in the tomb as rescuers tried for hours to reach him.

CNN's claim that 77 people — one Israeli and 76 Palestinians — died in one week of clashes at Joseph's Tomb is a gross inaccuracy. In truth, six Palestinians and one Israeli soldier had died during that week of clashes at Joseph's Tomb. In other words, CNN cited the total number of Palestinian casualties in all clashes, and juxtaposed that figure with the Israeli casualty of one isolated event.

If all this sounds discouraging, it helps to know that by being astute media observers, we can make a difference.

The first step is to become an analyst. Understand the subtle media distortions, and read the newspaper with a critical eye.

When discovering a piece of bias, immediately contact the news agency to complain. All major newspapers have websites with an e-mail address to contact the editor. Keep your remarks respectful. Stick to the facts. Avoid name-calling or charges of anti-Semitism. Newspapers are sensitive to such accusations and will immediately dismiss such criticism.

Finally, create a response network. Build a list of e-mail addresses of friends and colleagues, so when you discover a piece of media bias, you can alert the others to file a complaint, too. This will increase the impact exponentially.

Tom Gross

Jeningrad

May 2002

We are talking here of massacre, and a cover-up, of genocide.
(London Evening Standard, April 15, 2002)

Now that even the Palestinian Authority has admitted there was no massacre in Jenin — and some Palestinian accounts speak instead of a "great victory against the Jews" in door-to-door fighting that left 23 Israelis dead — it is worth taking another look at how the international media covered the fighting there.

The Palestinian Authority now claims that 56 Palestinians died in Jenin, the majority of whom were combatants, according to the head of Yasser Arafat's Fatah organization in the town. Human Rights Watch says 52 Palestinians died. Israel says that 46 Palestinians died, all but three of whom were combatants. Palestinian medical sources have confirmed that at least one of these civilians died after Israel withdrew from Jenin on April 12, as a result of a booby-trapped bomb that Palestinian fighters had planted accidentally going off.

TOM GROSS is former Middle East reporter for the *London Sunday Telegraph* and *New York Daily News*. He previously served as a United Nations human-rights adviser on Czech Roma (gypsies). He is now an independent journalist and commentator in New York.

Yet in April 2002, the media's favorite Palestinian spokesman, Saeb Erekat, spoke first of 3,000 Palestinian dead, then of 500. Without bothering to check, the international media lapped his figures up.

The British media was particularly emotive in its reporting. They devoted page upon page, day after day, to tales of mass murders, common graves, summary executions, and war crimes. Israel was invariably compared to the Nazis, to Al Qaeda, and to the Taliban. One report even compared the thousands of supposedly missing Palestinians to the "disappeared" of Argentina. Yasser Arafat's claim that Palestinians had suffered "Jeningrad" seems exaggerated — to put it mildly — considering that 800,000 Russians died during the three-year siege of Leningrad; 1.3 million died in Stalingrad.

Under the headline, "Amid the Ruins, the Grisly Evidence of a War Crime," the Jerusalem correspondent for the *London Independent*, Phil Reeves, began his April 16 dispatch from Jenin: "A monstrous war crime that Israel has tried to cover up for a fortnight has finally been exposed.... The sweet and ghastly reek of rotting human bodies is everywhere, evidence that it is a human tomb. The people say there are hundreds of corpses, entombed beneath the dust."

Reeves spoke of "killing fields," an image more usually associated with Pol Pot's Cambodia. Forgetting to tell his readers that Arafat's representatives, like those of the other totalitarian regimes that surround Israel, have a habit of fabrication, he quoted Palestinians who spoke of "mass murder" and "executions." Reeves didn't bother to quote any Israeli source whatsoever.

Even the right-wing *Daily Telegraph* — which some have dubbed the *"Daily Tel-Aviv-ograph"* because its editorials are frequently sympathetic to Israel — was hardly any less misleading, running headlines such as "Hundreds of Victims 'Were Buried by Bulldozer in Mass Grave.' "

In a story on April 15 entitled "Horror Stories from the Siege of Jenin," *Telegraph* correspondent David Blair quoted one woman telling him that Palestinians were "stripped to their underwear, they were searched, bound hand and foot, placed against a wall, and killed with single shots to the head."

The *Evening Standard*'s Sam Kiley conjured up witnesses to speak of Israel's "staggering brutality and callous murder." The *Guardian*'s Suzanne Goldenberg wrote, "The scale [of destruction] is almost beyond imagination." The (London) *Times*' Janine di Giovanni suggested that Israel's mission to destroy suicide bomb-making factories in Jenin (a town from which at the Palestinians' own admission 28 suicide bombers had already set out) was an excuse by Ariel Sharon to attack children with chicken pox.

On April 17, the *Guardian*'s lead editorial compared the Israeli incursion in Jenin with the September 11 attacks. "Jenin," wrote the *Guardian*, was "every bit as repellent in its particulars, no less distressing, and every bit as man-made."

While the *Guardian* compared the Jewish state to Al Qaeda, the *Evening Standard* compared the Israeli government to the Taliban. Writing on April 15, A.N. Wilson, one of the *Evening Standard*'s leading columnists, accused Israel of "the poisoning of water supplies" (a libel dangerously reminiscent of ancient anti-Semitic myths), and wrote that "we are talking here of massacre, and a cover-up, of genocide."

He also attempted to pit Christians against Jews by accusing Israel of "the willful burning of several church buildings," and making the perhaps even more incredible assertion that "Many young Muslims in Palestine are the children of Anglican Christians, educated at St. George's Jerusalem, who felt that their parents' mild faith was not enough to fight the oppressor."

Then, before casually switching to write about how much money Catherine Zeta-Jones is paying her nanny, Wilson wrote: "Last week, we saw the Israeli troops destroy monuments in Nablus of ancient importance: the scene where Jesus spoke to a Samaritan woman at the well. It is the equivalent of the Taliban destroying Buddhist sculpture." (Perhaps Wilson had forgotten that the only monument destroyed in Nablus was the ancient Jewish holy site of Joseph's Tomb, torn down by a Palestinian mob while Arafat's security forces looked on.)

Other commentators threw in the Holocaust, turning it against Israel. Yasmin Alibhai-Brown, a leading columnist for the *Independent*, wrote (April 15): "I would suggest that Ariel Sharon should be tried for crimes against humanity... and be damned for so debasing the profoundly important legacy of the Holocaust, which was meant to stop forever nations turning themselves into ethnic killing machines."

And the newspaper in Luton, an industrial town in the south of England, ran a double-page spread entitled "Jews in Jackboots."

In the wake of the media attacks came the politicians. Speaking in the House of Commons on April 16, Gerald Kaufman, a veteran Labour Member of Parliament and a former shadow foreign secretary, announced that Ariel Sharon was a "war criminal" who led a "repulsive government." To nods of approval from his fellow parliamentarians, Kaufman, who is Jewish, said the "methods of barbarism against the Palestinians" supposedly employed by the Israeli army were "staining the Star of David with blood."

Ann Clwyd, a Labour MP, on return from a fleeting fact-finding mission to Jenin, called on all European states to withdraw their ambassadors from Israel. Clwyd had joined a succession of VIP visitors parading through Jenin — representatives of the European Parliament, Amnesty International, and even Bianca Jagger.

Not to be outdone, Britain's esteemed academics went further. Tom Paulin, who lectures at Oxford University and Columbia University in New York, opined that he feels "nothing but hatred" for American-born Jews who live in the West Bank and that they should be "shot dead." (In the past, Paulin has referred to the "Zionist SS.")

Beyond this, the British press had closed their ears to Israelis themselves — a society with one of the most vigorous and self-critical democracies in the world. In the words of Kenneth Preiss, a professor at Ben Gurion University: "Please inform the reporters trying to figure out if the Israeli army is trying to 'hide a massacre' of Palestinians, that Israel's citizen army includes journalists, members of parliament, professors, doctors, human rights activists, members of every political party, and every other kind of person, all within sight and cell phone distance of home and editorial offices. Were the slightest infringements to have taken place, there would be demonstrations outside the prime minister's office in no time."

European readers might fair better believing the testimony

given by Palestinian bomb-maker, Omar, in the leading Egyptian newspaper, Al-Ahram:

"We had more than 50 houses booby-trapped around the [Jenin] camp," Omar said. "We chose old and empty buildings and the houses of men who were wanted by Israel because we knew the soldiers would search for them.... We cut off lengths of main water pipes and packed them with explosives and nails. Then we placed them about four meters apart throughout the houses — in cupboards, under sinks, in sofas.... The women went out to tell the soldiers that we had run out of bullets and were leaving. The women alerted the fighters as the soldiers reached the booby-trapped area."

Meanwhile, a video filmed by the Israeli army (and shown on Israeli television) showed Palestinians moving corpses of people who had previously died of natural causes into graveyards around the Jenin camp to fabricate "evidence" in advance of the (subsequently cancelled) UN fact-finding mission.

The systematic building up of a false picture of Israel as aggressor and deliberate killer of civilians, is slowly chipping away at Israel's legitimacy. How can ordinary people elsewhere not end up hating such a country? And contrary to the perceptions of some, Israel is not a major power able to withstand such international antagonism indefinitely. As Jews have learned only too well, acts of wholesale destruction and ultimately genocide did not just spring forth in a vacuum: they are the product of a climate. The British media is not an innocent bystander in this affair.

Lenny Ben-David

Why Are They Saying All Those Terrible Things about Israel?

September 2001

Since the start of violence in September 2000, media bias against Israel has proliferated. One question remains, however: Why have reporters and correspondents adopted these biases? Do they have a political agenda? Is it because they are anti-Israel or anti-Semitic? Is there a media conspiracy?

Here are six possible explanations for anti-Israel bias in the media:

1. Some reporters just don't know the facts.

Most reporters parachute into the region and have to learn the terrain quickly. It is relatively simple to pick up the conventional "shorthand" used by their colleagues. They can choose a few choice landmarks, such as the Palestinian press office at the American Colony Hotel, and start to navigate. But few journalists truly

LENNY BEN-DAVID served as Israel's "number two" diplomat in Washington from 1997 to 2000. Today he consults on government and business affairs and is program director for the Institute for Contemporary Affairs in Jerusalem.

know the area's history, religious background, and diplomatic record.

The correspondent thinks, "This Jerusalem neighborhood of Gilo was built over the 'Green Line,' right? Therefore it must be a settlement built on Palestinian land. And that's how my predecessor described it, right?"

Wrong. Few reporters know the background of UN Resolution 242 and other international laws dealing with the return of territory. They've bought the Palestinian line that 242 obligates Israel to return all the land, and that Israelis are prohibited from settling there. That, of course, is not the case.

2. Some reporters run in packs. But that doesn't mean there's a conspiracy.

For some reporters, it is easier to file the same story as their colleagues. They can share the research, the cab fare, the information, and the work — and in some cases the ignorance. This phenomenon is called "pack journalism." Reporters are not supposed to copy from handouts given by Palestinian sources or to plagiarize from each other, but it happens.

Veteran journalist Marvin Kalb described "pack journalism" this way:

> [Covering a] story where a horde of journalists rush after a single source can often yield the meager one-dimensional news product associated with "pack journalism." But, though a number of prominent news organizations may highlight similar stories, using virtually identical sources, this is not to be mistaken for conspiracy. It is only lazy journalism.

Perhaps it was just coincidence that led both Deborah Sontag of *The New York Times* and Suzanne Goldenberg of the *Guardian* (UK) to a Ramallah shrine in memory of Palestinians killed in the current uprising. In February 2001, on consecutive days, they both filed stories with identical use of the uncommon word "totem" to describe objects at the shrine. That might be a matter of coincidence, but note the nearly identical language of the reports:

Sontag: "Israeli critics would say that the exhibit, "100 Martyrs — 100 Lives," glorifies death and encourages the cult of
the shaheed, or martyr."

Goldenberg: "Israeli critics would argue that the exhibit glorifies violent death, and promotes a cult of martyrdom."

Coincidence?

3. Some reporters do have a political agenda.

Consumers expect media objectivity. In reality, while writers
and editors may attempt to be fair, they all have personal opinions
and biases. Particularly in European and Israeli newspapers, publishers, editors, and reporters frequently have a political message
they wish to convey. "Advocacy journalism" is their avocation.

Fiamma Nirenstein, an Italian journalist who covers the Middle East for *La Stampa*, filed a story on "The Journalists and the Palestinians" (translated in *Commentary*, January 2001):

> The culture of the press is almost entirely Left. These are peo-
> ple who feel the weakness of democratic values; who enjoy
> the frisson of sidling up to a threatening civilization that
> coddles them even while holding in disdain the system they
> represent.

The practitioners of biased political reporting will sometimes
even admit their prejudices. For example, Paul Foot writes in the
Guardian (UK) in praise of "indignant" journalism (February 2001):

> Anti-Arab, pro-Israel prejudice in the U.S. is as powerful as
> ever, but in Britain, I would say, it is on the wane. This is
> thanks at least partly to strong and indignant journalism, in-
> cluding the commentaries from David Hirst and the recent
> reports from the occupied territories by the *Guardian*'s Su-
> zanne Goldenberg. Robert Fisk of the *Independent* has been
> gloriously and contemptuously furious at the [Israeli]
> bombings....

4. Anti-Semitism may also play a role.

Of course, criticism of the actions of Jews or of Israel does not make the critic an anti-Semite. If, however, a reporter or editor denies Israel and Jews the same rights given to other nations and peoples, or if Palestinians and Arabs are given preferential treatment, then perhaps the discrimination is motivated by anti-Semitism.

In this respect, double standards — bending over backward to create a false sense of "even-handed" reporting — smacks of anti-Semitism. For example, many reporters equated a Palestinian gunman's premeditated sniper shooting of 10-month-old Shalhevet Pass with the accidental death of a Palestinian child at the hands of an Israeli soldier firing back at Palestinian gunmen.

Most reporters and correspondents would vehemently deny holding anti-Semitic prejudices. *La Stampa*'s Fiamma Nirenstein, however, argued: "The truth is that Israel, as the Jewish state, is also the object of a contemporary form of anti-Semitism that is no less real for being masked or even unconscious."

Surprisingly, even Jewish journalists can have an anti-Israel agenda. In fact, the correspondents' Judaism may be a conscious or subconscious factor in the writers' desire to be "even-handed." He may feel the need to show colleagues that religious background does not deter him from being critical of Israel. He may also feel that only by being critical of Israel can he "get the story" on the Palestinian side of the border. His job and life may depend on it.

5. Palestinian harassment leads to biased reporting.

Reporting from a war zone can be dangerous business. Around the world, correspondents have been harassed, wounded, kidnapped, and killed.

In the recent violence, a few journalists have been accidentally shot by Israeli soldiers. But here's the difference: The Israeli government does not have a policy of threatening or intimidating journalists. An Israeli soldier intentionally firing on an unarmed reporter would be court-martialed and sent to prison.

The Palestinian Authority, on the other hand, has a longstanding policy of intimidating journalists, dating back to its PLO antecedents in Beirut, when journalists were assassinated for writing articles critical of the PLO and Arafat. Today, at least four human rights watchdog groups — Amnesty International, Freedom House, U.S. State Department Human Rights Report, and the Palestinian Human Rights Monitoring Group — have all published reports on Palestinian harassment, arrest, and torture of journalists. All four reports conclude that for the sake of self-preservation, Palestinian reporters practice "self-censorship."

Over the course of the Palestinian uprising, foreign crews have had their film confiscated when covering events that put the Palestinians in a bad light. The film of the lynching of two Israeli reservists in Ramallah had to be smuggled out for broadcast, and another Italian journalist apologized to the Palestinian Authority after the film was broadcast.

In May 2001, a *Newsweek* correspondent and photographer were kidnapped by Palestinians in Gaza. Here is how the experience was described in Newsweek: "...Hammer says he never feared his captors would hurt him or Knight. 'They never threatened us or pointed their guns at us,' Hammer says. 'They actually fed us one of the best meals I've eaten in Gaza.' "

Is this not the voice of intimidation?

The problem was most evident on September 11, when Palestinians in Nablus and eastern Jerusalem exploded in street celebrations — rejoicing, dancing, and handing out candies. Then, to prevent the world from seeing these incriminating images, armed Palestinians — some in uniform — trapped photojournalists inside a Nablus hotel while festivities continued in the streets. One cameraman on assignment for Associated Press Television News was summoned to a Palestinian Authority security office and told that if his video footage was broadcast, the PA "cannot guarantee the life" of the cameraman.

Either subtly or overtly, reporters are restricted from doing a hard-hitting story on Palestinian corruption, brutality, or violations of agreements — without jeopardizing future access to Palestinian sources, and without risk to their lives.

6. Reliance on Palestinian stringers and cameramen means biased reporting.

A journalist can't just walk into Gaza and begin snapping pictures. Because of such restricted access to Palestinian sources, Western news agencies rely on their Palestinian staffers, stringers, researchers, facilitators, and film crews for translations, access to Palestinian leadership, and getting the stories and films that are too difficult or dangerous for the foreign correspondent.

Of course, the materials supplied by Palestinian sources are biased. Most of the "suppliers" are anti-Israel and fervent supporters of the Palestinian "cause." And all of them must practice self-censorship for their own safety.

Ehud Ya'ari, a veteran Israeli television analyst and Arab affairs expert, wrote in the *Jerusalem Report*:

> ...[O]ver 95 percent of the TV pictures going out on satellite every evening to the various foreign and Israeli channels are supplied by Palestinian film crews. These crews obviously identify emotionally and politically with the intifada and, in the "best" case, they simply don't dare film anything that could embarrass the Palestinian Authority.

Conclusion

Like an infectious disease, biased reporting cannot be eradicated. But at the same time, biased reporting should not be ignored or treated with placebos.

As consumers of news, we have the right to demand an honest product. But first we have to know spoiled milk when we smell it. That calls for educating ourselves about the history of the Arab-Israeli conflict, the political positions and claims of both sides, and current diplomatic complexities. Then we can demand a more satisfactory product or switch to a more reliable supplier.

Israel H. Asper

Dishonest Reporting

A s founder of the largest media corporation in Canada, I have an unshakeable commitment to three cornerstones of my personal value system. My first commitment is to my country, Canada. My second is to Israel as a symbol and teacher of excellence for all of humankind. And third, I am committed to the media as the most honorable and steadfast advocate, defender and distributor of truth, honesty, fairness, freedom, democracy, and human rights.

So it is with a combination of sadness, fear, and anger that I see how Israel and the media are under grievous assault. And even more painful for me, even though at first glance the two pillars of Israel and the media should be separate, I regret to say, they are both threatened by the same cancer and have thus become inextricably linked. This is because dishonest reporting is destroying the trust in and credibility of the media and the journalists — and the same dishonest reporting is biased against Israel, destroying the world's favorable disposition toward it.

I charge that much of the world media covering the Arab-Israeli conflict have abandoned the fundamental precepts of honest reporting. They have been taken captive by their own biases or

ISRAEL ("IZZY") H. ASPER is president of the Asper Foundation and founder of the Canadian media empire, CanWest Global Communications Corp.

victimized by their own ignorance. They have adopted Palestinian propaganda as the context for their stories. Thus dishonest reporting has made truth a casualty of the war, causing grievous damage to both Israel and the integrity of the journalistic profession.

Dishonest reporting occurs in several forms. One is through the selection of terminology which promote a presumed set of facts. Many biased media describe the Palestinian perpetrators of clear acts of terror against Israel merely as militants, resistance fighters, gunmen, or extremists. The terms "cycle of violence," "moderate Arab states," "peace process," "occupied territories," and "illegal settlements" have also become tools and weapons used by the journalistic propagandists.

Yet these phrases are false. The term "cycle of violence" is an insult to the truth, somehow equating terrorist with victim. And under the Oslo agreements there is no prohibition against Israel establishing new settlements in the territory it captured from Jordan.

The first and worst lie is what this war is all about. Dishonest reporting tells you that it's about territory, Jerusalem, Palestinian statehood, and alleged refugees. Honest reporting would tell you that it is a war to destroy Israel and kill or expel or subjugate all the Jews. But the media has reported relentlessly the big lie that this war could be ended by Israeli land concessions.

Another big lie is that the current conflict arises from Palestinian frustration over the slowness of the alleged "peace process." The central, and conveniently ignored, fact is that the current violence is merely the latest chapter in a war against the Jewish people. That war began in earnest 85 years ago, when in 1917, Britain and the League of Nations declared, with world approval, that a Jewish state would be established in Palestine. The region's Arabs have engaged in terrorist slaughter, riots, and military invasion against the Jewish nation ever since. The only periodic lulls in this savage and often barbaric assault, specializing in seeking women, children, and elderly victims, has occurred when the Arabs have been resoundingly defeated. Then, they sue for peace, issue "poor-me" hand-wringing pleas for international help, and use the lull in the battle to regroup, re-arm, and plot their next assault.

Any reportage or commentary that is not clothed in this context is, at best, misleading or ignorant, and plain dishonest at worst. I offer a handful of examples extracted from the hundreds available:

Recently a nationally syndicated American columnist, Georgie Ann Geyer, wrote a column laced with pure fabrications, such as "Prime Minister Sharon told his cabinet recently, 'Don't worry about American objections to our actions, I control America.' " When challenged, she admitted that the statement originated from a press release from the pro-Hamas American group, Islamic Association for Palestine. They claimed it had originated with an official Israeli government radio broadcast. On checking, it turned out that no such broadcast ever occurred.

When confronted with this information, Geyer cowered ignobly behind the standard liar's shield: Her sources, she whined, "were two anonymous Israeli individuals." Naturally, she refused to identify them.

As we all know, pictures can tell a story much better than words. In May 2002, when 100,000 supporters of Israel marched down Manhattan's Fifth Avenue to celebrate Israel's 54th birthday, *The New York Times* photograph was of a placard "end Israeli occupation." The same bias was repeated in the coverage of the huge Toronto rally in support of Israel where thousands of pro-Israel supporters marched. The few hundred anti-Israel protestors that dogged the parade got more media attention. Meanwhile, a Toronto Jewish doctor, standing on the street watching the parade, called out his support for Israel, and was beaten by Palestinian supporter thugs who broke his shoulder. This was not reported.

But if nothing else in this entire sad and sordid story irrefutably demonstrates the inherent media bias against Israel, it is the Jenin massacre myth on which the herd of ravenous reporters descended with vulture-like hysteria. Hyperbolical Palestinian propagandists shrieked "Massacre — 500 innocents slaughtered." Finally, when the UN commission declared that only 54 Palestinians had died, and over half of them were armed combatants, the myth exploded. However, few media apologized or retracted the charges of "genocide," "war crimes," and "heinous Israeli atrocities."

Contrast that with a true war crime that occurred shortly after. It is an offense, under the Geneva war conventions, for armed persons to occupy any church. Yet the whole world sat silently and did not condemn the crime when Palestinian terrorists in Bethlehem occupied the Church of the Nativity, took its occupants hostage, and refused to surrender to surrounding Israeli soldiers. Rather, the so-called world community, aided by a silent media, brought huge international pressure against Israel to give up its barricade and let the alleged terrorists go. There was no United Nations intervention, no Christian church intervention, and no condemnation of the war crimes committed by the terrorists.

Every one of us must do what we can to correct this travesty. It is time to say "Enough!" We must demand that the journalism schools do a better job of teaching integrity more forcibly. Then, we must demand that our media owners invest more money in educating their journalists and media operators. On the university campuses, we must demand that the administrators of higher education retake control of the teaching process, to ensure that hate is not taught, propaganda is not preached, and that the revered term "academic freedom" is never used as a license to libel, a podium for propaganda, and an advocacy of hate. And we should withhold our financial support for those institutions that fail this obligation of educational integrity.

And finally, the public must take action against the media wrongdoers. The issue here is not media bias against Israel. The issue is media bias, period. If we cannot trust the media in its reporting on Israel, how can we trust it on anything? And if we cannot trust our media, then democracy and our freedom are profoundly threatened. The public must be more vigilant and aggressive with letters to the editor, phone calls, cancellation of subscriptions, and refusal to patronize advertisers. The public should establish, in each community, response groups to call to account offending dishonest media. And the public must become politically active to demand a government policy that is consistent with fairness to and supportive of the only beacon of democracy in a swamp of hate, violence, and terrorism, the State of Israel.

Don't think that an individual is powerless. Remember that all it takes for evil to triumph is for good people to remain silent. We are witnessing the most virulent, vitriolic, and vicious explosion of anti-Semitism, rivaled only by the rise of Nazism in Europe in the 1930s. Left unchecked, it will consume all freedoms, for every attack of anti-Semitism in the history of mankind has always been a forerunner to the destruction of liberty in other sectors of human endeavor, not just for Jews. Do not repeat the errors of the previous generation, who passively and complacently witnessed government indifference to the rise of genocide in Europe during the 1930s. It is time to vigorously and vigilantly become activists.

As for me, I do not intend to be silent. I have carried on a love affair with the media all my adult life, and I have also been a staunch supporter of Israel. At the same time, I am an unashamed and unrelenting Canadian patriot. I am not going to stand idly by to watch any of the democratic ideals that made Canada the envy of nations be injured, sullied, or disgraced. At this time, our appropriate position should be to stand tall in support of honesty in reporting, as well as for the right of Israel to exist and to take whatever actions it needs to battle its savage attackers. And to demand that our media and our politicians act with honor in this quest.

Sara Yoheved Rigler

Can the Whole World Be Wrong?

April 2002

Speaking from Madrid, United Nations Secretary General Kofi Annan reiterated his demand that Israel immediately terminate its campaign against terrorism. Citing the opposition to Israel from China through Europe to the United States, Mr. Annan declared: "Can the whole world be wrong?"

I wish to remind Mr. Annan: Some 3,800 years ago, the whole world worshipped pantheons of disparate forces embodied as various gods. A single individual, Abraham, claimed that all existence emanated from one, indivisible, incorporeal God. Abraham was labeled *Ha'Ivri* ("the Hebrew"), meaning that he came from the other side.

While this appellation may have had a geographical origin (he came from the other side of the Euphrates River), Jewish tradition understands "other side" in the sense of an adversarial position: While the whole world adhered to polytheism, Abraham insisted on the truth of monotheism.

Can the whole world be wrong?

For biography of SARA YOHEVED RIGLER, see p. 28.

In the fourth century BCE, the Greek Empire stretched from Macedonia to India, the entire "civilized" world. With Greek political domination came the hegemony of Greek culture and philosophy. The whole world accepted the Greek worldview with man at the center and the physical world as ultimate reality. A small band of Jews, known as the Maccabees, refused to succumb. They insisted that God was the source and that a deeper spiritual connection was the goal of life.

Can the whole world be wrong?

In the ancient world, including the advanced civilizations of Greece and Rome, infanticide was universally practiced. Newborns who were unwanted because they were weak or handicapped (or girls) were killed by their parents or left to die of exposure. The Jews insisted that all life was sacred and condemned infanticide as murder.

Can the whole world be wrong?

Compassion for the poor and infirm, built into the commandments of the Torah, was scorned as weakness by societies from ancient Greece to modern Nazi Germany. The Nazis instituted a program called "T-4," which systematically set out to kill all physically and mentally disabled persons.

Can the whole world be wrong?

From 1939–1945, the whole world claimed that immigration quotas made it impossible to accept Jews trying to flee the Nazis. The British turned away shiploads of Jewish refugees trying to find shelter in Palestine. Even President Roosevelt, "a friend of the Jews," refused to order the bombing of the train tracks leading to Auschwitz, which would have saved the 400,000 Jews of Hungary.

Can the whole world be wrong?

In June 1981, a daring Israeli Air Force raid destroyed the Iraqi nuclear reactor at Osirak. Israeli intelligence maintained that the reactor was about to be loaded with highly enriched uranium, and that radioactive fallout of any later raid might have decimated Baghdad. International condemnation was fast and furious, and an emergency session was convened of the United Nations Security Council. A decade later as the Gulf War began, and a decade after that as America engineered a regime charge in Iraq, the strike at

Osirak was hailed as masterful military foresight.

Can the whole world be wrong?

In April 2002, after a rash of suicide bombings left 127 Israeli civilians (including babies and entire families) dead in a single month, the government of Israel launches a defensive campaign against Palestinian terrorists and their infrastructure. Israeli forces uncover scores of bomb factories, with suicide belts already prepared, and large stashes of illegal munitions and rockets. Kofi Annan and the whole world insists that Israel has no right to defend itself.

Can the whole world be wrong?

Jeff Jacoby

Peace at Any Price Equals War

April 2002

You cannot make sense of the Israeli-Palestinian war without first making sense of 1993.

That year found Israel in reasonably good shape. Its economy was the most powerful in the Middle East. Its military power was respected and feared throughout the region. Its enemies in the Arab and Muslim world, who for so long had dreamt of wiping Israel off the map, were at last coming to accept that the Jewish state was here to stay. To be sure, Yasser Arafat and his Palestine Liberation Organization still plotted to "liberate" Israel from the Jews, but they were in exile in Tunisia and their political and moral capital were close to nil.

Things were not perfect, of course. The Palestinian intifada of the late 1980s had petered out, but violence still flared in the West Bank and Gaza, where Israel's military presence — the result of the Arabs' 1967 war of aggression — was resented. In Israel proper, Arab terrorism sometimes sent innocent civilians to terrible deaths. Israelis longed for a more normal existence, one that didn't involve such a heavy burden of military service or the hostility of their neighbors or the onus of ruling over another people.

JEFF JACOBY is a columnist for the *Boston Globe*, where this article first appeared.

If these conditions weren't ideal, they were stable. Israel could have continued to shun the PLO as long as its charter called for Israel's extermination. It could have maintained indefinitely its tough-minded policy of deterring hostility by retaliating fiercely when attacked.

But Israel chose a different course. In 1993, following secret negotiations in Oslo, Norway, it embarked on a "peace process" designed to elevate Arafat and the PLO to heights of power, wealth, and respect they had never before known. In exchange for Arafat's promise of peace — "the PLO renounces the use of terrorism and other acts of violence," he had pledged in writing — Israel agreed to forget the PLO's long history of mass murder and terror and to treat it as the legitimate representative of the Palestinians. The deal was sealed at the White House on September 13, 1993, when Prime Minister Yitzhak Rabin gave Arafat his hand and affirmed his new status as Israel's partner in peace.

What followed was unprecedented in the history of statecraft. Arafat and thousands of PLO killers, now reconstituted as the "Palestinian Authority," entered Gaza and the West Bank in triumph. In short order, Israel transferred virtually every Arab city and town in the territories to Arafat's control. It allowed the Palestinian Authority to assume total control over the Palestinian people. It not only agreed to the creation of an armed Palestinian militia, it supplied that militia with weapons. It began paying Arafat a multimillion-dollar monthly allowance and lobbied internationally for additional financial support. It permitted the PA to build an airport, to operate radio and television networks, and to deal with other countries as a sovereign power.

But even after Israel saw that Arafat's hostility was undimmed, it went on making one concession after another.

Literally from the day the Oslo accord was signed, Arafat made it plain that his lifelong goal — Israel's liquidation — had not changed. He reaffirmed the PLO's "Plan of Phases," its 1974 program of eliminating Israel by stages. He repeatedly called for jihad and extolled Palestinian terrorists as "martyrs" and heroes.

The starting point of the Oslo peace process, the foundation on which everything else had been conditioned, was the Palestinians' unequivocal renunciation of terror and violence. But instead of ending, the terror and violence accelerated. The Israeli death toll soared. Arab snipers and bombers, many from Arafat's own wing of the PLO, murdered Jews at a faster pace than ever before. And each new atrocity was hailed by the Palestinian media, which poured out a flood of anti-Semitic venom and blood lust.

With every new concession, the Palestinians grew more certain that the Israelis were weak and on the run — and that hitting them even harder would bring even greater returns. When Prime Minister Ehud Barak offered Arafat nearly everything he had demanded, including a state with Jerusalem as its capital, Arafat's reply was to unleash a second intifada, more furious and lethal than the first.

Israel is at war today partly because it refused to see that dictators bent on conquest can never be appeased, only defeated. It craved peace at any price, craved it so madly that it was willing to overlook even the murder of its own sons and daughters. In so doing, it emboldened the murderers — and achieved not peace, but its opposite.

Dore Gold

"Occupied" Territories?

January 2002

At the heart of the Palestinian diplomatic struggle against Israel is the repeated assertion that the Palestinians of the West Bank and Gaza Strip are resisting "occupation." Speaking on CNN's Larry King Weekend, Hanan Ashrawi hoped that the United States war on terrorism would lead to new diplomatic initiatives to address its root "causes." She then went on to specifically identify "the occupation which has gone on too long" as an example of one of terrorism's sources.[1] In other words, according to Ashrawi, the violence of the intifada emanates from the "occupation."

Mustafa Barghouti, president of the Palestinian Medical Relief Committees and a frequent guest on CNN as well, similarly asserted that[2] "the root of the problem is Israeli occupation."[2] Writing in the *Washington Post* (January 16, 2002), Marwan Barghouti, head of Arafat's Fatah PLO faction in the West Bank, continued this theme with an article entitled: "Want Security? End the Occupation." This has become the most ubiquitous line of argument today among Palestinian spokesmen, who have to contend with the

DORE GOLD formerly served as Israel's Ambassador to the United Nations, and now heads the Jerusalem Center for Public Affairs (jcpa.org). He is the author of *Hatred's Kingdom*.

growing international consensus against terrorism as a political instrument.

This language and logic have also penetrated the diplomatic struggles in the United Nations. During August 2001, a Palestinian draft resolution at the UN Security Council repeated the commonly used Palestinian reference to the West Bank and Gaza Strip as "occupied Palestinian territories." References to Israel's "foreign occupation" also appeared in the Durban Draft Declaration of the UN World Conference Against Racism. The Libyan ambassador to the United Nations, in the name of the Arab Group Caucus, reiterated on October 1, 2001, what Palestinian spokesmen had been saying on network television: "The Arab Group stresses its determination to confront any attempt to classify resistance to occupation as an act of terrorism."[3]

Three clear purposes seem to be served by the repeated references to "occupation" or "occupied Palestinian territories." First, Palestinian spokesmen hope to create a political context to explain and even justify the Palestinians' adoption of violence and terrorism during the current intifada. Second, the Palestinian demand of Israel to "end the occupation" does not leave any room for territorial compromise in the West Bank and Gaza Strip, as suggested by the original language of UN Security Council Resolution 242 (see below).

Third, the use of "occupied Palestinian territories" denies any Israeli claim to the land: had the more neutral language of "disputed territories" been used, then the Palestinians and Israel would be on an even playing field with equal rights. Additionally, by presenting Israel as a "foreign occupier," advocates of the Palestinian cause can delegitimize the Jewish historical attachment to Israel. This has become a focal point of Palestinian diplomatic efforts since the failed 2000 Camp David Summit, but particularly since the UN Durban Conference in 2001. Indeed, at Durban, the delegitimization campaign against Israel exploited the language of "occupation" in order to invoke the memories of Nazi-occupied Europe during World War II and link them to Israeli practices in the West Bank and Gaza Strip.[4]

The politically loaded term "occupied territories" or "occupation" seems to apply only to Israel and is hardly ever used when other territorial disputes are discussed, especially by interested third parties. For example, the United States Department of State refers to Kashmir as "disputed areas."[5] Similarly, in its Country Reports on Human Rights Practices, the State Department describes the patch of Azerbaijan claimed as an independent republic by indigenous Armenian separatists as "the disputed area of Nagorno-Karabakh."[6]

Despite the 1975 advisory opinion of the International Court of Justice establishing that Western Sahara was not under Moroccan territorial sovereignty, it is not commonly accepted to describe the Moroccan military incursion in the former Spanish colony as an act of "occupation." In a more recent decision of the International Court of Justice from March 2001, the Persian Gulf island of Zubarah, claimed by both Qatar and Bahrain, was described by the Court as "disputed territory," until it was finally allocated to Qatar.[7]

Of course, each situation has its own unique history, but in a variety of other territorial disputes from northern Cyprus, to the Kurile Islands, to Abu Musa in the Persian Gulf — which have involved some degree of armed conflict — the term "occupied territories" is not commonly used in international discourse.[8]

Thus, the case of the West Bank and Gaza Strip appears to be a special exception in recent history, for in many other territorial disputes since World War II, in which the land in question was under the previous sovereignty of another state, the term "occupied territory" has not been applied to the territory that had come under one side's military control as a result of armed conflict.

Israel entered the West Bank and Gaza Strip in the 1967 Six Day War. Israeli legal experts traditionally resisted efforts to define the West Bank and Gaza Strip as "occupied" or falling under the main international treaties dealing with military occupation. Former Chief Justice of the Israeli Supreme Court Meir Shamgar wrote in the 1970s that there is no de jure applicability of the 1949 Fourth Geneva Convention regarding occupied territories to the case of the West Bank and Gaza Strip since the Convention "is based on the assumption that there had been a sovereign who was ousted and that he had been a legitimate sovereign."

In fact, prior to 1967, Jordan had occupied the West Bank and Egypt had occupied the Gaza Strip; their presence in those territories was the result of their illegal invasion in 1948, in defiance of the UN Security Council. Jordan's 1950 annexation of the West Bank was recognized only by Great Britain (excluding the annexation of Jerusalem) and Pakistan, and rejected by the vast majority of the international community, including the Arab states.

At Jordan's insistence, the 1949 Armistice Line, which constituted the Israeli-Jordanian boundary until 1967, was not a recognized international border but only a line separating armies. The Armistice Agreement specifically stated: "No provision of this Agreement shall in any way prejudice the rights, claims, and positions of either Party hereto in the peaceful settlement of the Palestine questions, the provisions of this Agreement being dictated exclusively by military considerations" (Article II.2).

As noted above, in many other cases in recent history in which recognized international borders were crossed in armed conflicts and sovereign territory seized, the language of "occupation" was not used — even in clear-cut cases of aggression. Yet in the case of the West Bank and Gaza, where no internationally recognized sovereign control previously existed, the stigma of Israel as an "occupier" has gained currency.

❧

International jurists generally draw a distinction between situations of "aggressive conquest" and territorial disputes that arise after a war of self-defense. Former State Department Legal Advisor Stephen Schwebel, who later headed the International Court of Justice in the Hague, wrote in 1970 regarding Israel's case: "Where the prior holder of territory had seized that territory unlawfully, the state which subsequently takes that territory in the lawful exercise of self-defense has, against that prior holder, better title."[9]

Here the historical sequence of events on June 5, 1967, is critical, for Israel only entered the West Bank after repeated Jordanian artillery fire and ground movements across the previous armistice lines. Jordanian attacks began at 10:00 a.m.; an Israeli warning to

Jordan was passed through the UN at 11:00 a.m.; Jordanian attacks nonetheless persisted, so that Israeli military action only began at 12:45 p.m. Additionally, Iraqi forces had crossed Jordanian territory and were poised to enter the West Bank. Under such circumstances, the temporary armistice boundaries of 1949 lost all validity the moment Jordanian forces revoked the armistice and attacked. Israel thus took control of the West Bank as a result of a defensive war.

The language of "occupation" has allowed Palestinian spokesmen to obfuscate this history. By repeatedly pointing to "occupation," they manage to reverse the causality of the conflict, especially in front of Western audiences. Thus, the current territorial dispute is allegedly the result of an Israeli decision "to occupy," rather than a result of a war imposed on Israel by a coalition of Arab states in 1967.

Under UN Security Council Resolution 242 of November 22, 1967 — that has served as the basis of the 1991 Madrid Conference and the 1993 Declaration of Principles — Israel is only expected to withdraw "from territories" to "secure and recognized boundaries" and not from "the territories" or "all the territories" captured in the Six Day War. This deliberate language resulted from months of painstaking diplomacy. For example, the Soviet Union attempted to introduce the word "all" before the word "territories" in the British draft resolution that became Resolution 242. Lord Caradon, the British UN ambassador, resisted these efforts.[10] Since the Soviets tried to add the language of full withdrawal but failed, there is no ambiguity about the meaning of the withdrawal clause contained in Resolution 242, which was unanimously adopted by the UN Security Council.

Thus, the UN Security Council recognized that Israel was entitled to part of these territories for new defensible borders. Britain's foreign secretary in 1967, George Brown, stated three years later that the meaning of Resolution 242 was "that Israel will not withdraw from all the territories."[11] Taken together with UN Security Council Resolution 338, it became clear that only negotiations would determine which portion of these territories would eventually become "Israeli territories" or territories to be retained by Israel's Arab counterpart.

Actually, the last international legal allocation of territory that includes what is today the West Bank and Gaza Strip occurred with the 1922 League of Nations Mandate for Palestine, which recognized Jewish national rights in the whole of the Mandated territory: "Recognition has been given to the historical connection of the Jewish people with Palestine and to the grounds for reconstituting their national home in that country." The members of the League of Nations did not create the rights of the Jewish people, but rather recognized a preexisting right, that had been expressed by the 2,000-year-old quest of the Jewish people to reestablish their homeland.

Moreover, Israel's rights were preserved under the United Nations as well, according to Article 80 of the UN Charter, despite the termination of the League of Nations in 1946. Article 80 established that nothing in the UN Charter should be "construed to alter in any manner the rights whatsoever of any states or any peoples or the terms of existing international instruments." These rights were unaffected by UN General Assembly Resolution 181 of November 1947 — the Partition Plan — which was a nonbinding recommendation that was rejected, in any case, by the Palestinians and the Arab states.

Given these fundamental sources of international legality, Israel possesses legal rights with respect to the West Bank and Gaza Strip that appear to be ignored by those international observers who repeat the term "occupied territories" without any awareness of Israeli territorial claims. Even if Israel only seeks "secure boundaries" that cover part of the West Bank and the Gaza Strip, there is a world of difference between a situation in which Israel approaches the international community as a "foreign occupier" with no territorial rights, and one in which Israel has strong historical rights to the land that were recognized by the main bodies serving as the source of international legitimacy in the previous century.

In the 1980s, President Carter's State Department legal advisor, Herbert Hansell, sought to shift the argument over occupation from the land to the Palestinians who live there. He determined that the 1949 Fourth Geneva Convention governing military occupation applied to the West Bank and Gaza Strip since its paramount purpose was "protecting the civilian population of an occupied territory."[12] Hansell's legal analysis was dropped by the Reagan and the first Bush administrations; nonetheless, he had somewhat shifted the focus from the territory to its populace. Yet here, too, the standard definitions of what constitutes an occupied population do not easily fit, especially since the implementation of the 1993 Oslo Agreements.

Under Oslo, Israel transferred specific powers from its military government in the West Bank and Gaza to the newly created Palestinian Authority. Already in 1994, the legal advisor to the International Red Cross, Dr. Hans-Peter Gasser, concluded that his organization had no reason to monitor Israeli compliance with the Fourth Geneva Convention in the Gaza Strip and Jericho area, since the Convention no longer applied with the advent of Palestinian administration in those areas.[13]

Upon concluding the Oslo II Interim Agreement in September 1995, which extended Palestinian administration to the rest of the West Bank cities, Foreign Minister Shimon Peres declared: "Once the agreement will be implemented, no longer will the Palestinians reside under our domination. They will gain self-rule and we shall return to our heritage."[14]

Since that time, 98 percent of the Palestinian population in the West Bank and Gaza Strip has come under Palestinian jurisdiction.[15] Israel transferred 40 spheres of civilian authority, as well as responsibility for security and public order, to the Palestinian Authority, while retaining powers for Israel's external security and the security of Israeli citizens.

The 1949 Fourth Geneva Convention (Article 6) states that the Occupying Power would only be bound to its terms "to the extent that such Power exercises the functions of government in such territory." Under the earlier 1907 Hague Regulations, as well, a territory can only be considered occupied when it is under the effective and actual control of the occupier. Thus, according to the main international agreements dealing with military occupation, Israel's transfer of powers to the Palestinian Authority under the Oslo Agreements has made it difficult to continue to characterize the West Bank and Gaza as occupied territories.

Israel has been forced to exercise its residual powers in recent months only in response to the escalation of violence and armed attacks instigated by the Palestinian Authority.[16] Thus, any increase in defensive Israeli military deployments today around Palestinian cities is the direct consequence of a Palestinian decision to escalate the military confrontation against Israel, and not an expression of a continuing Israeli occupation, as the Palestinians contend. For once the Palestinian leadership takes the strategic decision to put an end to the current wave of violence, there is no reason why the Israeli military presence in the West Bank and Gaza cannot return to its pre-September 2000 deployment, which minimally affected the Palestinians.

Describing the territories as "Palestinian" may serve the political agenda of one side in the dispute, but it prejudges the outcome of future territorial negotiations that were envisioned under UN Security Council Resolution 242. It also represents a total denial of Israel's fundamental rights. Furthermore, reference to "resisting occupation" has simply become a ploy advanced by Palestinian and Arab spokesmen to justify an ongoing terrorist campaign against Israel, despite the new global consensus against terrorism that has been formed since September 11, 2001.

It would be far more accurate to describe the West Bank and Gaza Strip as "disputed territories" to which both Israelis and Palestinians have claims. As United States Ambassador to the UN Madeleine Albright stated in March 1994: "We simply do not support the description of the territories occupied by Israel in the 1967 War as occupied Palestinian territory."

Notes

1. CNN Larry King Weekend, "America Recovers: Can the Fight Against Terrorism be Won?" Aired November 10, 2001, 21:00 ET (CNN.com/transcripts).

2. Mustafa Barghouti, "Occupation Is the Problem," *Al-Ahram Weekly Outline*, December 6–12, 2001.

3. Anne F. Bayefsky, "Terrorism and Racism: The Aftermath of Durban," *Jerusalem Viewpoints*, no. 468, December 16, 2001.

4. See Bayefsky, op. cit. United States and European officials may use the term "occupation" out of a concern for the humanitarian needs of the Palestinians,

without identifying with the PLO political agenda at Durban or at the UN.

5. United States Department of State, Consular Information Sheet: India (http://travel.state.gov/india.html), November 23, 2001.

6. 1999 Country Reports on Human Rights Practices: Azerbaijan, released by the Bureau of Democracy, Human Rights and Labor, United States Department of State, February 25, 2000.

7. Case Concerning Maritime Delimitation and Territorial Questions between Qatar and Bahrain, March 15, 2001, Judgment on the Merits, International Court of Justice, March 16, 2000, paragraph 100.

8. The Japanese Foreign Ministry does not use the language of "ending the Russian occupation of the Kurile Islands," but rather resolving "the Northern Territory Issue" (www.mofa.go.jp/region/europe/russia/territory). United States Department of State "Background Notes" describe the Turkish Republic of Northern Cyprus as the Island's "northern part [which is] under an autonomous Turkish-Cypriot administration supported by the presence of Turkish troops" — not under Turkish occupation.

9. Stephen Schwebel, "What Weight to Conquest," *American Journal of International Law*, 64 (1970): 345–347.

10. Vernon Turner, "The Intent of UNSC 242 — The View of Regional Actors," in UN Security Council Resolution 242: The Building Block of Peacemaking (Washington: Washington Institute for Near East Policy, 1993), p. 27.

11. Meir Rosenne, "Legal Interpretations of UNSC242," in UN Security Council Resolution 242: The Building Block of Peacemaking, op. cit., p. 31.

12. Under the Carter administration, Hansell's distinction led, for the first time, to a United States determination that Israeli settlement activity was illegal since it purportedly contravened Article 49 of the Fourth Geneva Convention which stated that "the Occupying Power shall not deport or transfer parts of its own civilian population into the territory it is occupying." Subsequently, the Reagan and Bush administrations altered the legal determination of the Carter period, changed the United States voting pattern at the UN, and refused to describe Israeli settlements as illegal, even if American political objections to settlement activity continued to be expressed. One reason was that the Fourth Geneva Convention applied to situations like that of Nazi-occupied Europe, which involved "forcible transfer, deportation, or resettlement of large numbers of people." This view was formally stated by the United States Ambassador to the UN in Geneva, Morris Abram, on February 1, 1990, who had served on the United States staff at the Nuremberg trials and, hence, was familiar with the legal intent behind the 1949 Fourth Geneva Convention.

13. Dr. Hans-Peter Gasser, Legal Adviser, International Committee of the Red Cross, "On the Applicability of the Fourth Geneva Convention after the Declaration of Principles and the Cairo Agreement," paper presented at the International Colloquium on Human Rights, Gaza, September 10–12, 1994. Gasser did not

state that in his view the territories were no longer "occupied," but he did point out the legal complexities that had arisen with Oslo's implementation.

14. Foreign Minister Shimon Peres' Address at the Israeli-Palestinian Interim Agreement Signing Ceremony, Washington, D.C., September 28, 1995.

15. Ehud Barak, "Israel Needs a True Partner for Peace," *The New York Times*, July 30, 2001.

16. The present intifada violence resulted from a strategic decision taken by Yasser Arafat, as admitted by numerous Palestinian spokesmen:

"Whoever thinks the intifada broke out because of the despised Sharon's visit to the Al-Aqsa Mosque is wrong.... This intifada was planned in advance, ever since President Arafat's return from the Camp David Negotiations," admitted Palestinian Communications Minister 'Imad Al-Faluji (*Al-Safir*, March 3, 2001, trans. MEMRI). Even earlier, Al-Faluji had explained that the intifada was initiated as the result of a strategic decision made by the Palestinians (*Al-Ayyam*, December 6, 2000).

Arafat began to call for a new intifada in the first few months of 2000. Speaking before Fatah youth in Ramallah, Arafat "hinted that the Palestinian people are likely to turn to the intifada option" (*Al-Mujahid*, April 3, 2000).

Marwan Barghouti, the head of Fatah in the West Bank, explained in March 2000: "We must wage a battle in the field alongside of the negotiating battle... I mean confrontation" (*Ahbar Al-Halil*, March 8, 2000). During the summer of 2000, Fatah trained Palestinian youths for the upcoming violence in 40 training camps.

The July 2000 edition of *Al-Shuhada* monthly, distributed among the Palestinian Security Services, states: "From the negotiating delegation led by the commander and symbol, Abu Amar (Yasser Arafat) to the brave Palestinian people, be ready. The Battle for Jerusalem has begun." One month later, the commander of the Palestinian police told the official Palestinian newspaper *Al-Hayat Al-Jadida*: "The Palestinian police will lead together with the noble sons of the Palestinian people, when the hour of confrontation arrives." Freih Abu Middein, the PA Justice Minister, warned that same month: "Violence is near and the Palestinian people are willing to sacrifice even 5,000 casualties" (*Al-Hayut al-Jadida*, August 24, 2000 — MEMRI).

Another official publication of the Palestinian Authority, *Al-Sabah*, dated September 11, 2000 — more than two weeks before the Sharon visit — declared: "We will advance and declare a general intifada for Jerusalem. The time for the intifada has arrived, the time for intifada has arrived, the time for jihad has arrived."

Arafat advisor Mamduh Nufal told the French *Nouvel Observateur* (March 1, 2001): "A few days before the Sharon visit to the Mosque, when Arafat requested that we be ready to initiate a clash, I supported mass demonstrations and opposed the use of firearms." Of course, Arafat ultimately adopted the use of firearms and bomb attacks against Israeli civilians and military personnel. On September 30, 2001, Nufal detailed in *al-Ayyam* that Arafat actually issued orders to field commanders for violent confrontations with Israel on September 28, 2000.

Rabbi Shraga Simmons

The Refugee Issue

The issue of Palestinian refugees is a sticking point in Middle East peace negotiations. How did this problem begin, and who is responsible?

In the 1948 war, approximately 600,000 Jewish refugees were persecuted and expelled from Arab lands including Iraq, Syria, Lebanon, Egypt, Libya, Tunisia, Algeria, and Morocco — leaving behind an estimated $30 billion in assets. These Jewish refugees were welcomed by Israel and with their descendants now comprise a majority population of the State of Israel.

In the same war, according to the UN, approximately 720,000 Palestinians refugees fled to Jordan, Egypt, Lebanon, and the West Bank and Gaza. The UN estimates that they and their descendents now number about 3.7 million.

The Arab League forbade any Arab country from accepting these refugees or settling them in normal housing, preferring to leave them in squalid camps. Former UNRWA Director Ralph Galloway stated in 1958: "The Arab states do not want to solve the refugee problem. They want to keep it as an open sore, as a weapon against Israel. Arab leaders do not give a damn whether Arab refugees live or die."

Again, it was Arabs who resisted efforts by Israel to settle the

For biography of RABBI SHRAGA SIMMONS, see p. 121.

refugees in normal housing from 1967–95, when Israel administered the lands.

And again in the late-1990s, when 97 percent of Palestinians in the West Bank and Gaza lived under full jurisdiction of the Palestinian Authority, the refugees continued to be confined to camps — despite the millions of UNRWA and international relief dollars which poured into PA coffers specifically for this purpose.

It is important to note, as Joan Peters documents in her seminal work, *From Time Immemorial*, that the vast majority of these refugees did not live for generations on the land, but rather came from Egypt, Syria, and Iraq as economic opportunities increased during the first half of the 20th century, the formative years of Jewish aliyah.

The United Nations' standard definition of a "refugee" is one who was forced to leave a "permanent" or "habitual" home. In the case of Arab refugees, however, the UN broadened the definition of refugee to include anyone who lived in "Palestine" for only two years prior to Israel's statehood in 1948.

The number of 3.7 million refugees is further inflated, given that the UN Convention Relating to the Status of Refugees does not include descendents in its definition of refugees, nor does it apply to a person who "has acquired a new nationality and enjoys the protection of the country of his new nationality." Under this definition, the number of Palestinians qualifying for refugee status would be well below half a million. Yet the UN has created a new set of rules for Palestinian refugees.

❧

A key question is the issue of responsibility: Since five Arab armies launched the 1948 war, logic dictates that they are responsible for the outcome. Yet it is still instructive to know: Did Israel forcibly evict these Arabs in 1948, or did they leave voluntarily?

Though historical sources vary, many statements from Arab leaders and the media support the contention that Arabs created the refugee problem:

The *Beirut Daily Telegraph* (September 6, 1948) quoted Emil

Ghory, secretary of the Palestine Arab Higher Committee:

> The fact that there are those refugees is the direct conse-
> quence of the action of the Arab states in opposing partition
> and the Jewish state. The Arab states agreed upon this policy
> unanimously....

The *London Economist* (October 2, 1948) reported an eyewitness account of the flight of Haifa's Arabs:

> There is little doubt that the most potent of the factors [in
> the flight] were the announcements made over the air by the
> Arab Higher Executive urging all Arabs in Haifa to quit....
> And it was clearly intimated that those Arabs who remained
> in Haifa and accepted Jewish protection would be regarded as
> renegades.

Habib Issa, secretary-general of the Arab League, wrote in the
New York Lebanese daily *al-Hoda* (June 8, 1951):

> [Azzam Pasha, Arab League secretary,] assured the Arab peo-
> ples that the occupation of Palestine and of Tel Aviv would be
> as simple as a military promenade.... Brotherly advice was
> given to the Arabs of Palestine to leave their land, homes,
> and property, and to stay temporarily in neighboring frater-
> nal states.

Former Prime Minister of Syria, Khaled al-Azem, wrote in his
memoirs, published in 1973 in Beirut:

> We brought destruction upon a million Arab refugees by call-
> ing on them and pleading with them to leave their land.

The PA's current prime minister, Mahmud Abbas ("Abu
Mazen") wrote in the PLO journal *Palestine a-Thaura* (March 1976):

> The Arab armies, who invaded the country in '48, forced the
> Palestinians to emigrate and leave their homeland and
> forced a political and ideological siege on them.

There is a common misconception regarding UN General Assembly Resolution 194 of December 1948. The resolution does not recognize any "right" of return for refugees, but recommends that they "should" be "permitted" to return, subject to two conditions: that the refugee wishes to return, and that he wishes to live at peace with his neighbors.

Even though the Arab states originally rejected Resolution 194, they now misquote it to back the demand of an unlimited right of return to within the borders of the State of Israel. In Yasser Arafat's January 1, 2001, letter to President Clinton, he declared: "Recognizing the Right of Return and allowing the refugees' freedom of choice are a prerequisite for ending the conflict."

In the summer of 2000, Palestinian negotiators submitted an official document at Camp David, demanding that the refugees automatically be granted Israeli citizenship, and that the right of return should have no time limit. Additionally, the PA demanded that Israel provide compensation amounting to $500 billion dollars. Abu Mazen said that compensation payments should be made by Israel alone, and not from any international funds.

Israel maintains that settling refugees in Israel is a crude political move to destroy the Jewish state through demographics. If the whole point of a Palestinian state is to provide an independent home for their people, why do they insist on going to Israel?

While the political outcome remains uncertain, one thing is tragically clear: Thousands of Palestinians remain in squalid camps, used as political pawns in the ongoing war against Israel.

As Jordan's King Hussein stated in 1960:

> Since 1948, Arab leaders have approached the Palestine problem in an irresponsible manner. They have used the Palestine people for selfish political purposes. This is ridiculous and I could say even criminal.

Sources: MEMRI, Ha'aretz, Joan Peters, Moshe Kohn, Professor Shlomo Slonim, Professor Ruth Lapidoth.

John Wiggins

Children Under Fire

*P*alestinian children are on the front lines, throwing rocks and bombs and getting injured. Who's to blame?

The media is awash in moral equivalence, blanketly comparing the intentional targeting of Israeli children by suicide bombers with Palestinian children killed while engaging in riots or injured as Palestinian terrorists act from within Palestinian civilian populations.

An October 2002 *Los Angeles Times* staff editorial blasts the moral equivalence myth:

> [Arafat] equated attacks against Israeli civilians with attacks against Palestinian civilians. But there is no moral equivalence between Israel's strikes on terrorist leaders that sometimes kill other Palestinians in the area, and the suicide bombers who enter a pizza parlor or vegetable market intending to kill and maim as many Israeli men, women, and children as possible in order to spread terror.

Justus Weiner at the Jerusalem Center for Public Affairs writes that early in the current intifada children acted as decoys, burning tires and shooting slingshots to attract TV cameras, while making

---

JOHN WIGGINS lives in London and is the founding editor of HonestReporting.com.

it harder for the world to identify the gunmen lying in ambush. Knowing that Israeli soldiers are ordered not to shoot live ammunition at children, Palestinian snipers hid among groups of youngsters, on rooftops or in alleys, often using children as shields when aiming at exposed IDF soldiers. On some occasions, these gunmen apparently inadvertently shot Palestinian children from behind.

USA Today correspondent Jack Kelley reported (October 23, 2000):

> Children serve as infantry in the confrontations between Israeli and Palestinian soldiers. In scenes reminiscent of Iranian children sent to the Iraqi front equipped with plastic keys to heaven, Palestinian children are sent close to Israeli positions with rocks and Molotov cocktails, while the gunmen and snipers fire from positions hundreds of yards back.

The Jordanian newspaper *Al-Rai* (citing a June 2002 interview with the Kuwaiti newspaper *Al-Zaman*), quoted Abu Mazen, current prime minister of the Palestinian Authority, who spoke of how Palestinian children are being exploited into carrying out terror attacks:

> At least 40 children from the city of Raphah have lost their arms as a result of the explosions of pipe bombs. They received five Israeli shekels (about one U.S. dollar) for throwing them.

The Palestinian Authority has provided children with military training. *The New York Times* (August 3, 2000) reported that 25,000 children were trained in the summer 2000 in PA camps in the use of firearms, the making of Molotov cocktails, the methods of kidnapping Israeli leaders, and conducting ambushes.

The use of children reflects a long-time Palestinian strategy in the fight against Israel. In June 1982, the PLO issued a military call-up order for all boys aged 12 and older whose fathers served in Fatah units. The children were promised $80 a month and were attached to regular PLO battalions, each serving in his father's company.

One Palestinian tactic is to encourage children to seek heroic *shahada* (martyrdom) — and then use the numbers of dead children in the PR war against Israel. Sam Kiley describes in the *London Times* (October 19, 2000):

> Since birth, Palestinian children have been pumped full of religious fundamentalism which promises paradise for those who die for the cause of free Palestine.... Approving or not, the Palestinian authorities have done nothing to stop children playing with their lives. Let's face it, dead kids make great telly.

The average Western mind has trouble comprehending a society that might intentionally seek death in order to advance a political cause. Reporters assume that if Palestinian children are being killed, it can only be Israel's fault.

Yet as Arafat adviser Bassam Abu Sharif told *Time* magazine:

> If [Arafat] knows he will achieve a political point that will get him closer to independence and if that will cost him 10,000 killed, he wouldn't mind.

Indeed, fault for most of these casualties lies strictly with Palestinians themselves. Hamas leader Salah Shehadeh operated from a heavily populated neighborhood, precisely because he knew the civilians would serve as a human shield against any Israeli attempt to assassinate him. Writing in the *New York Post* (July 24, 2002), John Podhoretz explains:

> The Fourth Geneva Convention goes into great and elaborate detail about how to assign fault when military activities take place in civilian areas.... Hamas is at war with Israel. But instead of separating themselves from the general population in military camps and wearing uniforms, as required by international law, Hamas members and other Palestinian terrorists try to use civilians — the "protected persons" mentioned in [The Fourth Geneva Convention] 3:1:28 — as

living camouflage. To prevent such a thing from happening, international law explicitly gives Israel the right to conduct military operations against military targets under these circumstances.

Speaking about another region of the world (Afghanistan), United States Defense Secretary Donald Rumsfeld said in 2001:

> Let there be no doubt, the responsibility for every casualty of this war, lies with the Taliban. They use civilians as human shields, and place their arsenal among their homes. We did not look to commence this conflict — the war was thrown at us, and we are defending ourselves.

How does Palestinian society promote a culture of martyrdom? In 2002, a nursery school in Gaza held a unique ceremony, where toddlers burned Israeli flags, marched in uniforms with toy guns to liberate Palestine, dressed up as Hizbullah leaders, and even raised their bloody hands in solidarity with the disembowelers of two Israelis in Ramallah.

In recent searches of Palestinian homes, the IDF has discovered disturbing "family photos": One shows a Palestinian baby with a semiautomatic pistol and machine gun, and another shows a baby wearing a pretend explosives belt with red wires strapped to his waist.

The Palestinian media is a primary vehicle used to promote the martyrdom of children. In September 2002, the PA renewed broadcasting of one of the most odious video clips, the "Farewell Letter." In the clip, a child writes a farewell letter to his parents, glorifying his desire to die, and then places himself in front of Israeli soldiers during a violent riot where he is shot and dies, achieving his goal.

Another Palestinian Authority TV clip, aimed at young viewers, features a boy killed in Gaza arriving in Heaven where there are beaches, waterfalls, and a ferris wheel. He is saying, "I am not waving goodbye, I am waving to tell you to follow in my footsteps." On the accompanying soundtrack, a song plays, "How pleasant is the smell of martyrs, how pleasant the smell of land, the land enriched by the blood, the blood pouring out of a fresh body."

Religious leaders also encourage the martyrdom of children. Sheik 'Ikrimi Sabri, the Palestinian Authority-appointed mufti of Jerusalem, declared:

> I feel the martyr is lucky because the angels usher him to his wedding in heaven.... The younger the martyr, the greater and the more I respect him.
>
> *(Al-Ahram Al-Arabi, October 28, 2000)*

Parents are also portrayed in Palestinian society as supporting their children's death. *Al-Ayyam* newspaper quotes a mother who encouraged her sons to sacrifice themselves for Palestinian beliefs (November 1, 2000):

> The danger of injury to Tzabar Ashkaram, age 18, paralysis and permanent disability, just added to his mother's determination to encourage her sons to participate in the intifada riots.... The fact of his injury by a live bullet did not cause her to mourn. She said she had previously lost her older son, Iyyad.

Another Palestinian mother was quoted in the *London Times*:

> I am happy that [my 13-year-old son] has been martyred. I will sacrifice all my [12] sons and daughters to Al-Aqsa and Jerusalem.

All this makes one wonder about the sanctimonious pronouncements of Palestinian spokeswoman Hanan Ashrawi who, when asked on "60 Minutes" about the Palestinian Authority dispatching children into battle with Israeli soldiers, angrily turned on her interviewer (October 24, 2000):

> They're telling us we are — we have no feelings for our children? We're not human beings? We're not parents? We're not mothers or fathers? This is just incredible.... I don't want to sink to the level of responding, or proving I'm human. I mean, even animals have feelings for their children.

Encouraging children to martyrdom extends into Palestinian classrooms and textbooks as well. Palestinian Brig. Gen. Mahmoud M. Abu Marzoug reminded a group of 10th grade girls in Gaza City that "as a martyr, you will be alive in Heaven." After the address, a group of these girls lined up to assure a *Washington Post* reporter that they would be happy to carry out suicide bombings or other actions ending in their deaths (*Washington Post*, April 24, 2002).

Here is an excerpt from the textbook, *Modern Arab History for Twelfth Grade Part 1*:

> With an understanding of the racist and aggressive character of the Zionist movement, please summarize the similarity between Nazism, Fascism, and Zionism.

The problem has infested all strata of Palestinian society. Under these cultural influences, many children voice a desire to become suicide bombers. In June 2002, a documentary on PA television presented a survey conducted by Dr. Fatsil Abu Hin, a lecturer in psychology in the Gaza Strip. He interviewed 996 children between the ages of nine and 17. Ninety percent expressed their desire to participate in intifada activities, and 73 percent expressed a desire to become martyrs.

Suicide bombing is considered a source of social pride. Palestinian streets are named after the perpetrators. Signs on the walls of kindergartens proclaim their students as "the *shaheeds* [martyrs] of tomorrow." It was reported that Palestinian children at the Balata camp have thrown away their Pokemon cards in favor of necklace pendants with pictures of Palestinian suicide bombers. The children spend their meager allowances to collect and trade them, hunting for prized martyr pictures like a vintage baseball card.

One Palestinian parent told the *Toronto Star* (June 17, 2002): "I opened my son's closet and found it full of martyrs posters and necklaces. I said to him... 'Ultimately, you'll be rewarded with your picture hanging from a necklace, and we will have lost a son.' "

"Muslim Fun," a CD-ROM produced in the UK, includes a game called "The Resistance," in which "you are a farmer in south Lebanon who has joined the Islamic Resistance to defend your land and family from the invading Zionists." The Islamic Fun website recommends the game for children ages five and up and says: "Your child will learn about Islam by playing lots of exciting games, full of colourful animations and cute sound effects."

Another reason Palestinian parents allow and even encourage their children to get involved is the financial incentive offered to families of "martyrs." The PA furnished cash payments — $2,000 per child killed and $300 per child wounded. Saudi Arabia announced that it had pledged $250 million as its first contribution to a billion-dollar fund aimed at supporting the families of Palestinian martyrs.

In addition, the Arab Liberation Front, working through Saddam Hussein, paid generous bounties to the injured and the families of the dead according to the following sliding scale: $500 for a wound; $1,000 for disability; $10,000 to the family of each martyr; and $25,000 to the family of each suicide bomber — lavish sums, given the chronic unemployment and poverty of the majority of the Palestinian residents of the West Bank and Gaza Strip.

Yet not everyone agrees with this method of Palestinian child abuse.

Fox News quoted Atta Sarasara, a father of a 16-year-old suicide bomber, who Fox says "is angry with not just the Israelis, but also with the Al Aqsa Martyrs' Brigades for preying on impressionable teenagers and giving his son a bomb. 'They used a child. He was very kind, handsome, smart. They used him,' Sarasara said" (August 14, 2002).

Sweden's Queen Silvia raised the issue at a meeting of the World Childhood Foundation at the United Nations. She strongly criticized Palestinian parents and leaders for "exploiting them [the children] and risking their lives in a political fight.... As a mother, I'm very worried about this. I'd like to tell them to quit. This is very dangerous. The children should not take part" (*Jerusalem Post*, November 27, 2000).

Appearing on NBC's Meet the Press, Condoleezza Rice said:

What does that picture of a baby dressed as a suicide bomber say about the hopes of Palestinians for life with the Israeli people as good neighbors? You know, we've all, in our lives, had experiences with hatred. I certainly have in Birmingham, Alabama. And it all starts with recognizing that the other person is human and deserves a future. If you're going to send your babies and your teenagers to kill other teenagers, something has broken down in this concept of humanity.

The editorial board of the Fort Worth *Star-Telegram* wrote (July 9, 2002):

> According to the AP, polls repeatedly have recorded majority Palestinian backing for suicide bombings, with a recent survey indicating more than 60 percent approval. In such an atmosphere, amid accounts of parents piously sanctioning the idea of their offspring becoming instruments of civilian death, perhaps the idea of an infant swaddled in guerrilla's clothes should not be so shocking after all.

Some Palestinian parents are speaking out as well. Abu Saber, the father of one suicide bomber, wrote a letter to the London-based Arabic-language daily *Al-Hayat* (October 8, 2002):

> I ask on my behalf, and on behalf of every father and mother informed that their son has blown himself up: By what right do these leaders send the young people, even young boys in the flower of their youth, to their deaths? Who gave them religious or any other legitimacy to tempt our children and urge them to their deaths?... The sums of money [paid] to the martyrs' families cause pain more than they heal; they make the families feel that they are being rewarded for the lives of their children.... Do the children's lives have a price? Has death become the only way to restore the rights and liberate the land?
>
> And if this be the case, why doesn't a single one of all the sheikhs who compete amongst themselves in issuing fiery religious rulings, send his son? Why doesn't a single one of the leaders who cannot restrain himself in expressing his joy and

ecstasy on the satellite channels every time a young Palestinian man or woman sets out to blow himself or herself up send his son?"

It is incumbent upon all lovers of humanity to protest this incitement of children for political purposes, a flagrant violation of basic human rights.

For more info, refer to www.opsick.com, a website dedicated to stopping abuse of children in the Mideast conflict.

Source material from IMRA.org.

Ben Blicker

One Hundred Years in a Nutshell

*H*ere's a brief look at the major geopolitical, historical, and diplomatic events from the last century relating to Israel.

1917 — Balfour Declaration — After the fall of the Ottoman Empire, British Foreign Secretary Lord Balfour declares: "His Majesty's Government views with favor the establishment in Palestine of a national home for the Jewish people."

1922 — British Mandate — After World War I, the League of Nations affirms the British Mandate to create two distinct entities in the territory both east and west of the Jordan River, one Arab and one Jewish. 78 percent of the original Mandate is then lopped off to create the Hashemite Kingdom of Jordan, which is closed to Jewish settlement.

1929 — Arab riots — Arabs protest the growing Jewish presence in Palestine, murdering 133 Jews in Hebron and elsewhere, and pressuring the British to impose restrictions on Jewish prayer at the Western Wall.

BEN BLICKER, originally from Russia, now lives in Minneapolis, Minnesota.

1937 — Peel Commission — The British Peel Commission recommends that the future Jewish state be confined to a tiny sliver of land along the Mediterranean coast and a small piece abutting the Sea of Galilee.

1939 — Immigration Quotas — In order to appease the Arabs, a British "White Paper" severely restricts Jewish immigration to the Holy Land to a token number for five years, even to the point of turning away boatloads of Jews fleeing Hitler.

1947 — UN Partition Plan — On November 29, 1947, the UN authorizes Resolution 181, calling for separate Arab and Jewish states west of the Jordan River. The plan is accepted by Israel, but rejected by the Arab League.

1948 — War of Independence — On May 15, 1948, following Ben-Gurion's Declaration of Independence, the armies of five Arab states join local Arab militias to invade Israel, with the goal of aborting the newly declared state. Jordan conquers and annexes the "West Bank" (the lands heretofore called "Judea and Samaria" on all British mandate maps), expelling all Jews from the Old City of Jerusalem, and destroying 57 synagogues and Mount of Olives tombstones. One percent of the Israeli Jewish population is killed in the war.

1949 — Refugee Issue — In the ensuing war, approximately 650,000 Arabs flee Israel as refugees. In the war's aftermath, approximately 600,000 Jewish refugees flee from Arab countries, when massacres, arrests, and ostracism made life impossible. The Jewish refugees are integrated into Israeli life; the Arab refugees are placed in squalid camps by their Arab hosts, supported by the UNRWA.

1956 — Suez War — After Egypt blockades Israel's shipping and Nasser assumes command of the Syrian and Jordanian armies, Israel attacks Egypt and captures the Gaza Strip and much of the Sinai. International pressure forces Israel to withdraw without obtaining any concessions.

1964 — Palestine Liberation Organization — While Jordan and

Egypt hold the "territories," the PLO forms with the goal of annihilating the State of Israel through violence and terror. In the ensuing years, a rash of airplane hijackings and bombings and the Munich Olympic Massacre bring the Palestinians media attention.

1967 — Six Day War — Egyptian President Nasser closes the Straits of Tiran to Israeli shipping, and Syrian Defense Minister Hafez Assad declares that "the time has come to enter into a battle of annihilation." Israel responds with a preemptive strike and captures the Golan Heights, West Bank, Gaza Strip, and Sinai Peninsula. Israel immediately offers to return the conquered land in exchange for peace. Meeting in Khartoum, the Arab League issues the infamous three noes: "No peace with Israel. No negotiations with Israel. No recognition of Israel."

1973 — Yom Kippur War — On the holiest day of the Jewish year, Egypt and Syria launch a surprise attack. In the Golan, 180 Israeli tanks face an onslaught of 1,400 Syrian tanks. Along the Suez Canal, 500 Israeli soldiers are attacked by 80,000 Egyptians. Israel suffers heavy casualties, but wins the war.

1978 — Camp David Accords — Egyptian President Anwar Sadat meets with Israeli Prime Minister Menachem Begin to negotiate a settlement. Israel agrees to return the entire Sinai Peninsula — constituting 80 percent of Israel's land mass — in exchange for normalization of relations with Egypt.

1993 — Oslo Accords — Following a historic handshake between Yitzhak Rabin and Yasser Arafat on the White House lawn, the Oslo accords call for Israeli recognition of the PLO, and a Palestinian commitment to cease violence and terror.

1994 — Peace with Jordan — King Hussein reverses decades of belligerence and signs a formal peace treaty with Israel. The treaty involves minor border changes and includes a guaranteed supply of water by Israel to Jordan.

1995 — The assassination of Yitzhak Rabin shocks the nation and the world.

2000 — Palestinian Violence — Israeli Prime Minister Ehud Barak offers 95 percent of the territories, including eastern Jerusalem, for the creation of a Palestinian state. Yasser Arafat refuses, and Palestinians launch thousands of violent attacks against Israeli targets. Six months after the violence begins, Ariel Sharon comes to power in a landslide victory.

2003 — Road Map — The international Quartet proposes a road map for peace, calling for an end to Palestinian violence and a limiting of Israeli settlement activity, as a precursor to an independent Palestinian state. Israeli and Palestinian leaders accept the road map in principle, triggering a new round of diplomatic efforts to resolve the conflict.

Ephraim Shore

15 Things I Don't Understand about the Peace Process

September 2003

1. If Palestinians want to live side-by-side with Israel, then why do their government logos (fateh.net) show Palestine encompassing all of Israel, with Israel nonexistent?

2. If a primary point of the road map is "confronting all those engaged in terror and dismantlement of terrorist capabilities and infrastructure," then why do the Palestinians demand that Israel release thousands of terrorists from prison, an item not even included in the road map? Instead, shouldn't the Palestinians be arresting terrorists themselves? And shouldn't we be outraged that the two suicide bombers who murdered 15 Israelis on Sept. 9, 2003 (Hillel Cafe and Tzrifin bus stop) were among a group of Palestinian prisoners released by Israel this year? (*Jerusalem Post*, Sept. 12, 2003).

RABBI EPHRAIM SHORE is the Israel Director for HonestReporting.com and the Hasbara Fellowships for campus Israel activism. Prior to making aliyah, he was Executive Director of Aish HaTorah in Miami and Toronto.

3. If Israel is supposedly allowed to "take all necessary steps to defend its citizens," then why is Israel condemned for building bypass roads so drivers can avoid ambushes, condemned for building a fence to keep suicide bombers out, condemned for targeted killings of terrorist leaders, condemned for operating road blocks to screen for suicide bombers, condemned for clearing areas used for launching rockets, and condemned for keeping terrorists in jail? How exactly is Israel expected to defend itself?

4. When the PLO first demanded a state in 1964, it wanted every part of Israel except the West Bank and Gaza (which were then in the hands of Jordan and Egypt). Is it reasonable to assume that they now want only the West Bank and Gaza, or is that more likely a Trojan Horse — as Palestinian leader Faisal al-Husseini described it in 2001 as a first step to destroy Israel?

5. Why is the targeted killing of terrorists and their supporters lauded when done by the United States in Iraq, but not when done by Israel whose civilians face a daily threat of terror attacks?

6. Why has the United Nations passed far more condemnations against Israel than any other country — including Iraq, Iran, Sudan, Chechnya, Saudi Arabia, Liberia, North Korea, and China combined — while millions were massacred in these other places? And then how does the UN expect Israel to accept it as an impartial mediator?

7. Why — if the Palestinian Authority has little freedom of speech and freedom of the press, little religious tolerance, is oppressive of Christians and other minorities, is corrupt at all levels of government, and is rife with vigilantism — is the creation of a Palestinian state a favorite "liberal" cause?

8. Why — after Yasser Arafat has proven for 40 years to be one of history's most incorrigible terrorists, while loyally backing dictators like Saddam Hussein — does the European

Union still strongly support Arafat's leadership?

9. Why does the media call it "terror" when Al Qaeda strikes at Western targets, but not when Hamas strikes at Israelis (or even American citizens in Israel)?

10. If the Palestinians truly want peace, why do their school textbooks vilify Israel and glorify suicide bombers? Why does the government-controlled TV station broadcast virulent anti-Semitic messages? Why do mosques regularly incite followers to jihad? Why are (UN-supported) children's paramilitary training camps — masquerading as summer camps — named in honor of the most "successful" Palestinian terrorists (an indoctrination process that has resulted in 60–80 percent support for suicide bombings)?

11. Why does the world call the West Bank "occupied" if it never belonged to the Palestinians? [Jordan controlled the West Bank for 19 years after conquering it in a war of aggression. It previously belonged to the Mamelukes, the Crusaders, the Ottoman Turks, and then Britain.]

12. What other country would give control of its holiest spot (the Temple Mount) to another religion (which arrived 1,500 years later), and then permit them to systematically destroy ancient remains (to eliminate evidence of a 3,000-year-old Jewish presence) and allow that religious body to prohibit access to non-Muslims for three years?

13. Why does anyone doubt Israel's sincerity for peace, after offering 97 percent of the West Bank and Gaza in the Taba Talks 2001, and having given back the Sinai Peninsula to Egypt — a territory three times the size of Israel constituting 91 percent of the territory Israel took control of in the 1967 war?

14. Why does the world demand the uprooting of Jewish settlements — effectively making those areas *Judenrein* (empty of Jews)? Would anyone tolerate a similar form of ethnic cleansing if Israel would not allow Arabs to live in areas under Israeli control?

15. If, during Oslo, Israel gave tens of thousands of machine guns and 40 percent of the West Bank and Gaza to the Palestinians (giving them control over 97 percent of their population), in return for the promise that "all future disputes would be handled without violence," and instead Israel got 18,000 terrorist attacks that killed 870 and wounded 5,794 people, a collapsed economy, intolerable daily life for its citizens, and its holy sites desecrated, why is Israel again being asked to negotiate with that same Palestinian leadership, trust their future promises, and place its security in their hands?

Am I imaging things — or is this situation truly insane?

COMING
HOME

Sol Jakubowicz

Still Crazy:
Why We Made Aliyah

I am finally home. I live amongst my own people. I am living
the dream. A new life in the Land of Israel.

Ever since my first visit to Israel back in 1983, I knew that
one day I would live here. I visited several times since. Each time as
I boarded the plane to return to Canada, I got a sick feeling in my
stomach. When would I return? How would I return? How can I
leave knowing that so many exciting things are happening in Israel? Somehow, I managed to stifle these questions.

But not for long.

I settled down — got married, had three children, a good nine-
to-five job, a minivan (and second family car), and a modest but attractive home in the suburbs of Toronto, in a thriving Jewish community. I lacked for nothing materially and I was growing spiritually. We had started to keep Shabbat, kashrut, and other mitzvot to
the best of our ability. But I still did not feel complete.

Every time there was strife in Israel, I watched the events un-
fold from the safety of my home in Canada. The 1991 Gulf War
had a tremendous impact on me. On the first night of the war, I

SOL JAKUBOWICZ and his family made aliyah from Toronto in 2000. Sol
works as a knowledge manager in hi-tech and lives in Ramat Beit Shemesh.

wanted to get on a plane to Israel — to be part of the trials and tribulations of the Jewish people, and not just an "armchair analyst" 7,000 miles away. I knew that when it was all over, I would not be able to say I was part of it.

At that point my wife and I began to seriously consider the idea of aliyah, "going up," in a spiritual sense, by living in Israel.

We knew it was the right thing to do. For 2,000 years of exile, Jews had cried and prayed to return to the land. Now we could do it just by hopping on a plane. How could we not?

We knew that such a move would be better for us, our children, and even the Jewish people. But it was hard to ignore the "sacrifice" that this move would entail.

I would have to quit my secure job and find a new one in a different country. We would have to leave our beautiful community in Canada, where we had great and loving friends to support us. We'd have to uproot our kids from their good schools and find a community where we would fit in and a school where our children would fit in. We'd have to learn a new language and adjust to new cultural subtleties.

The decision was very difficult, and even more so for my wife. She knew that our material status would likely suffer, most definitely in the short term, and likely in the long term — the average Israeli does not have a four-bedroom, two-story house with a front and back lawn, and a car, much less two cars. She worried about not having the support of family and friends. What would happen if and when difficulties set in? Who would be there to help us?

And what about the family we would leave behind? How would we be able to help them when they need us?

We knew that spiritually, aliyah was the right thing to do, but it seemed to require leaving so much physical and emotional comfort behind. We were forced to confront ourselves and to honestly analyze our most basic Jewish values.

We took the plunge.

Although we have been in Israel only a short time, and we are still getting adjusted, most of our fears have been allayed. I have found employment. We drive on modern highways, and stores are filled with all the name brands. There are many types of communities and many streams of schools, enabling most people to find their place here. My wife is happy in our community, and with the new friends she is making. We live in a beautiful, bright, four-bedroom apartment. Although it is much smaller than what we had in Canada, we feel that our quality of life has increased, not decreased.

Life here isn't as rough as we feared. We may no longer have a basement, a minivan, or a dishwasher. But we do have many parks and other areas where the children can run and play safely all day. My wife can walk around at night without fear. And I can have a cup of coffee on my balcony and enjoy a beautiful, picture-postcard sunset.

And it is profoundly satisfying to live in a place where being Jewish is "normal." On Passover, everywhere we went, we saw people, religious and secular alike, eating matzah. Just last year, while still in Canada, we went to the zoo on Passover and felt so uncomfortable eating our strange-looking matzah sandwiches while everyone else bought their food at McDonald's.

⬥

When I first revealed my intentions to move here, almost everyone told me I was crazy — friends, family, work associates, and neighbors. During a brief pilot trip to Israel, I met with Rabbi Noah Weinberg, Dean of Aish HaTorah. In addition to discussing some technical matters, I wanted a "spiritual checkup."

I sat down and said to the rabbi, as if confessing, "I want to make aliyah."

"Of course you should want to make aliyah," he responded. "This is where the Jewish people belong. Why wouldn't you want to make aliyah?"

"Rabbi, I'm so relieved to hear you say that! Everywhere I turn people tell me I'm crazy."

"Of course they say you're crazy," he replied. "To be crazy is to run from reality, to run away from true meaning. Everybody does it. But now that you're getting in touch with reality, people perceive that as crazy!"

Rabbi Weinberg explained that Jews have always had ideas that others considered "crazy." We brought monotheism to a pagan world and guaranteed women's rights in marriage. We brought concepts like world peace, social responsibility, and education to the world. They were rays of sanity. But back then people thought we were crazy!

Mark Twain visited Israel in the late 1800s and commented that nothing would ever come of this place. Any sane person would have agreed. Except for the crazy Jews. And today we have a country of 6 million people, with skyscrapers, hotels, shopping malls, yeshivas, and schools teeming with young children.

If we pray for the ingathering of exiles so consistently, it may be crazy, but it can't be wrong. And even if everyone around us is saying it can't be done, then it is our job as Jews to demonstrate that, with God's help, we can do it.

I don't want to give the false impression that moving here is easy and that Israel is a perfect country. It is a very challenging process. Yes, there are problems that must be solved. But being involved in these problems is a labor of love when realizing that one is building the foundation for the Jewish homeland.

This promises to be the last and final stop in our journey through exile. In every other place, our investment is temporary. One day, sooner or later, we'll all end up in Israel. It may not be today or tomorrow, but Jewish tradition tells us that in the End of Days, the Jewish people will be gathered from the four corners of the earth, to rebuild the Temple and Jerusalem, to once again become a true light unto the nations.

By being here today, I believe that my decisions and actions can influence that future. It's my way of showing myself, my God, and the world that we do really believe in what we are praying for. And that we really believe our dreams will come true.

Even if we do seem a little crazy.

Nathan Morris

Should I Stay or Should I Go?

May 2001

With Holocaust Day, Israel Memorial Day, and Independence Day all coming together in one week, it's gotten me thinking.

What am I doing here?

Israel is a tiny country, the size of New Jersey. At one spot, it's just nine miles wide. We are 5 million Jews surrounded by 250 million Arabs — implacable enemies in possession of enormous oil reserves and 640 times greater land mass.

These Arab neighbors have launched wars of annihilation against Israel in 1948, 1967, and 1973. They have orchestrated a massive economic boycott. They have ostracized Israel at the United Nations. They have repeatedly threatened — both in word and in deed — "to push the Jews into the sea," to exterminate the Jewish presence from the Land of Israel.

Which leads me back to my question: What am I doing here?

I do not live in a provocative neighborhood, "a small enclave amidst thousands of angry Arabs." No, I live in the center of the country, close to the '67 border in suburban Modi'in. But my precise location doesn't seem to be the salient issue. All of Israel —

NATHAN MORRIS is a biochemist by trade. He works in the Israeli hi-tech sector.

Netanya, Hadera, Jaffa, and, of course, Jerusalem — continues to be a target of Arab terror.

The issue is our very existence. Muslim fundamentalists are waging holy war to forcibly remove the infidels from the land. It doesn't matter to them, apparently, that there are 22 Arab countries and only one of us. One is too many.

Birzeit University, a leading Palestinian institution of higher education, recently conducted a poll of 1,234 Palestinians in 75 locations throughout the West Bank and Gaza. They were asked: "If East Jerusalem comes under Palestinian sovereignty, will you accept Israeli sovereignty over West Jerusalem?" Seventy-four percent of respondents said "no."

I feel war in the air and imagine hordes of Arab youth rampaging down my street. It's hard to fall asleep at night with so many thoughts racing through my head. I make a mental note to stock up on canned food and bottled water. And I wonder if our gas masks, left untouched since the Gulf War, still retain their effectiveness.

At the outbreak of the latest wave of violence, my cousin's neighbor, while at work in Jerusalem, was murdered by Palestinian terrorists. I visited the newly mourning widow and it hit close to home.

But last week, when machine gun fire was sprayed in my direction, hitting homes 100 meters from mine, I could no longer avoid the question.

What am I doing here?

Should I stay or should I go?

I am reminded that leaving Israel is no guarantee of security. If a war breaks out in Israel, life for Jews will be difficult everywhere. And of course, sociopolitical volatility can erupt anywhere, anytime. Before the '67 war, one man I know fled with his family to safe haven in Chile — arriving days before the bloody Pinot revolution.

Here, we have an Israeli army whose sole purpose is to protect and defend Jews. That's a big step forward from unarmed resistance in the Warsaw Ghetto.

And, of course, Diaspora Jewry has been highly supportive of the Jewish state, contributing both political and financial resources. My friends and relatives e-mail from abroad, saying how infuriated they are at the media's treatment of Israel. They tell me they're monitoring events closely.

I treasure this support and encouragement, though I would like to see less worry and more activism.

I recently received a phone call from a journalist at a Jewish newspaper in a major American city. She asked my opinion of the security situation in Israel, and I said that, in my estimation, the Arabs are likely to start a war, with its goal the annihilation of the Jewish state. She was somewhat surprised, and asked what American Jews could do about it.

I told her they could lobby their representatives in Congress, they could write op-ed pieces for local newspapers, they could work to fight anti-Israel bias in the media, they could raise money for civil defense in Israel....

The journalist, silent until then, interrupted me. "Oh well," she muttered uncomfortably. "Have a nice day." Then she hung up.

When push comes to shove, I wonder how many Jews in the Diaspora would drop everything to come fight. Israel, I feel, is alone on the front lines.

So if we are threatened, and ultimately alone, the question keeps arising: Why should I stay?

First of all, because Israel is not just another piece of land. It isn't Uganda, which Herzl once proposed for the Jewish state. Nor is it Grand Island, New York, suggested as a suitable spot for a Jewish homeland by American Jewish diplomats in 1820.

Israel is not simply "land." Israel is our home, intrinsic to our Jewish destiny, as it has been since God made His covenant with Abraham.

It is holy land, where God's presence can be felt more intensely than in any other place on Earth. As the Torah says, "The eyes of God are upon it always, from the beginning of the year until the end of the year."

A friend once tried to articulate the difference between Israel and the Diaspora. "In Israel," he said, "everything seems to matter more." Or as someone else wrote: "In Israel, life doesn't go by you, it goes through you."

I recall attending two demonstrations in the 1980s, both in support of Soviet Jewry. The rally in Tel Aviv was attended by 10,000 people; the other, in New York, by 10 times that number.

Somehow, the rally in Tel Aviv generated a far greater sense of urgency. It was not merely about aiding some far-off land; it was about bringing Jews home to us here.

In Israel, I am not an observer looking from afar. I am creating Jewish destiny.

A strong Jewish presence in Israel strengthens Jewish life throughout the world. When Jews here exhibit weakness, our enemies are emboldened to act against us.

As well, my presence here strengthens the resolve of those around me to continue their own struggle.

The Torah provides military exemption for those who are afraid, yet this only applies before the onset of battle. Once a person commits himself to taking part in the communal effort, he is not allowed to demoralize others by backing out. As the Talmud says: "The beginning of defeat is flight."

In considering all the factors, I mustn't presume that regular sociohistorical standards apply to the Jewish people. Because in reality, our entire existence has been miraculous.

There is the basic miracle of Jewish survival, despite millennia of harsh exile and persecution: Jews in the Crusades and Inquisitions choosing death over conversion, Jews staving off blood libels and pogroms, Jews in the Holocaust preserving their humanity under the most inhumane conditions.

Zechariah chapter 14 speaks of the fateful War of Gog and Magog, when the entire world will descend upon Jerusalem and try to oust the Jews from their land. Rabbi Moshe Cordovero, the great 16th century kabbalist, wrote:

All the nations will unite together against Jerusalem, for they shall make a peace treaty among themselves to turn against Israel and annihilate her, because Israel will have established a sovereign state for themselves. It will be "a time of crisis for Jacob [Israel]," but they shall not be broken, rather, "They shall be saved from it."

It is precisely now, when the stakes are so high, that spiritual forces work their hardest against us. That is one of the surest signs that we are in the midst of a bona fide battle for our own souls, and the soul of the Jewish people, and of humanity.

Is this the beginning of that apocalyptic war? I don't know. But today, as the bullets whiz past my window, I am trying to be realistic.

And realistically, I've decided to stay. And if need be, to fight.

Sure, I'll continue to monitor the political situation and to fight bias in the media. But above all, I will work to strengthen my connection to the Almighty Guardian of Israel.

Because Israel is our challenge, and it is our destiny. It's where I belong.

Tefilla Buxbaum

Israel Now

In 1939, my father, Joe Kupfer, was on his way back to college in Belgium when the Nazis caught him at the Polish border. He spent the next six years in a series of labor camps, culminating in Auschwitz.

"I was as shocked when the Nazis grabbed me as you'd be if it happened in America today," my father always told me. "It happened overnight. One day, life was normal. Then suddenly everything changed."

For Jews, it's an unfortunate but familiar story. From Egypt to Babylon, from Spain to Germany, the pattern repeats itself: Jews establish themselves in a country, prosper, and then begin to assimilate. Never was this pattern more clearly exemplified than by the Jews in early 20th century Germany, who called Berlin "the New Jerusalem."

We all know the terrible end of this story. So you would think that by now, Jews would have gotten the message. And yet we continue to make the same mistake. We miss the proverbial writing on the wall.

What exactly is the message we're missing?

Berlin is not Jerusalem. Miami Beach and Long Island are not

TEFILLA BUXBAUM, a mother of five, lives in Jerusalem and works for Sulam, a school for special children.

the Garden of Eden. And America isn't "the Golden *Medina*."

God wants the Jewish people to be a light unto the nations, to teach, by example, what it means to live by the highest standards in all areas of life. That means being different, unique — in our customs, diet, and view of the world.

That explains, in part, why we were sent into exile. When we moved away from Torah, the light became too small. So we had to be dispersed throughout the world, as little flames to teach humanity the Torah's values.

In some cases we succeeded, and in others we failed. In either case, the time has come to return to our destiny, united in the Land of Israel.

In the Torah, God tells Abraham to go to the Land of Israel — "*Lech lecha*." The Midrash translates these words as "Go for yourself." God was telling Abraham that moving to Israel would be the best possible thing not only for the future of his people, but for him and his family as well. On one hand, yes, Israel has its difficulties. On the other hand, it offers the greatest source of personal fulfillment.

Anyone who visits Israel can attest to an intangible quality that touches the recesses of every Jewish heart and brings out the latent spiritual potential of every Jew. In the Holy Land, everyone feels closer to God. No matter who you are, or what your level of observance, Israel is where a Jew can best feel his essence.

It goes beyond self-fulfillment. For a Jew, living outside of Israel is by definition a way-station. Things may prosper for a few decades, or even centuries, but it is never permanent.

The story is told of Rabbi Berel Wein, who was building a new synagogue in Monsey, New York. The contractor told him that he could either order American lumber — which was guaranteed to last 90 years, or special Finnish lumber — guaranteed for 150. Rabbi Wein replied, "We'll take the American lumber." Because Jewish permanence in America, Rabbi Wein explained, is not the goal. And historically, very few buildings have remained in Jewish hands for more than 90 years. (Rabbi Wein has since made aliyah.)

Unquestionably, America has been a remarkably kind and generous host to the Jews. Yet America is not our permanent home.

Things may be bigger and fancier than in Israel, but they are indeed less permanent.

Rabbi Chaim Brovender tells the story of the famous Apollo Theater in New York. Originally, this building was a magnificent synagogue that held 600 people. Every Shabbos, it teemed with children and adults coming to pray together as a vibrant Jewish community. But the neighborhood changed, Jews moved out, and the once-beautiful shul became an empty, dilapidated building. It was eventually sold and converted into the Apollo Theater.

In Israel you won't come across such phenomena. The shul you pray in, says Rabbi Brovender, will be the shul you show your grandchildren. It will never turn into the Apollo Theater.

If we trace the steps of previous exiles, we can see the pattern repeating itself in our generation. The Durban circus opened a Pandora's box of worldwide anti-Semitism, as did Bin Laden, with his assertion that Israeli policy is responsible for terror in America.

When American interests and Israeli interests collide, as when President Bush told Israel, "America's war comes first," American Jews are in the most awkward position. Since the September 11 attacks, some American Jewish military officials have sensed a new mistrust and antagonism directed their way, and their Jewishness is the only apparent reason.

North American universities have become a hotbed of anti-Israel and anti-Semitic activity, with pro-Palestinian riots and vandalism alarmingly frequent.

If America should decide, in conjunction with the UN, to impose a military solution on the Israeli-Palestinian dilemma, every American Jew will be a target of the infamous dual-loyalty question: "Whose side are you on?"

As the heat is turned up, we need to step back and take a look at the big picture. Where is all this leading us? If this were 1933 — at which point there had already been some warning signs, but no real trouble yet — what would you have done?

Leah Rabin, the wife of Yitzhak Rabin, recalled that after Hitler's rise to power in 1933, her father said, "He's going to kill all of us." So the family packed up everything and moved to pre-state Israel. That decision saved their family. Her father's friends thought he was crazy to give up the comforts of Europe for a barren desert. Yes, crazy in 1933. A man of vision in 1943.

Now is the time to look beyond our current comforts and see the possibilities before our eyes. If it were, in fact, 1933, what would you do? Sell all your things and pack? Buy real estate in Israel?

Perhaps it is unrealistic to think about dropping it all and packing up. So what should you do?

Take a step in the right direction. If you've never visited Israel, plan a trip now. For 7, 10, 14 days. Can't afford it? One couple I know saved their pennies — literally — for 15 years and were finally able to fulfill their dream of visiting Israel for the first time.

If you've already been to Israel, plan to stay longer the next time. Spend the summer and send the kids to camp in Israel. Or arrange for a year-long leave of absence in Jerusalem.

If you ever have contemplated aliyah, set a target date.

And at the very least, concretize your commitment to Israel as the land of Jewish destiny.

We hope and pray for peace in America, Israel, and every corner of the world. But we must be realistic. The sands of history are shifting. God loves us and won't let us disappear into the oblivion of assimilation.

My father, after surviving Auschwitz and weighing 76 pounds, used to say, "There are two ways to go to Israel. You can get on an airplane, or you can try to swim." One way or another, we all make it home.

Jenna Ziman

Mom, I'm Moving to Israel

T here is nothing easy about telling your mom that you're moving to Israel. It might have been easy two years ago, but not now.

Even though my mom knew I'd been planning this trip ever since last summer, once the intifada began, she assumed I had abandoned the idea. She was wrong. I'd just gotten quieter about my planning.

So, after too many months of stalling and time spent practicing my response to Mom's inevitable freak-out, I thought I was finally ready to tell her. I drove over to her condominium one sunny Monday afternoon. We sat down together in her living room and began a light conversation.

Periodically rubbing my sweaty palms during our chat, I waited for a door to open for my announcement. My mom started talking about the political situation in Israel. A perfect segue. My cue.

I took a deep breath and waited for her to finish her sentence. Just as I was about to say it, Mom enthusiastically declared, "Thank God you're not going to Israel. I would just kill myself if you were there right now!"

So I decided I should probably tell my friends first before telling my mom. Their reactions could help me gauge exactly what

JENNA ZIMAN, formerly of Los Angeles, is a freelance writer, reporter, and fine arts painter.

her anxiety would look like and how best to counter her attempts to dissuade me. My speech to my friends was direct and simple: "I just wanted to let you know that I am moving to Israel to study Torah for an indefinite amount of time."

Their responses covered a wide spectrum: from dread to humor, from hesitation to encouragement.

Graham: "You're going where? To study what?"

Jeff: "Selfish and dumb. So how much time do we have left to hang out before you die?"

C.J.: "If anyone else told me they were going to Israel now, I would go to great lengths to talk them out of it. But I think your going to Israel may mean peace in the Middle East."

Storm: "Fret, fret, fret. I can't help but fret. Just know that I'll be doing a whole lot of fretting while you're away."

Dennis: "Now I'm gonna have to start caring about what's going on in the Middle East. Thanks a lot."

But the most common response I received, and the only question my dad had for me, was, "Now? Are you sure you want to go there now?"

For the Jewish people, there is no such thing as a bad time to go to Israel. Israel lives inside of us, no matter where we live throughout the world. Our souls are all in Israel, waiting for our bodies to catch up. It's not a question of if we choose to go; it's only a question of when. When Israel calls, you have to go; you can think of nothing else until you do. For some of us, the time to go is now, because our homeland is hurting; our people are angry, frustrated, and afraid.

I am going to Israel because of my love for Torah, the land, and the people that protect the Torah's teachings. As the only observant Jew in my circle of family and friends, this is a hard idea to explain and an even harder one for them to understand. Put simply: The times I feel closest to God are when I feel love and when I am studying Torah.

For the Jewish people, the Torah is the blueprint to our physical realm, our role and purpose therein, and to all the dimensions of the universe. Jews believe that the very essence of God seeps through each and every letter of Torah. In that way it acts as a portal through which the Divine ideal touches, however slightly, our earthly reality.

Many Jews believe that if more of us made the choice to embody the teachings of Torah and brought that love to Israel's wounded people, inevitably a solution to the social crisis in the region would be found. For those of us choosing to go to Israel now, during such a dangerous time, we are hoping to be part of that healing, part of the solution.

We are trying to realize the core essence of Judaism: to love thy neighbor as thyself. And this desire transcends all notions of fear for one's own safety.

Time to tell Mom.

I didn't know my "open door" would come during Mother's Day lunch. But when my mom looked at me from across the table and said, "Jenna, tell me what's going on with you. What's new?" I just knew I had to tell her.

"I'm moving to Israel to study Torah," I said without blinking.

There are very few things I can say to my mom that could make her turn instantly pale.

She stared at me, stunned. In her eyes I saw a stream of terrifying images: burnt out buses, suicide bombers, police checkpoints, political demonstrations, the burning of American and Israeli flags. I recognized that this conversation was the very one countless mothers around the world would give anything to have again, so that they could forbid their child from going to Israel out of fear they'd never come back.

I saw in my mom's stare pictures of all of those mothers weeping for our faith, for their lost children, for the sacrifices we make as Jews, and the suffering we know as a people who are often hated. But I also saw that my mom understood, maybe for the first time, that her daughter had come to understand her role in the world, as a woman and as a Jew. The debate in my mom's eyes ended there, and she surrendered.

And in perfect Jewish-mother fashion, she finally replied, "Well, do you have the right clothes? Should we go shopping?"

Fifty-five Ways to Help Israel

F or many around the world, one of the most frustrating aspects of the violence in Israel is the seeming inability to help — even in some small way. And while we may not be able to stop the suicide bombers, we can still take action to lift Israel's spirits and help it contend with an increasingly uncertain situation.

Even if our actions do not appear to influence the overall outcome of events, at the very least we succeed in changing ourselves. And that, in itself, is an important victory.

In conjunction with Israel's 55th birthday, we present "55 Ways to Help Israel" (in no particular order). Each of these strengthens Israel's economic, religious, and social structures. Thanks to the hundreds of Aish.com readers who submitted ideas.

1. Buy Israeli products and services. With the Israeli economy suffering, go out of your way to support Israel's export trade. When in the grocery store, look for brands like Elite, Telma, Osem, and Ahava beauty products — even if you have to pay a few more dollars. Buy Israeli wine to bring as a gift when you visit friends. Ask store managers to order these items specifically. Make a list of local merchants that carry Israeli products, and distribute the list; let the merchants know you are doing this. Israelexport.org helps businesses find and import Israeli products. Many websites sell Israeli products

directly; see the on-line gift shops at Shopinisrael.com and Shorashim2u.net.

2. Speak out! The next time you hear an anti-Israel statement, don't wonder to yourself, "I hope someone does something about it." No Jewish organization or Israeli consulate can fight the propaganda war on every front, so don't assume they will. You be the "anyone" and pick up your pen or keyboard and write a piece for your local newspaper. Or set up an "Israel Information Table" at local religious, cultural, and educational centers. Send your friends articles that are short and to the point. Be a roving ambassador for Israel by explaining the facts to everyone you meet. Even the cashier in the supermarket needs good information. You never know how your contribution may ultimately affect the situation. The worst thing is to remain quiet.

3. Get the facts. The Internet is a great resource for getting an accurate picture of what's really happening. Get your news from a variety of sources so you'll see different perspectives. You can receive a daily news update at Jcpa.org/daily. For excellent background information, read books like *Israel: A History* (by Martin Gilbert), *From Time Immemorial* (by Joan Peters), and *Myths and Facts* (by Mitchell G. Bard) — on-line at Us-israel.org/jsource/myths/.

4. Pray. Regardless of your level of observance, you can add a request for Israel to your regular (or even irregular) prayer regimen. Pray for a peaceful resolution to the conflict. Pray for Israel's leaders, who need wisdom and courage to do what is best for Israel in spite of international pressure. Pray for the safety of Israeli civilians who are targeted by suicide bombers. Pray for the protection of IDF soldiers as they root out terrorists. Ask God to heal Israel's wounded and to thwart future attacks. And pray that Arabs realize the need to choose leaders who oppose hatred and murder. Most importantly, pray from the heart; this is not a contest with other religions to see who can flood God's office with the most

signatures on a petition. (You can send prayers via the Western Wall at Thewall.org.)

5. Contact Israelis. Show Israelis your support, love, and friendship by writing letters, postcards, and e-mails as often as possible. Pick up the phone and make a solidarity call to your Israeli friends and relatives. (If you don't know any Israelis personally, ask someone who does.) Assure them that you share their pain and understand what they're going through. Commend them for having the courage to live in Israel now. Let them know they are not alone!

6. Protest bias in the media. The media has a powerful influence on public opinion and government policy. When you discover a piece of bias, immediately contact the news agency and complain. Keep your remarks respectful and stick to the facts. Build a list of e-mail addresses of friends and colleagues so that when you discover bias, you can also alert others to complain. There is power in the number of responses, even if your specific letter is not printed. You can join a media watch e-mail list at HonestReporting.com, which has tens of thousands of subscribers protesting media bias against Israel.

7. Empathize with terror victims. As you are lying in bed at night, imagine what it's like to be the cousin, child, or parent of someone who yesterday was full of life, and today is nothing but scattered bones and flesh. It's a mitzvah to cry and feel another's pain. You can get a group together to adopt a family that has fallen victim to terror; then take turns calling, writing e-mails, sending letters and care packages. A list of terror victims — and suggestions to help — is on-line at: Projectonesoul.com and Walk4israel.com, where you can order a free poster of all the faces of Israelis who have died in recent terror attacks.

8. Visit Israel. Go to Israel on vacation, to study, or to visit family. Encourage your local organizations to sponsor study tours, religious tours, or bar/bat mitzvah tours. It can be for

three days or three weeks. Despite the tension in certain areas, you can still visit the beautiful sites of Jerusalem, the Galilee, the Dead Sea, and more. Spend as much money as you can afford in order to help the economy. Hotels, stores, and restaurants are lacking tourists — precisely what the terrorists seek! Encourage others as well, by talking about the beautiful Israeli landscape and about the depth of thousands of years of Jewish life there. Visiting Israel will show Israelis that you really care and will make a tremendous difference to your own sense of connection. Visit Goisrael.com for things and do and see. Make your motto "Tourism against terrorism!"

9. Fly the Israeli flag. Put an Israeli flag in front of your home. Let everyone know that you are proud of Israel. Put an "I support Israel" bumper sticker on your car. Wear a combined American/Israeli flag pin on your lapel. If you can't find an Israeli flag, make one yourself, or ask your children to draw one, and display it in your car window or office.

10. Conserve energy. Dependence on oil drives much of the pro-Arab sentiment throughout the world. American foreign policy is also heavily influenced by the need for imported oil. To conserve energy, take simple measures like making sure your tires are properly inflated, using compact fluorescent light bulbs in your home, and buying energy-efficient cars and appliances. What about hanging up those car keys and walking or riding your bicycle for a change? If millions would cut down on fuel consumption, political realities would change. Visit Fueleconomy.gov for suggestions on how to reduce oil consumption. On a public policy level, urge your representatives to allow drilling for oil (while taking appropriate measures to protect the environment), and to pass energy conservation measures.

11. Thank God for His many miracles. With all the practical efforts to help Israel — media watch, education, economic assistance, political lobbying, etc. — don't forget the spiritual

component. The very existence of the Jewish people after 3,500 years — and the return to the land after a long exile — is miraculous. Understand the significance of Abraham's covenant with God. And remember: God is in ultimate control. He has done miracles before and will do so again. Almost every day suicide bombers and attacks are averted. Thank God.

12. Support ZAKA. These dedicated volunteers at the scene of a terrorist attack, identified by their bright yellow vests, patiently scrape all the remaining bits of flesh and blood off the sidewalks and buildings so that the victims can be buried in full accordance with Jewish tradition. Show your appreciation for this self-sacrifice at Zakaisrael.org.

13. Rally for Israel. Hold a rally in your city. When thousands of people turn out for a public display of support, it affects all segments of your community — the politicians, the media, and general public opinion. Not only will you be making an important statement, but it also engenders unity and pride within the Jewish and pro-Israel community.

14. Know your enemy. The Arab world tends to say one thing in English, but a very different message in Arabic. Blood libels and fabrications of Israeli-sponsored massacres are common. To be able to counter misinformation, you need to know your opponents. Memri (memri.org) provides important translations of the Arabic media. And the Center for Monitoring Impact Peace (edume.org) tracks Palestinian compliance with peace agreements. For direct Palestinian perspectives, see the Palestine Media Center (palestine-pmc.com) and Electronicintifada.net.

15. Promote unity. When Jews stop arguing amongst ourselves and work together, we can stand united against the enemy, and the Almighty with us. Jerusalem was destroyed because of Jews speaking negatively about each other; reversing that is the way to rebuild Jerusalem. Abstain from saying (or listening to) anything bad about any Jew, group of Jews, the

Land of Israel, or the Israeli government unless it is constructive critique. The only way to defeat our enemies is to lay down our differences and work together, just as we stood as one people at Mount Sinai.

16. Increase Holocaust education. With the rise of anti-Semitic incidents around the world, and state-sponsored anti-Semitism in Arab countries, it is important to see the warning signs before a crisis happens. Learn about the Holocaust to appreciate the depth of anti-Semitism and its root causes. Stand up against this terrible hatred, no matter what the consequences. Excellent information is on-line at Antisemitism.com.

17. Visit your congressman. Form a concerned citizen's group, and then make an appointment to sit with your congressman for an hour in his Washington office. Then rent a bus and go! Your legislator will see how seriously his constituents are about Mideast issues. Find e-mail addresses at Congress.org, or send snail-mail to: Name of U.S. Representative/Senator, United States Capitol, Washington DC. And check the resources at Aipac.org.

18. Educate the Palestinian public. With all the hatred in Palestinian media and textbooks, an entire generation is being raised for war, not peace. Find ways to introduce democratic values into Palestinian society. Jews cannot realize their dream for peace until Arabs desire the same.

19. Talk at the dinner table. Discuss Israel every night at the dinner table. Involve your children. Ask: Why is Israel important? What happened in the news today? What can we do to help?

20. Divert some of your gifts to Israel. If you're having a bar/bat mitzvah, a graduation, or even a wedding, you can request that in lieu of gifts guests make a donation to a worthwhile cause in Israel — whether to support terror victims, or medical or educational institutions. Doing so will help Israelis in

a practical way and will add special meaning to your life-cycle event.

21. Post on the Web. There are hundreds of Palestinian websites devoted to spreading propaganda — with pictures of starving Palestinian children or blood dripping down the screen describing the "horror of massacres orchestrated by the fascist Israelis." Pro-Palestinian activists have flooded chat rooms, bulletin boards, on-line comments sections — even radio talk shows. Do your part to neutralize this offensive.

22. Strive to be a better person. Before you go to sleep each night, go through your day, review your behavior, and resolve how you can be better. If you've had an argument with someone, simply forgive them. Ultimately, by setting an example of higher moral and ethical standards, we can strengthen the nation of Israel — and bring the redemption one step closer.

23. Donate blood. When you are in Israel, donate blood. With all the recent attacks, there is a great shortage. To give blood is to give life and shows a deep solidarity with Israel and the Jewish people.

24. Fight child abuse. Palestinian children are being brainwashed into sacrificing their lives for the promise of "martyrdom." A group called SICK — Stop Inciting Children to Kill (opsick.com) — is working to stop this child abuse.

25. Become a virtual tourist. If you won't be visiting Israel anytime soon, find someone who is, and give them your tourist dollars to spend for you. Then, when they are in Israel and buy a falafel, have them pay for it twice — once for them "and once for my friend back home who wishes she could be here." Same with taxi rides and museum fees. You'll both be amazed at the overwhelming reaction when Israelis realize how much Diaspora Jews care.

26. Plant a tree. Ilan Ramon looked from outer space, observed that Israel is not green enough, and called for 14 million new

trees to be planted in Israel — one for each Jew in the world. (*Ilan* means "tree.") To help fulfill this dream, call the Jewish National Fund at 800-542-8733.

27. Organize an Israeli products fair. With tourism virtually nonexistent, many Israelis are suffering financially. If you're going to buy a gift, try to buy something (art, clothing, jewelry) by an Israeli artist. Cities across North America have sponsored a "Ben Yehudah Street Fair," where shop owners in Jerusalem send some of their inventory and it is sold for them. This helps Jerusalem merchants keep their shops open and provides a living for their families during this difficult time.

28. Add the merit of a mitzvah. Before you do any one of the 613 mitzvot, have in mind that God should use this merit to help protect Israel.

29. Support Israeli medical institutions. Magen David Adom, Israel's medical emergency service, is financially strapped and in need of ambulances. Months of terror have stretched MDA to its maximum capacity, while exposing its rescue workers to extreme danger and great sacrifice. Get your synagogue or school to start a campaign to defray the cost of an ambulance, or contribute on-line at Magendavidadom.org. Support as well the major hospitals in Israel, whose emergency rooms are stretched to the limit. Jewish lives depend on it.

30. Make aliyah. You can have a great effect on Israel by making it your home. A large influx of educated, entrepreneurial Jews from Western countries will give Israel a major boost. Israel is the place where a Jew is truly at home and can maximize his/her Jewish potential. Start making plans to move when things quiet down (or even now if you're brave). Nefeshbnefesh.org provides financial assistance to Americans wanting to make aliyah. Even if you can't make aliyah, raise children whose dream it is to one day live here. Send your children to Jewish camps and instill in them a sense of

responsibility and commitment toward Israel.

31. Learn Hebrew. Call your local synagogue and find out about Hebrew classes. This will build your bond with the Jewish people and the Land of Israel.

32. Get the Israeli viewpoint. There's a lot of misinformation out there. Check with an on-line Israeli newspaper once a day. For news, visit the Jerusalem Post (jpost.com) and IMRA (imra.org.il). When an incident happens in Israel, visit the websites of the Israeli Ministry of Foreign Affairs (mfa.gov.il) and the Israeli Defense Forces (idf.il/newsite/english).

33. Learn Torah. The traditional Jewish response to adversity has always been enhancing Jewish knowledge, and hence Jewish pride and commitment. Increase the amount of time you learn Torah each day. The impact of a few extra minutes is enormous. Attend a class about Judaism, or pick something from the recommended reading list at Aish.com/literacy/reference/.

34. Contact the president. Call or e-mail the president daily or weekly to commend his support for Israel in the common fight against terrorism. Write a short, personal e-mail with a subject line like: "Thank you for standing with Israel." Every call, letter, and fax is counted. Send e-mail to: president@whitehouse.gov, or call the White House comment line at 202-456-1111.

35. Support Israeli soldiers. Write a letter and express appreciation for the soldiers' self-sacrifice in valiantly defending our people and our land. Go to PizzaIDF.org to send a fresh hot pizza to soldiers on the front lines.

36. Fight terror. For the civilized world to survive, terrorism must be stopped. Call on government leaders to make policy decisions based on what is morally correct, not economically expedient. Promote the PBS video documentary "Jihad in America" by Steven Emerson. It's a real eye-opener.

37. Distribute literature on college campuses. There is an urgent

need to counter the virulent wave of anti-Semitism and pro-Palestinian activism on college campuses. Print and distribute literature highlighting Israel's humanitarian achievements, democracy, and ethnic diversity. Fight against the "divestment" movement. Urge faculty members to take active steps to support Israel. One group working on the campus front is IsraelActivism.com.

38. Recite Psalms. It is a time-honored Jewish tradition to recite Psalms in times of distress. King David composed stirring words that seem to be written for our exact situation today. You can say a few Psalms every day (recommended are Psalms 20, 83, 121, 130, and 142), or organize a group of friends to share saying the entire book together. Communal prayers are more powerful than any individual can muster. Rabbi Elyashiv in Israel has requested that all Jews worldwide take 15 minutes out of their hectic daily schedules to say Psalms. An English translation is available at Artscroll.com/itehillim.html.

39. Reach out. At such difficult times, Jews need to reach out to one another. Invite an unaffiliated Jew to Shabbat dinner or to attend a class. As the future of Israel is being threatened, people feel the need to connect and are more open to their heritage.

40. Register and vote. Elected officials carefully analyze voter registration and voter turnout, and make decisions accordingly. If you are not already registered to vote, contact your local Board of Elections and ask for a voter registration application. And be sure to vote in the next elections.

41. Invest. Buy stocks on the Tel Aviv Stock Exchange. Help Israeli companies obtain venture capital funds (israelseed.com). Israel has more scientists and engineers per capita than any nation in the world. Usaisrael.org has information on Israeli companies that do business with American ones. You can even buy an Israel Bond, to support infrastructure projects, for as little as $136 (israelbonds.com).

42. Stop carnage on the roads. Work to end the terrible traffic accidents in Israel which claim 600 lives each year. It is absurd that while we fight against terror, there are preventable tragedies killing so many of our people.

43. Sponsor educational forums. Offer a crash course in the Mideast conflict at your local JCC, synagogue, or community college. Bring "regular" Israeli citizens to speak. This will impact on the Israelis as well by strengthening their own clarity on the issues and giving them encouragement through seeing support for Israel abroad. And they'll go back home and spread the positive message to other Israelis.

44. Show both sides of the refugee issue. In conversations and in the media, emphasize how Arab states have mistreated the Palestinians — refusing to grant them citizenship in order to use the "refugees" as a political pawn against Israel. Raise the issue of how 600,000 Jews were driven out of Arab lands during Israel's independence and forced to abandon their property, with no right of return or compensation ever offered. Read *The Forgotten Millions: The Modern Jewish Exodus from Arab Lands* by Malka Hillel Shulewitz.

45. Hold governments accountable. Write and call (and boycott if necessary) any government that is complicit in anti-Semitic and anti-Israel activities. Educate the public about the inconsistency of the United Nations and the European Union. Why would democracies — who support human rights — not speak out against virulent Arab hate speech? Why do they condemn Israeli incursions, but remain silent on Palestinian bombings of civilians? Protest at the consulates of those countries who have not acted effectively against the anti-Semitic activities taking place in their countries. Get the European view of the conflict at Bbc.co.uk.

46. Promote articulate spokespeople. Palestinian spokespeople are persuasive and articulate, but Israeli spokespeople are sometimes less so. Compile a list of Israeli spokespeople and run an on-line poll, asking people to vote for their favorite.

Then publicize the results so the Israeli government knows who to get the networks to interview in the future. Study the Luntz Guides for effective pro-Israel communication.

47. Get a clear definition of terrorism. September 11 united the civilized world against terrorism. "Terrorism" is defined as intentionally targeting civilians. Yet many in the media refuse to label Palestinian suicide bombers as terrorists. Let the media and political leaders know that you do not agree with this double standard. And do not allow the media or politicians to draw a moral equivalence between people killed while rioting and people killed in terror attacks. Get involved at TerrorPetition.com.

48. Watch key videos. "Relentless: The Struggle for Peace in Israel" depicts raw footage from Palestinian TV that reveal shocking images of incitement and examines how the peace process unraveled in a surge of Palestinian violence. See Honestreporting.com/relentless/.

49. Learn Israeli geography. Buy a map of Israel and frame it. Put it up where you and your kids will look at it. When there is a terror attack, look where it is. Familiarize yourself with the green line, and how the territories factor into Israel's security needs. Learn the cities of Israel. Learn the proximity of Arab countries. Figure out the size of Israel relative to your state.

50. Sign up for solidarity. Israelis can often feel lonely and isolated surrounded by 250 million Arabs, and a world which routinely issues condemnations in the UN. IsraelPetition.com enables people around the world to express support for Israel in its fight against terror and as the lone vanguard of democracy in the Middle East. The petition will be presented to world leaders and published in the media.

51. Say the Shema. The Shema is a kind of Jewish "pledge of allegiance," a declaration of faith in One God and an affirmation of commitment to Israel and the Jewish people. It is the first prayer that Jewish children are taught to say, and the

last words a Jew says prior to death. Say the Shema twice each day: once in the morning and once at night.

52. Give *tzedakah*. Give some charity every day for Israel. Encourage others to give charity for Israel, too. One person wrote, "Because our church has been forced to cancel their annual trip to Israel, we are sending our money anyway to the tour guides and bus driver."

53. Volunteer. Volunteers For Israel is an opportunity to work for two to four weeks in a hospital, on an Israeli army base performing noncombat duties, or in your professional field matched to Israel's needs. Details at Vfi-usa.org.

54. Yearn for redemption. The Torah says that for the Jews in Egypt, it wasn't until "We cried out to God, that He heard our voice and saw our affliction." Cry out for God's compassion; the gates of tears are never closed. Yearn for the redemption and the fulfillment of Isaiah's vision of "swords beaten into plowshares."

55. Brainstorm. Get a group of friends together and spend one hour brainstorming for more ideas how to help Israel. Start something really big. Remember the MIA bracelets for the soldiers missing in action in the Vietnam war? Think of all the ribbons worn to symbolize awareness of various causes. Perhaps lapel buttons with the faces of Israeli terror victims? Come up with a high-impact way to create more awareness.

Rabbi Shalom Schwartz

To Live as Jews

What will be the end of the murderous situation in the Middle East? Political experts are skeptical of any diplomatic solution on the horizon. Military sources offer only stopgap measures to curb terror and can find no practical way to win this war. Israel is even losing most of the political and media battles, as many sympathize with the Arabs.

In October 2002, when a sniper began gunning down innocent citizens in Washington D.C., millions of people felt terrified for their lives. The security they needed to live a normal life was undermined. In the past thousand days, hundreds of Israeli citizens have been murdered and thousands seriously injured. Buses, stores, restaurants, and hotels are under constant attack. Clearly, the Jewish state faces a threat to its very existence. How will its people carry on their daily lives?

This is the very goal of Israel's enemies, to cripple the will of the nation through fear and suffering. With the feeling of paralysis that accompanies each terror attack, we ask: How much more can we bear? How much longer can we risk the lives of our children?

At this time we must look back. Surely we Jews have been here before. Our ancestors have faced massive threats of extinction, yet

For biography of RABBI SHALOM SCHWARTZ, see p. 46.

they survived. We, who are alive today, are descended from those survivors.

How did they view such circumstances?

- They saw the events of their time as the unfolding of their God-given destiny.

- They considered their spiritual response as equally important to whatever political, military, or media strategies they employed against their oppressors.

- They believed that radical personal and communal change was the catalyst to avert any impending threat.

Since Camp David, 2000, it has become painfully obvious that this conflict is not primarily about land. It is about Jews.

Polls taken in October 2002 reported that 70 percent of Israelis and 80 percent of Palestinians view this as a battle over the existence of the Jewish State.

Many of us were born into a world where the State of Israel always existed. But what if Israel's enemies unite? What if the Arab armies join the 40,000-strong Palestinian "police force" and try to "liberate" Jerusalem from the "Jewish infidels"?

The Jewish people's response to "Death to the Jews!" has always been to "Live as Jews!" If evil targets us because we envision a world built on moral values, then our answer must be to live even more passionately according to those values.

Today there is an increase of anti-Semitism, but it has donned the cloak of anti-Zionism. This attack on the continued existence of the Jewish state must prompt us to do some serious personal and national soul-searching.

In 1948, the world looked on as the Jews returned to Zion — the Jewish people emerging from the ashes of the Holocaust, back in their own land. What would they create?

Facing repeated attacks, the citizens of the young state spent most of their waking hours worrying about survival. And when there was time to come up for air, they had to build a country: roads, schools, infrastructure, and institutions. Who had time to think about a higher national purpose? It was enough to know that

Israel would be a place of refuge for Jews around the world if another holocaust threatened.

Modern Zionism saw Israel as a safe haven from anti-Semitism. Today that safe haven no longer exists. Who could imagine that the next threat of the destruction of millions of Jews would actually occur within the borders of Israel?

But Israel was meant to be something much more than an escape hatch. It was meant to be the springboard from which the Jewish people would carry out its destiny.

Believing Jews around the globe must ask themselves: Have we so lost track of Israel's purpose that Israel will be taken away from us? Have we so squandered our opportunity to build a Jewish homeland that we will end up losing that land?

Elie Wiesel compared modern Jewry to a messenger that was hit on the head and knocked out. When he woke up, he couldn't remember the message, who had sent him, to whom he had been sent, nor the very fact of his being a messenger.

Perhaps we have lost sight of the very uniqueness of our destiny. Judaism is much more than a religion, much more than a national identity. It is to be a light unto the nations, to repair the world, and to be a source of blessing to humanity. And this is to come about by the Jews living according to their tradition in their ancestral land, the Land of Israel.

How can the tiny Jewish nation be a catalyst for world repair? Christian scholar and historian Paul Johnson wrote in his bestseller, *History of the Jews*:

> One way of summing up 4,000 years of Jewish history is to ask ourselves, what would have happened to the human race if Abraham had not been a man of great sagacity; or if he had stayed in Ur and kept his higher notions to himself, and no specific Jewish people had come into being. Certainly the world without the Jews would have been a radically different place.
>
> All the great conceptual discoveries of the intellect seem obvious and inescapable once they have been revealed, but it requires a special genius to formulate them for the first time.

The Jews had this gift. To them we owe the ideas of equality before the law, both divine and human; of the sanctity of life and the dignity of the human person; of the individual conscience, and so of personal redemption; of the collective conscience, and so of social responsibility; of peace as an abstract ideal, and love as the foundation of justice; and many other items which constitute the basic moral furniture of the human mind.

Imagine a country whose moral fabric was so woven with those values that you could palpably feel them when first setting foot on its land. Imagine an economy, a social and health system that derived from and breathed those commitments. Imagine an educational and legal system built on this moral foundation. Imagine a nation that took upon itself the fulfillment of a 4,000-year-old covenant to be a light unto the nations.

We have always been a people with boundless faith and hope in the future.

We believed in our unique purpose even when exiled from one country to another.

We suffered cruelty and abandonment even as we continued to teach the world about a loving God.

We strove to bring goodness to the world, thereby becoming the target of the world's greatest evil.

What will be the end of the murderous situation in the Middle East? It will surely not end until we heed its message, a message that is calling out to each and every concerned Jew. Whether in Israel or in the Diaspora, whether Jewishly knowledgeable or Jewishly unschooled, whether religious or not — this is a wake-up call to reexamine our ties to our people. To reaffirm our Jewish identity and divine mission.

Just as our enemies have never differentiated between Jews, so too must we make no exceptions. Wake up! We're all in this together.

Sara Yoheved Rigler

Loving the Land of Israel

May 2003

I have a confession to make: I'm in love with the Land of Israel. After nearly 18 years living here, through two intifadas, two Gulf Wars, the ups and downs (mostly downs) of Israel's turbulent economy, and the current wave of terror which fills me with dread and heartbreak, my ardor for Israel has not abated.

Why do I love Israel? Because I have been to half the world's holy sites. I have meditated in Varanasi, immersed in the sacred headwaters of the Ganges, visited the Vatican, circumambulated the Buddhist stupa in Sarnath, bathed in the waters of Lourdes, trekked to the shrine of the Weeping Madonna in 10 feet of snow in the French Alps, and visited remote ashrams in the Himalayas. I felt a sense of exaltation in all of these places.

But only in Israel do I feel the palpable presence of God when I'm looking for a parking space, when I'm cooking dinner, when I'm hanging laundry, when I'm caught in a traffic jam, when I'm wondering how we'll pay the phone bill.

This should come as no surprise. God explicitly promised in the Torah that He would have a constant, 24/7 connection with the Land of Israel and those who dwell here: "A land that the Lord

---

For biography of SARA YOHEVED RIGLER, see p. 28.

your God scrutinizes constantly; the eyes of the Lord your God are on it from the beginning of the year until the end of the year" (Deuteronomy 11:12).

Most of my friends here in Jerusalem have myriads of stories about how the constant, direct Divine intervention (in Hebrew, *hashgacha pratit*) reveals itself in their lives. To share just a couple of my own:

When my husband (a musician), and I made aliyah, the law was that new immigrants were entitled to bring in three "lifts" tax-free. This meant that we could ship major appliances and furnishings from America without having to pay the usual 100 percent customs — an opportunity too good to pass up. For our third and final lift we bought a microwave, a Maytag dryer, a self-cleaning oven, and everything else we thought we might need for the rest of our lives. When, back in Israel, we calculated the cost of all we had bought plus the shipping charge and insurance, we were $2,100 short.

I prayed to God to cover the shortfall. After all, we had made the purchases for the sake of our life in Israel.

A few days later, an envelope came in the mail from the American Federation of Musicians, Local 47, to which my husband had formerly belonged. The computer printout informed him that re-runs from "Face the Music," a TV show he had worked on some 10 years before, had been sold to the Christian Broadcasting Network. Enclosed was a check for $2,100.

Another story: In Israeli apartments, space is always at a premium. Therefore, when we moved into our apartment 14 years ago, I considered myself fortunate that I found two clothes hampers which, in terms of size and shape, exactly fit into the narrow passage between my bedroom and the bathroom where the washing machine is located. After many years of use, one of the two plastic hampers cracked, until it was barely holding together. Its twin was still in perfect condition.

One day I looked at the broken hamper and said to myself: "It's not befitting *tifferet Yerushalayim* (the splendor of Jerusalem) to have broken stuff in our apartment." But where was I to buy a replacement to match the good hamper? Certainly they weren't making the same hampers anymore. Even the store where I had bought the hampers had gone out of business. And what was my chance of finding two new hampers to fit the narrow space?

The next day, a pruning project in my courtyard garden left me with a carton of debris to dispose of. Where I live in the Old City of Jerusalem, we put our garbage in closed garbage rooms, one for every several families. I had not been to our garbage room for many weeks, because my husband takes out the garbage. When I opened the door to the garbage room to dump my carton of prunings, I couldn't believe my eyes. Sitting there was a hamper identical to mine, in mint condition.

Do I mean to say that the Almighty God of Heaven and Earth involves Himself in my finances and my hampers? Absolutely yes! That is the quality of the Land of Israel: Total engagement. Constant, immediate, detailed Divine supervision. Unrelenting intimacy with the Infinite.

No wonder it's so difficult to live here.

❧

God loves the Land of Israel more than the most fervent Zionist. How do I know? He says so in His Book. Over and over again. No Israeli Ministry of Tourism brochure extols Israel as much as the Torah. According to the Torah, Israel isn't simply a great place to visit — or live, but a piece of earth inextricably bound up with the soul of the Jewish people.

God's very first pronouncement to the first Jew, Abraham, is a command to move to Israel. "Go from your land, from your birthplace, from your father's house, to the land that I will show you" (Genesis 12:1).

The Hebrew word for "go" — *lech* — is followed by the word *lecha*, meaning "to yourself." The classical biblical commentator Ohr HaChaim asserts that going to the Land of Israel entails moving toward oneself, one's truest, deepest self.

The covenant which God made with Abraham, Isaac, and Jacob promised two things to their descendents: the eternality of the Jewish people and the Land of Israel.

During God's first revelation to Moses, at the Burning Bush, He declares that He is aware of the pain of the Children of Israel in their Egyptian bondage. Then God reveals to Moses His plan of redemption: "I have come down to rescue them from the hand of Egypt and to bring them up from that land to a good and expansive land, to a land flowing with milk and honey..." (Exodus 3:8).

The Exodus was not only from a state of slavery to a state of freedom, but from a place called Egypt to a place which would later be called the Land of Israel. Coming to Israel was an integral part of the Redemption. A people who had entered into a special relationship with God and who had witnessed open miracles and who had been given the Torah could reside only in this particular location, Israel.

Throughout the Torah, Israel is referred to as "*eretz rechavah,*" meaning a land that is spacious or expansive. This is almost amusing, because Israel is a tiny land, about the size of the state of New Jersey. Even in ancient Mesopotamia, Israel was a sliver of land mass surrounded by large empires. Our Sages tell us that *rechavah* is not meant as a geographical description, but rather as a spiritual description. Israel is "expansive" because it expands the person who lives there.

◈

Judaism is the only religion in the world connected to a specific country. Other religions have sacred sites, rivers, and springs, but Judaism maintains that every inch of Israel within the biblical borders (which does not include Eilat and most of the Negev) is holy.

This has immense practical ramifications for the practice of Judaism. For instance, all the agricultural mitzvot (the commandments to tithe produce, let the land lie fallow every seven years, and so on) apply only in the Land of Israel. As Rebbetzin Tziporah Heller is fond of saying: "A tomato which grows in Israel is holier than the manna which fell in the desert." Why? Because mitzvot apply to that tomato. And mitzvot are a Jew's direct way to bond with God.

In bestowing many mitzvot of the Torah, God begins by saying, "When you come into the land...." Nachmanides, the great 13th century sage, claimed that the mitzvot of the Torah could be properly fulfilled only in Israel. Performing mitzvot outside the land, he wrote, was merely for the sake of keeping in practice, so that when the Jewish people return to the land, they will know what to do.

The *Kuzari* describes God's plan to cultivate the Jewish people as a "kingdom of priests and a holy nation" as akin to planting a vineyard. A vineyard needs four things: vines, land, sun, and rain. The *Kuzari* explains that the vines are the Jewish people, the land is Israel, the sun is Divine providence, and the rain is the Torah. Clearly, if one plants French vines in the Napa valley, they will yield different grapes. Just so, the Jewish people anywhere outside of Israel cannot fully achieve its Divine purpose and potential.

The very soil of Israel possesses a certain spiritual vitality. Many Jews from the Diaspora feel a soul-awakening when they come to Israel, or to Jerusalem, or to the Western Wall. The Wall, which sits at the base of the Temple Mount and is the remaining vestige of the Second Temple, has not a single spiritual trapping. No frescos, no incense, no music, no awesome architecture. Yet the *Shechinah*, the Presence of God, is so tangible there that few fail to feel it.

Imagine a lover taking his beloved to his "special place." Carrying a basket packed with wine and bread, as they walk along he regales her with descriptions of his secret trysting place. "It's so beautiful, so quiet, so remote, like another world. You'll love it."

Finally they reach the spot, an isolated clearing in the forest. She takes one look and sneers, "This? This is your special place? There's nothing here! Not even a bench to sit on! Not even a picnic table! Do you expect me to sit on the ground and get my skirt dirty? And there are insects crawling on the grass. I hate insects!"

If the beloved rejects the lover's special place, what are the prospects for their relationship?

The Torah recounts how in the second year after the Exodus, the Israelites arrived at the borders of the Promised Land. Ten of the 12 spies sent to reconnoiter the Land gave a negative report, and the people refused "to make aliyah." The Sages say that this sin, the rejection of the Land of Israel, was in some ways more grievous than the sin of worshipping the Golden Calf. After the incident of the Golden Calf, Moses went back to the summit of Mount Sinai to plead for Divine forgiveness, which was granted. However, we have never been forgiven for the sin of rejecting the Land of Israel.

If the beloved rejects the lover's special place, what are the prospects for their relationship?

⟩∞⟨

One way to reject Israel is to refuse to live here. There is another, more pernicious way to reject God's special place: to treat it as a piece of real estate like any other.

Imagine that the lover brings his beloved to his special place of rendezvous. She looks at it and exclaims: "It's beautiful! We can turn it into a real estate development. We could probably divide it into a dozen plots, 50 by 60 each."

The Land of Israel is not about nationalism. The goal of "making Israel a country like all other countries" violates its very essence. Imagine the city planners of Florence deciding to do away with the priceless works of art throughout the city in order to make Florence "a city like all other cities." The priceless treasure of Israel is its unique Jewish identity, its spiritual power, its holiness.

The Land of Israel is not about having a refuge from anti-Semitism. That goal has backfired. Israel is the only country in the world today where many Jews are being killed because they are Jews.

The Land of Israel is not about having a place where Jews are in charge. Yes, Israel has a Jewish president, a Jewish prime minister, Jewish legislators, mayors, and bureaucrats. It also has Jewish criminals and Jewish drug addicts.

The Land of Israel is the place that God has designated for His rendezvous with the Jewish people.

How can we spurn this opportunity?

We would like to thank the following individuals for their generous support in making the publication of this book possible:

Michael Evans, Denver

Rabbi Sholom and Leah Mark, Jerusalem

Valerie and David Smilovic & Family, Paradise Valley, AZ

Alan and Claudia Ainsley, Palm Beach

Anthony Ansell, London

Marilyn Berger, Santa Monica

Marion Davis, Boca Raton

Diana Diehl, Columbus

Allison Haas, New York

Paul Harney, Bermuda

David Hes, Toronto

John, Beverley, and Brett Jenkins, Conyers, GA

Deborah Martin, Springfield, MO

The Neumann Family, Brooklyn

Linda Oliver, Dallas

Joan Pressman, Atlanta

C. Tzvi Schwartz, Brooklyn

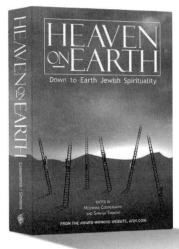